CHEVELLE
PERFORMANCE PROJECTS

1964-1972

Cole Quinnell

CarTech®

CarTech®

CarTech®, Inc.
838 Lake Street S.
Forest Lake, MN 55025
Phone: 651-277-1200 or 800-551-4754
Fax: 651-277-1203
www.cartechbooks.com

© 2012 by Cole Quinnell

All rights reserved. No part of this publication may be reproduced or utilized in any form or by any means, electronic or mechanical, including photocopying, recording, or by any information storage and retrieval system, without prior permission from the Publisher. All text, photographs, and artwork are the property of the Author unless otherwise noted or credited.

The information in this work is true and complete to the best of our knowledge. However, all information is presented without any guarantee on the part of the Author or Publisher, who also disclaim any liability incurred in connection with the use of the information.

All trademarks, trade names, model names and numbers, and other product designations referred to herein are the property of their respective owners and are used solely for identification purposes. This work is a publication of CarTech, Inc., and has not been licensed, approved, sponsored, or endorsed by any other person or entity.

Edit by Paul Johnson
Layout by Chris Fayers

ISBN 978-1-61325-583-4
Item No. SA226P

Library of Congress Cataloging-in-Publication Data

Quinnell, Cole.
 Chevelle performance projects : 1964-1972 / by Cole Quinnell.
   p. cm.
  ISBN 978-1-934709-79-5
1. Chevelle automobile–Customizing 2. Chevelle automobile–Performance. I. Title.
TL215.C48Q56 2012
629.28'722--dc23

 2012011040

Printed in the U.S.A.

Title Page:
A scattershield and clutch are mounted to the LS engine and the scattershield is clearly nestled between the headers. The headers are not torqued down to spec, so the scattershield can be easily mounted. With a swivel socket and a long extension, you can reach every bolt from the underside of the car. If you have rubber or polyurethane engine mounts, do not let the engine tilt unsupported with the transmission removed. This can damage the motor mounts. On this engine, we have a lift plate attached to the intake, and we are using an engine hoist to keep the engine close to its installed driveline angle.

Back Cover Photos

Top Left:
To install the brakes, tighten the rotor onto the axle. Install the caliper and tighten it onto the bracket. Using dial calipers, measure the gap from the rotor to the caliper body at the top inside, top outside, bottom inside, and bottom outside. Record all four of these numbers.

Top Right:
When installing headlights, the remaining wires to connect are the primary positive and negative wires, which should be routed directly to the battery. The white signal lead connects to the negative side of the coil, and the tach connection to supply a signal to your tachometer. Finally, you can hook up the throttle cable.

Middle Left:
This radiator is not a direct fit for the Chevelle; it is actually a bit wider than the original. To start the installation, slide the mounting brackets into the side channels of the side tanks and snug them so they don't move too much. Flex-a-lite includes rubber isolators, which should be used between the radiator and the core support. Gently lower the radiator into place and make broad notes about the general placement of the radiator.

Middle Right:
To set up the American Powertrain hydraulic clutch system properly, measuring the distance between the face of the throwout bearing and the fingers on the pressure plate is critical. This determines the gap between the two components when the clutch is released. Make sure that the throwout bearing is fully seated on the transmission collar and that it is fully compressed. Bolt the bellhousing onto the transmission. Use a straightedge as shown to measure the distance between the face of the throwout bearing and the face of the bellhousing. You need to be very precise in this measurement, and check it at three different places on the throwout bearing. The measurement should be the same at all three places. If not, the throwout bearing is not seated correctly or is partially extended.

Bottom Left:
With the pinion gear and the carrier installed, there are two critical measurements to check: backlash and mesh pattern. This is how much the gears rock back and forth between engagement. The ring and pinion gear manufacturer determines acceptable backlash, and it is printed in the setup instructions.

Bottom Right:
There is an easy way to improve the performance of your headlights, whether you have stock 35-watt headlights or have upgraded to 65-watt sealed halogen or xenon bulbs. The original circuit design has power traveling from the fuse block through the headlight and dimmer switches and then to the headlights. Along with a long length of wire that reduces amperage through resistance, the headlight switch also reduces the available amperage slightly. Painless Performance offers headlight relay kits for both 2- and 4-headlight systems that remove these drops in amperage, providing more power to the headlights for brighter operation. This route also removes a relatively high amperage circuit from the dashboard and through an old light switch for safer operation and to extend the life of the switches.

CONTENTS

Acknowledgments 4
Introduction 5

Chapter 1: Chassis Upgrades 6
   Frame 6
   Suspension 7
   Handling 9
   Project 1: Frame Boxing 12
   Project 2: Tubular Control Arm Kit Installation ... 14
   Project 3: Mini Tub Kit Installation 17
   Project 4: Suspension Kit Installation 22

Chapter 2: Building a Performance Steering System ... 24
   Steering Box 25
   Steering Linkage 25
   Steering Column 26
   Steering Wheel 28
   Project 1: Quick-Ratio Steering Box Installation ... 29
   Project 2: Steering Column Installation 32

Chapter 3: Wheels and Tires 35
   Appearance 35
   Performance 36
   Project 1: Wheel and Tire Fitment 39

Chapter 4: Building a Performance Rear Axle 43
   Upgrades to Your Original Axle 44
   Project 1: Setting Up a Ford 9-inch Differential ... 50

Chapter 5: Brake Upgrades 53
   Performance Factors 54
   Proportioning Valve 55
   Master Cylinder 55
   Roll Control Solenoid 57
   Project 1: High-Performance Brake System Installation 58

Chapter 6: Engine Upgrades 62
   Ignition System 63
   Exhaust System 63
   Intake System 63
   Cylinder Head and Camshaft 64
   Project 1: Performance Ignition System Installation ... 65
   Project 2: Fuel-Injection System Installation 67

Chapter 7: Engine Swaps 70
   Gen I vs LS 70
   LS-Series Benefits 71
   Engine Sources 72
   Budget Requirements 73

   Project 1: LS Engine Installation 76
   Project 2: Water Pump and Front Accessories Installation 81
   Project 3: Engine Installation 83

Chapter 8: Performance Fuel System 88
   Fuel Tank 88
   Fuel Line 89
   Fuel Filter 90
   Fuel Pump 91
   Project 1: Fuel Line Installation 93

Chapter 9: Performance Cooling System 96
   Overheating Diagnosis 96
   Electric Fan 97
   Belt-Driven Fan 98
   Radiator 99
   Project 1: Radiator Installation 101

Chapter 10: Performance Exhaust 105
   Headers or Manifolds 106
   Tailpipes 106
   Exhaust Tubing 107
   Mufflers 107
   Project 1: Performance Exhaust Installation 108

Chapter 11: Overdrive Transmission Swaps 113
   Automatic Transmissions 113
   Manual Transmissions 117
   Project 1: Clutch Installation 120
   Project 2: Transmission Installation 124

Chapter 12: Wiring Upgrades 127
   Wiring Harness 127
   Battery 128
   Starter Solenoid 128
   Relays 131
   Master Disconnect Switch 131
   Project 1: Wiring Harness Installation 132
   Project 2: Trunk-Mounted Battery Tray Installation ... 136
   Project 3: Master Disconnect Switch Installation ... 138

Chapter 13: Performance Interior 140
   Seating 140
   Safety Cage 141
   Dash 141
   Sound Deadening 142
   Project 1: Roll Cage Installation 145
   Project 2: Interior Installation 153

Source Guide 158

DEDICATION

To my wife, Julie, and my daughters, Julie, Analise, and Amelia, for their patience and support while I worked on this book.

ACKNOWLEDGMENTS

Even though I've eaten, lived, and breathed performance Chevelles for more than 20 years, this book is more than just a collection of my memories and experiences. I tapped into my resources to make sure that I could bring you an extremely broad, technical book to help you build your Chevelle.

One person who inspired me as a young man to like hot rods in general and Chevelles specifically, is Jeff Smith. He has been the editor of several magazines, including *Hot Rod*, and is currently the Senior Technical Editor at *Car Craft*. While most kids idolize rock stars or pro athletes, I was enamored by Jeff's work in the magazines, and especially with the stories he did on his collection of Chevelles. Just a few years later, he mentored me as I started my career at Petersen Publishing, and I spent quite a few evenings and weekends wrenching on his cars in his backyard. I appreciate all of the help he has provided over the years, and he still inspires me to work on my Chevelle!

I'd like to thank Tony and TJ Grzelakowski at Advanced Body & Color and its sister company, ABC Performance. They worked long hours on one of the cars used for multiple projects in this book, bringing their expertise and dedication to each piece. They also developed several new products for Chevelles during the course of the book, which I'm happy I was able to include. While their companies are relatively new to the sport, I think that you'll see more and more great Chevelle performance products from ABC Performance, and some great performing cars built by Advanced Body & Color.

I'd also like to extend a special thanks to these additional companies that helped me directly in creating this book: American Powertrain, Baer, CARS, FAST, Flaming River, Flex-a-lite, Flowmaster, Holley, Kirkey, Moser, MSD, Painless Performance, Stewart Warner, TCI, Trans-Dapt, and Tremec.

I had a great group of several thousand supporters and encouragers along the path to completing this book that I stayed connected to on my Facebook page. I would bounce ideas off of them, poll the Chevelle owners among them about specific topics, and share progress and sneak peeks of some of the photography and topics I was working on.

Finally, I'd like to thank the team at CarTech for their patience and help in converting a life-long magazine writer and editor into a published book author.

INTRODUCTION

There are few cars as closely associated with the muscle car era as the Chevelle. The model was launched in 1964, as factory-backed drag racing was strong and growing. It was right-sized, positioned between the "compact" Chevy II and the extra-large Impala. It was large enough for a family, which kept its sales strong. It was also large enough for hot rodders and racers to stuff larger engines into, readily change out engine parts, add headers, change transmissions, and so on. It also had the basic architecture of a great suspension at both the front and rear. Chevrolet also launched it with the high-performance SS model. It didn't take long for Chevrolet performance enthusiasts to embrace the all-new model. It had plenty of performance potential.

Everything that made the Chevelle good during its run of 1964–1972 is still true today. It's large enough to take your family and small enough to be competitive in drag racing, road racing, and autocrossing. You can mix and match drivetrain components with factory-original and aftermarket parts to create just about any type of performance combination you want. And there are more performance parts available for these cars today than ever before. One of the companies I talked to that makes parts for about a dozen different types of cars says that they sell more parts for Chevelles now than they ever have, and the popularity of the cars is continuing to grow.

During the eight years of production that I focus on here, there were three distinct changes that divide the cars from a styling standpoint and, to a lesser extent, a functional standpoint. The early era was the 1964–1965 cars, while 1966–1967s are known as mid-year Chevelles, and the 1968–1972s are classified as round bodies. We know that the Chevelle name was used on later models and eventually transitioned to the Laguna, and these are also popular to build into performance cars, but this book focuses on the core muscle car era.

While you usually see chassis and drivetrain parts for these cars that fit the entire run, there are subtle differences. For example, the engine crossmember and steering linkage are closer to the engine in the 1964–1967 Chevelles than they are in the later cars. The 1968–1972 cars also have slightly taller shocks in the front. The latter example doesn't affect parts dramatically, as the difference is slight and one shock fits all Chevelles. But the other point is important for engine swaps and fitting larger oil pans. I address these differences in this book where I found them to be important to building a modern performance Chevelle.

This is the golden era for the Chevelle, with more of these cars being built and more performance parts available than ever before. This is partially because of the muscle car heritage of the car, but it's also because the chassis is such a great foundation for creating a pro-touring car. For the most part, you can bolt on suspension, brakes, and drivetrain components to build a Chevelle that rivals a brand-new Corvette in handling, stopping, and acceleration, but has the classic looks and styling from the muscle car era.

CHAPTER 1

Chassis Upgrades

The original frame under 1964–1972 Chevelles is not a bad foundation for building a solid-performing car. Most of the modifications in this chapter focus on greatly increasing the handling capability of the vehicle, which also improves control, making the car much more enjoyable to drive on the street. The frame and rear suspension upgrades also help in drag racing, while the front suspension modifications don't hurt drag racing. For ultimate performance, however, you need to strengthen the frame rails and change quite a few of the bolt-on suspension components.

There's good news and bad news when it comes to the chassis under your 1964–1972 Chevelle. The good news is that it's a fantastic foundation for a solid performing chassis. The suspension location points are in good places and the basic double A-arm front suspension is a sound design, as is the rear four-link. The bad news is that the frame rails are really the only pieces of the original chassis that you won't be unbolting and replacing, although you can replace them too, if you want. More good news, though; almost everything you need to convert your Chevelle into a modern-handling machine can be done through bolt-on components.

Frame

While many people begin their research and modifications with the suspension components, it's best to start with the frame itself. The frame design is pretty good as muscle car production frames go. The biggest drawback is that the center sections of the frame rails are C-channels. The lack of fully-boxed frame sections

CHASSIS UPGRADES

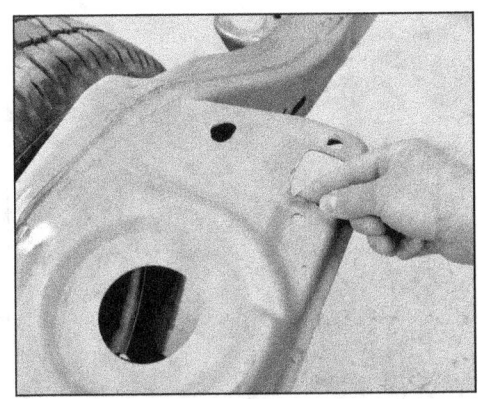

In addition to upgrading the frame, you need to inspect the original frame for damage and fatigue. It's very common for the shock absorber mounts at the front and rear to be damaged by a shock coming loose. At the rear, a lot of cars were "upgraded" to air shocks at some time during the 1970s, which put additional pressure on the upper shock mounts and often resulted in damage. Check the frame near all suspension mounts for cracks. It's easier to do this with the body removed and the frame media-blasted, but you can also find damage with the body still on the frame.

here introduces flex. While driving under the conditions these cars were originally designed for, this isn't an issue; but when you double or triple the power and expect the car to launch hard on the dragstrip or turn corners with grace at anything over 40 mph, this weak link becomes an issue. ABC Performance makes a do-it-yourself Frame Boxing Kit including CNC laser-cut sections you can weld in place and box your frame. The kit results in a frame that is four times as stiff as the original. Boxing the frame center sections should be considered mandatory if you have aspirations of turning your car into a performance Chevelle.

You also want to inspect the frame carefully. After all, the newest original frame is at least 40 years old. Even regular road use can cause cracks in the frames near suspension attachment points, including the A-arm mounts in the front and the upper shock mounts at the rear of the car. If your car is from the "Rust Belt," inspect it very carefully to make sure that it has not been compromised by corrosion.

Another option to overcoming open-channel frame rails and frame damage is to upgrade to a completely new chassis. Art Morrison Enterprises and Schwartz Performance, Inc., make all-new chassis for these cars that bolt in place, complete with front and rear suspension. Schwartz Performance makes a G-machine chassis to fit 1964–1967 and 1968–1972 Chevelles. The chassis is made from mandrel-bent 2x3-inch main rails, which boast torsional flex that is 200 percent less than that of a stock frame. The front suspension uses Schwartz-fabricated spindles and strut-rod-style lower control arms and upper control arms. The springs and shocks are Ridetech single-adjustable coil-overs. Schwartz fits the chassis with a 1-inch splined sway bar with billet arms and adjustable links. Teflon-lined spherical rod ends are used in the front suspension for much less bind than polyurethane bushings. Teflon is self-lubricating, so the rod ends are quieter than standard rod ends. The steering is a Ford-style Fox platform rack-and-pinion system. Brakes include Wilwood Engineering, Inc., six-piston front calipers with 13-inch rotors and Wilwood four-piston rears, also with 13-inch rotors. Baer brake packages are also available.

The Art Morrison GT-Sport chassis is also available for 1964–1967 and 1968–1972 Chevelles. The chassis is a unique design with mandrel bends and a special inner-angled frame rail that tucks under the floor for better ground clearance. It comes with Sport IFS control arms, C6 Corvette spindles, Strange Engineering adjustable coil-over shocks, front and rear sway bars, rack-and-pinion steering, triangulated rear four-bar suspension, and a 9-inch rear end housing. You can also order the chassis with front and rear brakes and a rear axle for a complete chassis.

Suspension

Moving on from the frame, there's quite a bit you can do with the front and rear suspension on a Chevelle to make the car perform better on the street and dragstrip, and turn corners better than the engineers at General Motors could have even imagined was possible in the 1960s and early 1970s.

If you keep an original frame, the front double A-arm suspension architecture is a very good system. There are a number of areas you can improve for better control and handling. The biggest drawback of the original Chevelle suspension is that the camber curve goes positive on the outboard tire in a corner. What that means is that the top of the tire actually leans out, reducing the effective contact patch of the tire to only a couple of inches during cornering.

Global West Suspension was one of the first companies to identify a cure for this, creating a redesigned tubular upper control arm for these cars in the early 1980s. This arm works in conjunction with a taller spindle to change the camber curve from positive to negative during cornering. This keeps the maximum tire contact patch on the ground. As a

CHAPTER 1

One option is to simply replace the entire chassis. Art Morrison Enterprises and Schwartz Performance offer complete chassis that bolt to the body. They are completely different, but offer many of the same features and fix the same issues found in the factory frame. These new chassis are far stiffer than the originals, providing far superior performance for drag racing and turning corners. They come with unique front suspension designs that can accept late-model Corvette brakes. They also convert the steering to rack-and-pinion. (Photo Courtesy Schwartz Performance)

side benefit, the spindles come from second-generation F- and B-cars, which had 10- or 11-inch disc brakes.

There are now several companies making their own versions of a negative-camber front suspension system, including ABC Performance, Detroit Speed, Inc. (DSE), Global West, and Hotchkis. They all have their own unique features and attributes, making it easy to find a system that fits the way you use your car and how you want it to perform. Most of these offer their own version of a taller spindle, some incorporating late-model Corvette-style spindles and accepting massive aftermarket brakes up to 14 inches in rotor diameter and with six-piston calipers. They also offer lower control arms, which are strong replacements for old and potentially cracked original arms.

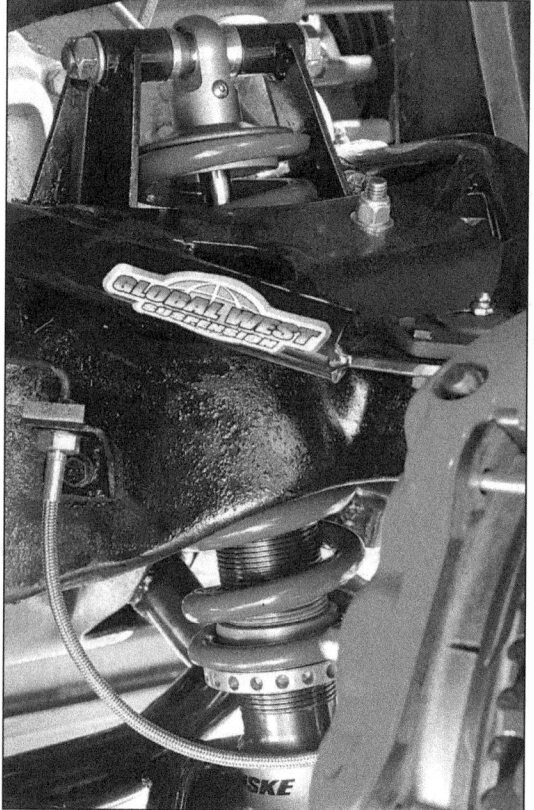

Several companies now offer conversions for the front suspension that place a coil-over in the stock shock and spring location. This conversion is quick and easy, and doesn't require any modification. However, the coil-over should be used with an aftermarket lower control arm designed to distribute the load over the circumference of the spring pocket, rather than just the two shock mounts. Global West Suspension has designed an extended-travel front suspension for A-Bodies allowing you to lower the car farther, but still have good suspension travel when using a coil-over. The kit includes a new upper mount welded into the frame to raise the upper coil-over mount. (Photo Courtesy Global West)

Many of the lower control arms shift the ball joint location forward to improve the caster in the suspension, and the design of the arm can make room for wider tires. The ABC Performance lower arms also offer a lowered spring pocket to lower the car without using a shorter spring; it can also be used in conjunction with a shorter spring for a much lower car that still has adequate suspension travel. ABC has also relocated the lower spring and shock mount to eliminate bind in the shock during suspension movement. This is especially beneficial when converting to a bolt-in coil-over shock, such as those offered by Ridetech and QA1.

Handling

Once you have the basic geometry of the front suspension keeping the tire planted on the ground through corners, you can turn your attention to more traditional means of improving handling, namely bushings, springs, shocks, and sway bars.

Bushings

Bushings may sound like a boring subject, but there are entire engineering teams dedicated to developing optimum bushing design. And in the aftermarket, the full gamut of technologies is being utilized.

Rubber bushings were used by General Motors in these Chevelles. Rubber is usually soft and absorbs some harshness and vibration from the road. Unfortunately, it also lets the control arms move several degrees under load, losing control over critical suspension geometry and making the suspension unpredictable under extreme use.

Polyurethane is a common upgrade from rubber, as it is stiffer and holds the control arms in place

Every company that makes a suspension kit for Chevelles offers slightly different solutions to providing great handling, and I don't want to oversimplify the differences. However, this DSE Speed Kit shows the concepts that are the same with most systems. The key change to the front suspension geometry is the use of a taller spindle and a shorter upper control arm. This changes the camber curve from positive to negative during a corner, making an unbelievable difference in handling capability and overall vehicle control. The kits usually also include tubular lower control arms, matched springs and shocks, and a sway bar that bolts on like the original one. (Photo Courtesy DSE)

better, yet still has some give. Rubber and polyurethane bushings can be made in an infinite range of hardness, measured with a durometer, so not all rubber and polyurethane is the same. Rubber and polyurethane bushings are installed in a way that resists movement in the control arm. The outer circumference of the bushing grips the control arm, while the inner circumference is held tight by the bolt. This is why you are supposed to torque the bushing bolts in place with the car sitting at ride height. Any movement of the control arm away from this position creates tension in the bushing, and the bushing tries to bring the arm back to this position. This can make the suspension feel stiff, regardless of the spring rate or shock valving.

Variations of solid bushings are another option. A solid bushing removes all play and movement, but can actually provide a better ride quality because there is no bind in the bushing, and the resistance to movement is managed completely by the shock and spring. Global West pioneered the use of Delrin as a bushing material. Using Delrin and aluminum, the company developed the Del-a-lum bushing, which removes virtually all deflection from the bushing and lets the control arms move smoothly without any resistance caused by the bushings. The material is also extremely durable and, in most cases, never needs to be replaced. ABC Performance and DSE also use Delrin bushings in their control arms.

CHAPTER 1

The last type of bushing isn't a bushing at all, but a spherical rod end. Purpose-built race cars use rod ends on their control arms to eliminate deflection, and they also make the link adjustable in length. The drawbacks are that rod ends typically make noise, and they wear.

Springs and Shocks

Springs and shocks should be considered as a matched package. In fact, coil-overs are a popular upgrade, and companies literally package the spring and shock together as one component. The primary function of the springs is to hold the weight of the car, while the job of the shocks is to control the movement of the suspension. The original coil springs in these cars were tall and soft, which gave the cars a family car ride quality. This also allows tons of body roll in a corner, which is not good for handling.

Higher spring rates and shorter springs lower the car and reduce body roll, contributing to better handling characteristics. Significant changes in the spring rate also reduces ride quality. This is where you start to make compromises if you want ultimate performance. The same is true of shock choice, but there are quite a few adjustable shocks on the market that let you reduce the firmness of the valving for street driving and tune them for optimum performance on the track.

Looking at the rear suspension, the basic four-link system that General Motors designed is pretty good. The shortcomings in this system are the open-channel control arms and the rubber bushings, both of which allow deflection. When you're trying to launch a Chevelle hard or toss it into a corner, the control arms twist and move in ways they are not supposed to, causing a loss of traction. Traction is impossible until you have better control over the rear axle.

There are quite a few companies making control arms from round and rectangular tube stock that eliminate the possibility of the control arm twisting, including all of the companies listed earlier that make front suspension components. Many of them also offer adjustable-length upper control arms, which let you dial in the pinion angle of the rear axle. This is very important if you have lowered the ride height of the car. With a four-link system, the pinion angle changes as you raise or lower the car, and changing the permanent ride height requires adjusting the pinion angle for traction, driveline smoothness, and U-joint durability. Bushings in the rear control arms include all of the variations mentioned for the front suspension systems.

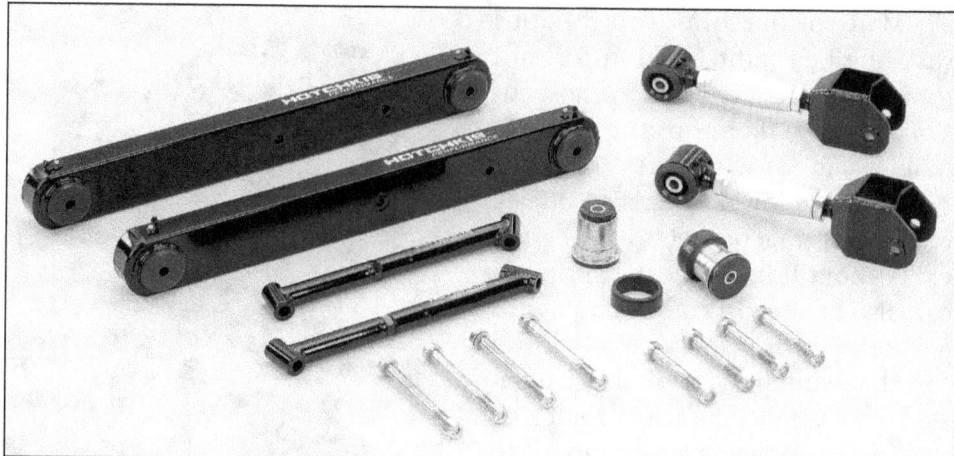

For the rear suspension, available kits tackle the issues slightly differently, but have many similarities. This rear suspension system from Hotchkis Sport Suspension includes tubular upper and lower control arms. The Hotchkis arms are rectangular, while many others are made from round tube. These control arms remove flex and uncontrolled movement from the rear suspension to let the rear suspension work the way it was designed to. This increases traction during straight-line acceleration and cornering. Hotchkis and others also include trailing-arm-mount braces that reinforce the upper control arm chassis mounts. (Photo Courtesy Hotchkis)

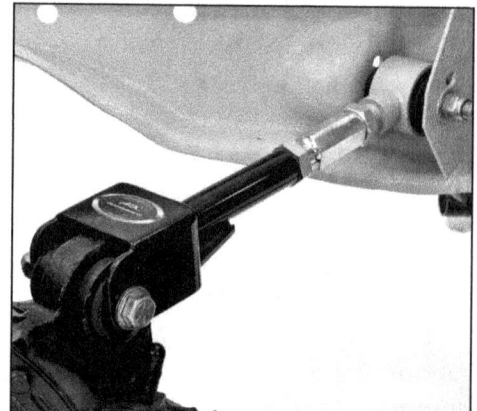

ABC Performance, DSE, Global West, and Hotchkis offer adjustable upper control arms for the rear suspension. These let you adjust the pinion angle, which is critical when you change the ride height of the vehicle or switch to a Ford 9-inch rear, which drops the pinion location. In addition, DSE makes adjustable lower control arms that give you the ability to move the axle slightly forward or rearward in the chassis and further tune the rear suspension.

CHASSIS UPGRADES

Air Ride

All of the suspension companies included in this chapter have unique aspects to their product line. Ridetech, however, has a completely different approach when it comes to springs and shocks. Yes, it offers coil-overs for Chevelles, but it also offers an air suspension system designed with performance in mind.

The system includes air springs that can be adjusted with air pressure, changing the ride height and the spring rate. In the front suspension, Ridetech ShockWaves are used, which are like a coil-over with the air spring and adjustable shock integrated into one unit. At the rear, they are separated so that each mounts in place of the original spring and shock.

The air system is powered by an onboard compressor, air tank, and control system called the Air-Pod RidePRO e3. The system lowers the ride height 3 inches in the front of the car and 4 inches in the rear, and lets you drop the car another 2 to 3 inches when it's parked.

The Level 3 kit includes StrongArms, Ridetech tall spindles, and MuscleBar sway bar for a complete suspension system. (Photo Courtesy RideTech)

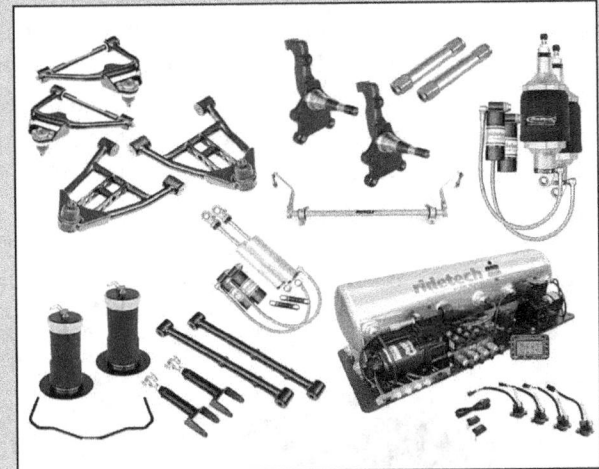

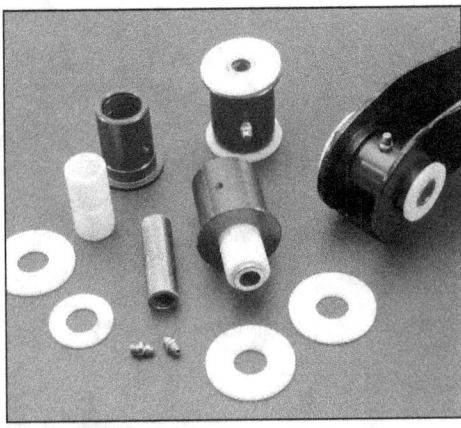

Another area of suspension where opinions vary widely is bushing material. Rubber was the original bushing material through the entire chassis in a Chevelle, and it is pretty much shunned now because it lets the suspension mounting points move too much (called deflection) under load. Polyurethane is popular, as it is stiffer than rubber and limits deflection. Del-a-lum bushings are an innovation of Global West. They combine a solid aluminum bushing (blue) with a nylon material called Delrin (white). The result is a bushing with virtually zero deflection and zero noise, but the design of the bushing eliminates bind in the bushing as the suspension moves. The result is an improvement in ride quality with the least amount of bushing deflection. (Photo Courtesy Global West)

In addition, ABC Performance uses sealed and greased spherical bushings. These allow the suspension to move through its full range of motion without binding.

If you want to retain the original coil spring and separate shock arrangement at the rear, there are lots of options for you. Each of the companies included in this chapter have a variety of combinations that have been found to work well to lower the car and provide a good compromise between ride quality and handling to meet most expectations.

Another option is to convert the rear to a coil-over system. There is a little more involved at the rear of the car than there is at the front to do a coil-over conversion. The natural location for a coil-over at the rear is where the original shocks mounted, but the upper and lower mounts need to be strengthened in order to now manage load-carrying as well as shock-absorbing duty.

Kits range from bolt-on conversions like DSE's, which includes upper and lower mounting brackets. The ABC Performance kit includes bolt-on brackets and an upper-mount support brace. The Global West system has weld-on brackets to move the coil-overs in front of the axle and mount them to the original upper spring pocket in the frame.

Sway Bars

The last part of the suspension system to cover is sway bars. Even though they're covered at the end of the chapter, they should be considered part of the ride and handling

CHEVELLE PERFORMANCE PROJECTS: 1964–1972

CHAPTER 1

Beyond tubular rear control arms, which should be considered a must, many companies offer a coil-over conversion for the rear. The methods vary, with differing opinions on the best mounting locations for strength versus ease of installation. The bottom line, though, is that it's now possible to do a completely bolt-on coil-over conversion on the front and rear of your Chevelle, providing adjustable ride height and shock valving.

package, and they should be selected at the same time you decide on the spring rate and shock valving for your Chevelle. The sway bars create resistance to body roll, applying pressure to the opposite side of the chassis when body roll is experienced. A stiff sway bar can take the place of extremely high spring rates and shock valving to provide a better ride quality with good handling characteristics.

There are lots of bolt-on sway bar options available for Chevelles that meet the needs of most people building a good-performance car. For more extreme capability, splined sway bars are popular and a few kits are available to install them on Chevelles. These use larger-diameter bars and longer levers, and they typically offer a range of adjustment to fine-tune the chassis.

Project 1: Frame Boxing

Choose Frame Boxing Kit

1 One of the most important things you can do to strengthen your chassis is to box the open-channel frame rail. For years, people have used race fabrication shops to make plates and weld them in place to box the frame. ABC Performance now makes a Frame Boxing Kit that provides CNC laser-cut plates specifically for this purpose. You can either use the company's two-piece kit that boxes the center of the frame, or the four-piece kit that also boxes the rear section behind the axle. The center section is most critical for chassis integrity.

Straighten Rear Section of Frame

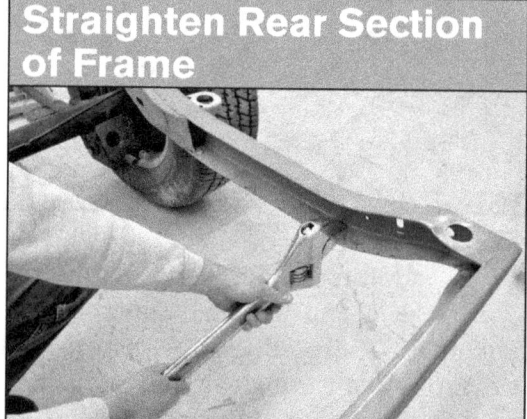

2 Remove the fuel tank to box the rear sections. It is easiest if you remove the body, although you could theoretically do this if you just raised the body off the frame far enough to weld and grind the top part of the frame. Since the original frame is at least 40 years old, you probably need to straighten out the upper and lower sections. A very large adjustable wrench works well for this.

CHASSIS UPGRADES

Fit and Tack Weld Box-in Plates to Frame

3 Use the box-in plates from ABC Performance as a template and work the open frame sections until they meet the plates uniformly along the top and bottom. The installation looks much better if you spend extra time getting the fitment as close to perfect as possible. The plates are made to allow you to make corner welds with a MIG welder along the top and bottom sections of the frame. This provides very good welding penetration for a strong frame section when finished. Make sure the original frame metal is clean from paint, grease, and rust before you start welding. When you are ready to weld the plate in place, start by tacking it about every 6 inches around the entire plate.

Work Box-in Plates into Position

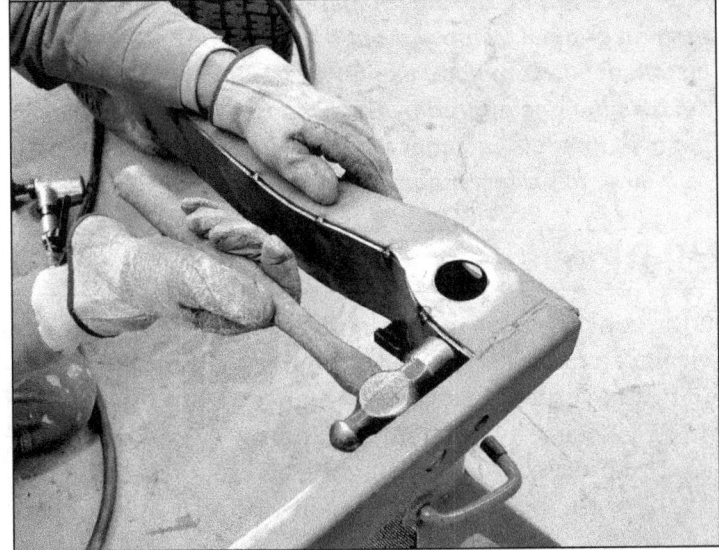

4 The rear sections are CNC-pressed to follow the curve of the rear frame around the body-mount bolt near the rear bumper. With the rest of the rear box-in plate tacked in place, you may have to tap the end with a hammer to get it to perfectly match your frame. Access to the body bolt is preserved through an opening in the bottom of the frame once the box-in plate is installed.

Determine Brake and Fuel Line Routing

5 You need to decide what you want to do with the brake and fuel lines before you box in the center section. The original brake and fuel lines ran on the inside of the open-channel frame. Some people may want to leave them there, where they are hidden and protected. Realize, however, that you won't be able to access them once the frame is boxed. The alternative is to remove them and route new brake and fuel lines on the outside of the fully boxed frame. The installation process for the center sections is exactly like the rear.

Grind Off Excess Welds on Frame

6 Once the box-in plates are completely welded in place, use an abrasive disc on a grinder to finish the welds. You may have to fill in sections with more weld to get the look you want, and you can round the edge to make it look similar to the outer section of the frame.

Apply Frame Powdercoating or Paint

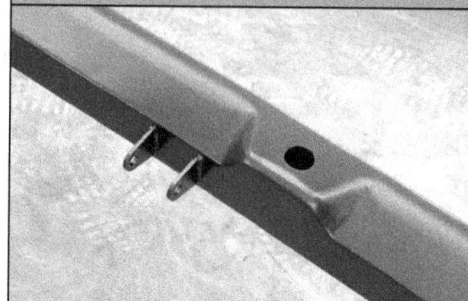

7 This is what the center section looked like on this car after the frame was painted. In addition to relocating fuel and brake lines, boxing the center of the frame also required a new transmission crossmember. ABC Performance makes a tubular crossmember for these Chevelles that comes with chassis tabs to mount the crossmember on the inside of the boxed frame rails. The company has done testing and found that a factory frame with its four-piece Frame Boxing Kit installed is four times stiffer than an original frame without the frame boxed. Once the installation is complete, use an internal frame coating, such as the one offered by Eastwood. This comes with a hose kit that lets you coat the inside length of the closed frame rail to protect it against rust.

Project 2: Tubular Control Arm Kit Installation

The Chevelle's stock suspension is based on antiquated technology, and its stamped-steel control arms were designed to cope with forces generated from moderately aggressive street driving with bias-ply tires on 14- and 15-inch wheels. Upgrading to large aftermarket brakes and larger 17- to 20-inch wheels and sticky radial tires places more force on the suspension, and therefore, a high-performance suspension kit is a suitable addition to a high-performance chassis package. Front suspension kits are available from a number of aftermarket manufacturers, such as ABC Performance, Detroit Speed, Global West, and Hotchkis, just to name a few. These kits, when used with complementary brake, steering, and chassis-strengthening components, produce a balanced chassis and suspension performance that rivals or exceeds new car standards.

Assembling the front suspension under a 1964–1972 Chevelle is fairly straight-forward. The process is very similar for nearly all of the performance kits available from various manufacturers. In this project, we are showing the installation of a Hotchkis Performance front suspension system, including upper and lower tubular control arms, performance-lowering coil springs, shocks, and bushings.

Attach Lower Control Arm to Chassis

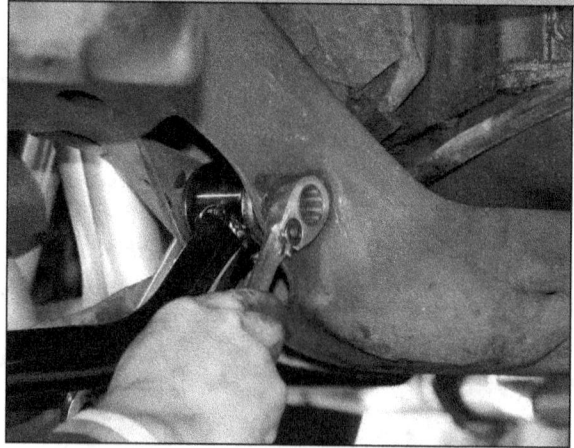

1 The first step is to bolt the lower control arm into place. Inspect the mounting tabs on the frame to make sure they are not bent and that the mounting holes are not elongated. Thread the nuts onto the bolts to hold the lower control arm in position, but do not tighten them yet. (Photo Courtesy Hotchkis Sport Suspension)

CHASSIS UPGRADES

Attach Upper Control Arm to Chassis

2 As with the lower control arms, bolt the upper control arm on the frame, also leaving the fasteners loose. Place the polyurethane spring cushion on top of the coil spring. It may help to tape the cushion to the spring for installation. Position the spindle on the lower control arm ball joint. While holding the spring in position, use a jack under the lower control arm to rotate the arm and spindle upward. *(Photo Courtesy Hotchkis Sport Suspension)*

Bolt Ball Joint into Spindle

3 With most lowerering coil springs, you are able to compress the spring sufficiently with the jack and the weight of the vehicle to insert the upper ball joint stud into the spindle. If you are doing this with the engine out of the car, reducing the weight of the vehicle, or have taller springs, you will need to use spring compressors to reduce the height of the coil spring enough to bolt the upper arm to the spindle. You can usually rent these from a local auto parts store. *(Photo Courtesy Hotchkis Sport Suspension)*

Align Spring and Install Castle Nuts

4 Ensure that the coil spring is sitting in both spring pockets: inside the framerail on the top of the spring and in the lower control arm on the bottom of the spring. Tighten the upper and lower ball joint castle nuts and install the cotter pins. You can now install the new shocks, slipping them in place through the lower control arms. *(Photo Courtesy Hotchkis Sport Suspension)*

CHAPTER 1

Reinstall Brake Caliper

5 If you are not changing the spindle or brake system, you don't need to take this assembly apart or re-assemble it to change the suspension components shown here. The brake caliper is the only thing that needs to be removed, allowing you to remove the spindle and rotor from the car. Fill the ball joints and control arm bushings with grease using a grease gun. Tighten the upper and lower control arms once the car is sitting on all four tires at ride height. (Photo Courtesy Hotchkis Sport Suspension)

Mount Sway Bar

6 This car was upgraded to a Hotchkis Extreme Performance Sway Bar. The sway bar frame brackets thread into captured nuts inside the frame rails. Check that the nuts are still welded in place. It's a good idea to run a tap through them to clean the threads before installing a new sway bar. (Photo Courtesy Hotchkis Sport Suspension)

Grease Sway Bar Bushings

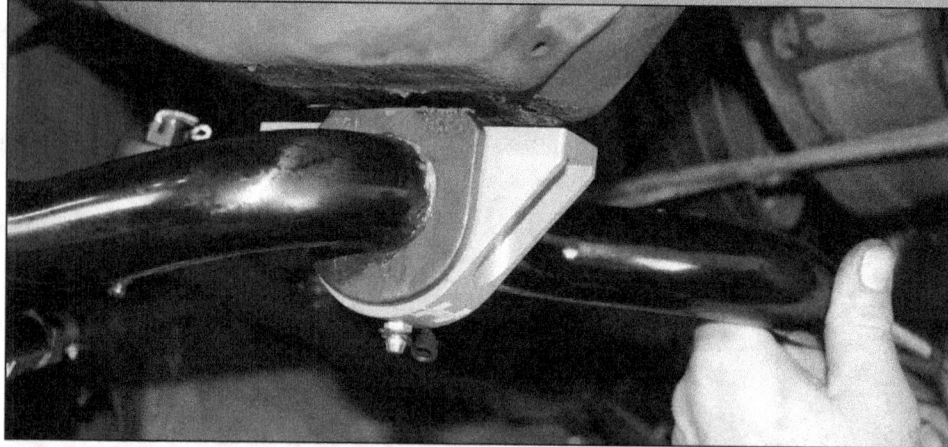

7 This is a tubular 1 3/8-inch front sway bar that is both durable and lightweight. A larger-diameter sway bar dramatically limits body roll without reducing ride quality. The frame mounts for the bar are Hotchkis heavy-duty billet brackets, machined from 7075 aluminum. Grease the bushings after bolting the brackets in place. (Photo Courtesy Hotchkis Sport Suspension)

Attach Sway Bar Endlinks to Control Arms

8 Bolt the endlinks to the lower control arms and then to the sway bar. You can adjust the length of the endlinks to accommodate various ride heights and to ensure that the sway bar and endlinks clear the suspension and tire. (Photo Courtesy Hotchkis Sport Suspension)

Project 3: Mini Tub Kit Installation

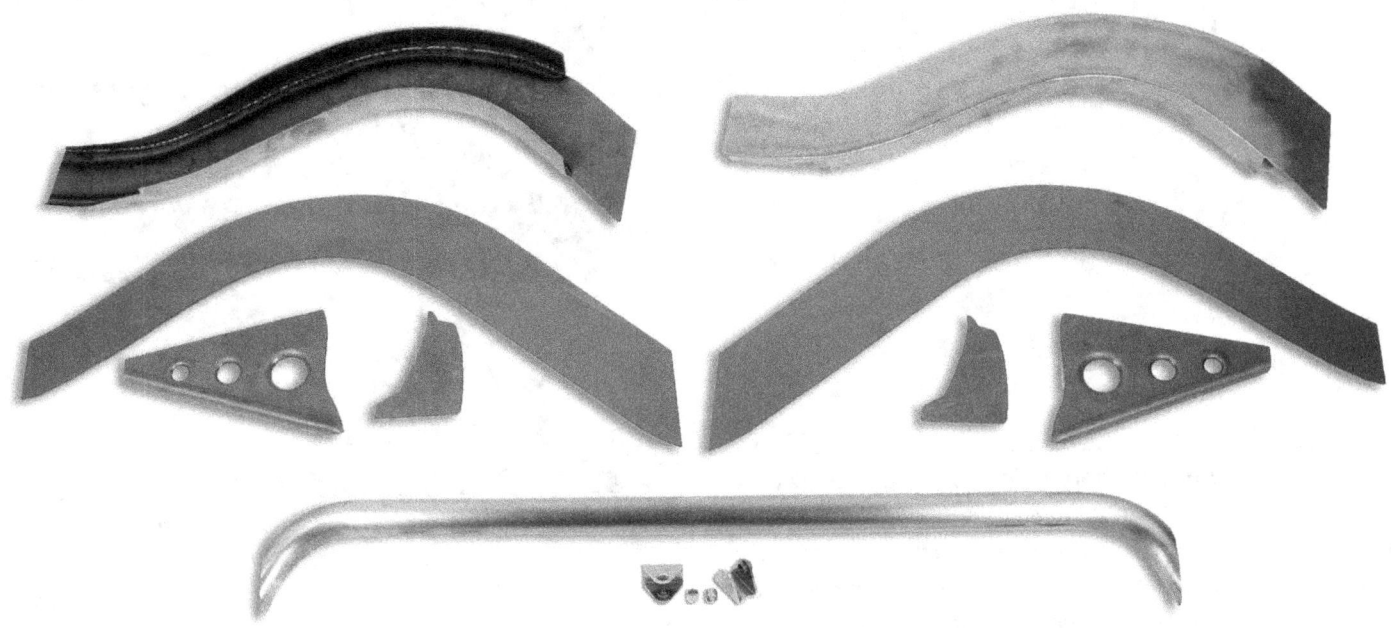

ABC Performance now makes a Mini Tub Frame Kit to fit 335/30ZR18 tires under the rear of a 1966–1967 Chevelle and 315/30ZR18s under a 1964–1965 Chevelle by moving the frame rails inward approximately 2 inches. In addition it's now offering a kit for 1968–1972 Chevelles. The kit lets you keep your rear control arms and does not require a narrowed rear axle. It includes 3/16-inch outer plates, 1/8-inch C-channel inner sections, and reinforcement gussets to create new frame sections that are stronger than the originals. A new upper shock-mount crossmember further strengthens the chassis and provides mounts for coil-overs. The new frame sections and gussets are CNC laser-cut, and the crossmember is formed in a CNC tubing bender.

Level and True the Frame

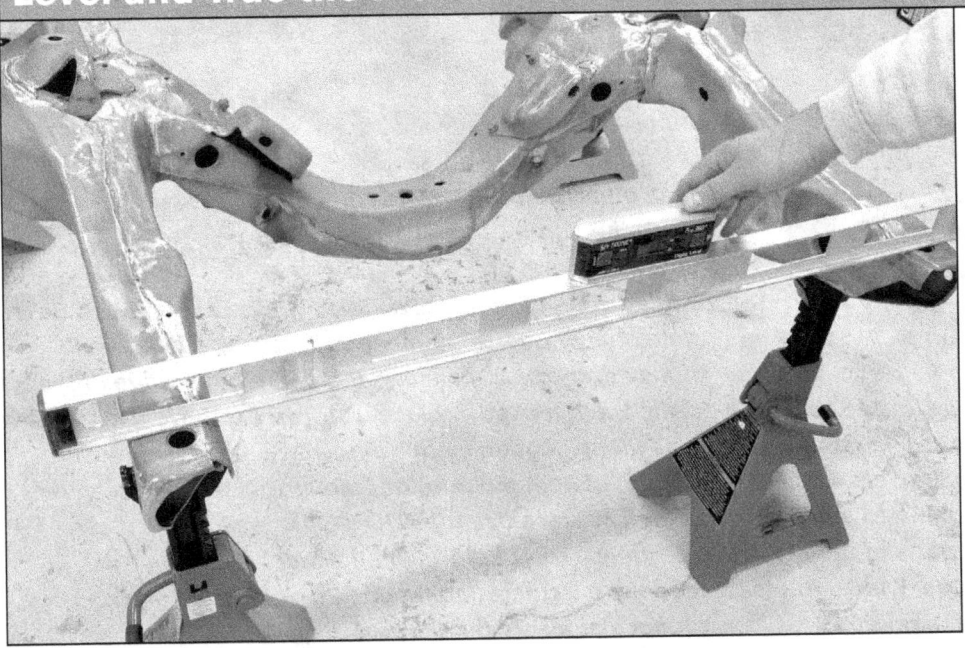

1 Before you start the installation of the ABC Performance Mini Tub Frame Kit, level the chassis at the front and rear. Write the distance on the floor between the frame and the floor in several places on both sides of the frame and check these measurements before doing your final welding. If the frame is not straight, have it straightened before you start installing this kit.

CHAPTER 1

Mark to Cut Frame Rail

2 The kit comes with frame dimensions and a drawing showing all mounting holes and height measurements so you know exactly where to cut. The process can be intimidating because you cut and weld the frame over the rear axle, but working slowly and double-checking your work results in a chassis that is stronger than it was originally. Coat the general area to be cut with machinist's die. This makes it easy to scribe a mark where you will be cutting. Also cut off the original upper shock and spring mount, but keep the upper control-arm crossmember and the body mount above the rear axle in place.

Cut Frame

3 Before you start cutting, weld steel tubing or strapping to the inner side of the frame rail in front of and behind the sections you cut. This retains the shape over the rear axle while you are reconstructing the frame rails. Do one side of the frame at a time to leave as much structure in place as possible. A high-speed cut-off wheel is the best way to cut the frame rail. The body mount behind the rear wheels must be relocated later. For now, cut the mount off the frame, but do so carefully so it can be welded back on later.

Cut Frame (Continued)

4 At the forward section of the frame rail, cut a section of the original frame approximately 4 inches long along the top and bottom. Use a C-clamp to pull the section against the new upper and lower parts of the frame rail. Use a cut-off tool to trim the area. Weld it to the top and bottom to form the new inner frame rail.

Tack Weld Box Plates

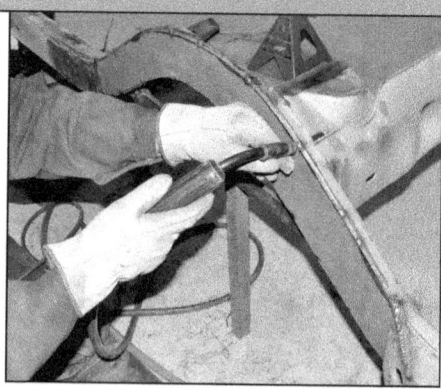

5 The outer section is made from 3/16-inch steel, and it is important that the two sections meet each other uniformly along the edges where they are welded. The outer plate should be held in place with tack welds approximately every 6 inches along the entire outer edge of the plate. Once tacked in place, you can finish-weld it, working in sections about 6 inches long at a time to limit the amount of heat put into the frame. This entire kit can be welded in place using a MIG welder, as long as it can adequately weld 3/16-inch mild steel. Typically, this requires a welder running on 220-volt power and can produce at least 160 amps of output.

CHASSIS UPDATES

Weld C-channel Plates into Place

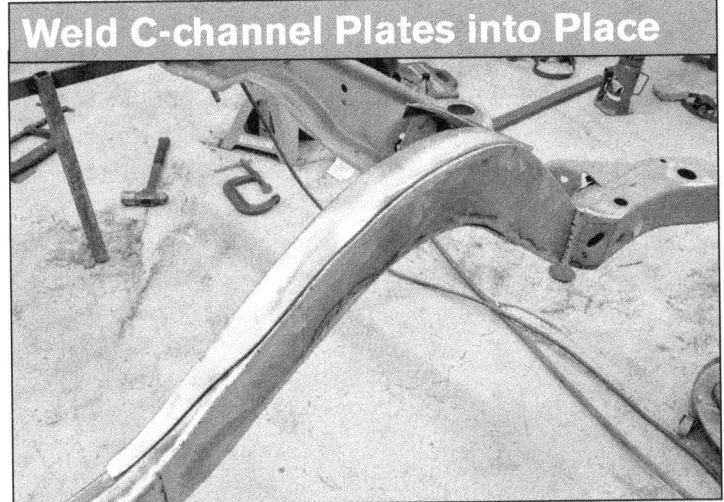

6 With the outer plates welded in place and the welds ground smooth, you can slip the new inner C-channel section in place. It should be a snug fit, and you may need to grind a little here and there to get it into position. Use C-clamps on the top and bottom of the frame section to get it to lay flat. Weld it in place, using the same technique of tack welds and finish-welding that you used for the outer frame section. Grind the welds smooth, and you're finished with one frame rail; repeat the process on the other side.

Weld Gussets to Frame Rail

7 The Mini Tub Frame Kit includes gussets to weld between the top of the frame rail and the upper control arm cross-member. This triangulates and reinforces the frame rail in this section and the crossmember. This gusset is tucked up against the floor when you set the body back in place.

Reposition Rear Frame Rails

8 Move the finished frame rail is moved inboard approximately 2 inches, making room for massive tires under the rear of the Chevelle. On this specific Chevelle, a wide wheel and tire combination placed the tire so close to the frame that it rubbed occasionally during corning. Note the additional space after the Mini Tub Frame Kit was installed. You do not need to move the lower control arm mount on the rear axle or build a new narrowed axle.

Move Body Mount Plate Rearward

9 Remove the mounts on the body by drilling out the spot welds. Move the mounts on the body and the corresponding mounts on the frame rearward approximately 3 inches. This positions them behind the modifications made to the frame and wheel tubs.

Mark Position of Body Mount Plate

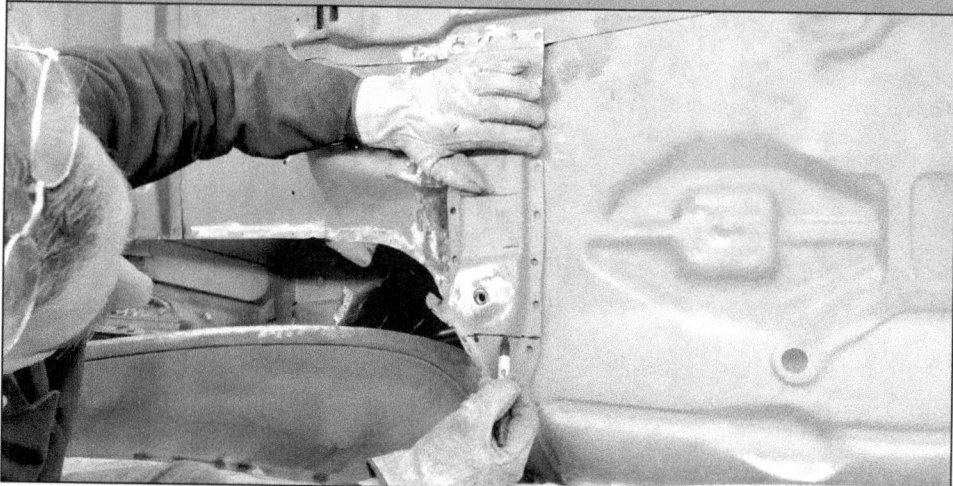

10 Mark the body mount where it can be trimmed, and position it rearward on the underside of the body. Install the mount on the frame the exact distance rearward, and match the position on the left to the right side of the body.

Cut Out Wheel Well

11 Moving the frame rails in by 2 inches means that the inner part of the wheel tubs must also be moved 2 inches inward to fit the larger tires. By the time you read this, ABC Performance will have its new, stamped-steel, wider wheel tubs available, which changes the next few steps slightly. Decide whether to install new, wider wheel tubs or stretch your stock ones. Precisely measure and mark where the new tubs or wheel well extensions will be placed. Use a cut off tool to remove the inner section of the wheel tub from the car. This also requires removing the trunk springs from the hinges and cutting the lower part of the hinge mounts off of the inner wheel tubs.

Weld Metal Strip to Inner Wheel Tub

12 Weld a 2-inch-wide strip of sheet metal to the inner wheel tub that was cut out. Use the new wheel tub as a template to trim the floor section to fit the new, wider wheel tub. The new wheel tub has 14½ inches of clearance at the wheel lip. The inner lip of the wheel tub is right above the frame rail. This fixes the tire clearance at the frame rail, but the outer section of the wheel tub comes inward toward the tire.

CHASSIS UPDATES

Trim Outer Wheel Tub

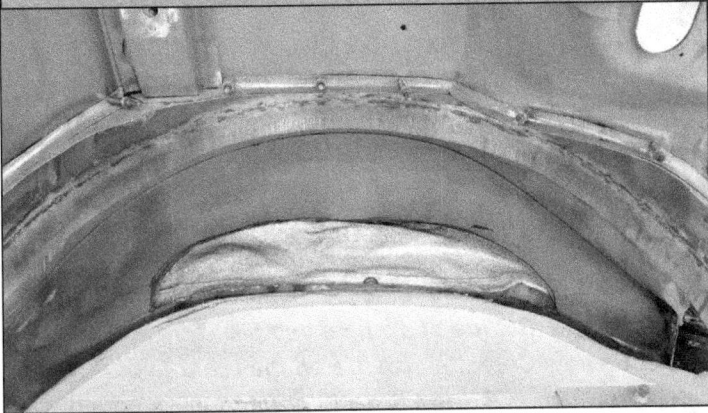

13 Mark the entire section of the outer wheel tub where it protrudes unnecessarily into the tire opening and cut it out. Cut this area very carefully, as the quarter panel is on the other side of the outer wheel tub, and it is very close to it near the wheel lip. Form a new section of metal that curves outward, away from the tire, to maximize tire clearance.

Inspect Finished Wheel Tub

14 Here is the finished wheel tub as seen from the trunk. You could grind and finish the welds on this side of the wheel tub to make it look completely factory. This wheel tub will be coated with trunk splatter paint, which will make this seam disappear. Straighten the trunk hinge mounts and attach them to the relocated inner wheel tubs.

Here is the finished frame with the ABC Performance Mini Tub Frame Kit installed and painted in Eastwood Chassis Black. The tubular upper coil-over crossmember mounted aft of the rear axle section is also part of the kit.

CHAPTER 1

On a 1966–1967 Chevelle, this conversion allows you to use a 12-inch-wide wheel. The earlier Chevelles are a bit more limited in outer tire clearance and do not use quite as wide of a wheel and tire. This kit lets you put a new Corvette-size tire on the rear of your Chevelle, which is a great benefit for ultimate handling, and also helps straight-line acceleration.

Project 4: Suspension Kit Installation

Remove Front Suspension

1 The front suspension systems covered in this chapter bolt onto the original frame using the factory locations. That means installing one of these kits is as simple as removing the old parts, installing the new ones, and having the front end aligned when you're finished. A complete kit includes new spindles, which means a brake upgrade, even if you have a later car with factory disc brakes. Use a spring compressor to decrease the tension on the A-arms before releasing the upper ball joint to disassemble the original suspension.

Spread Lower Control Arm Bracket

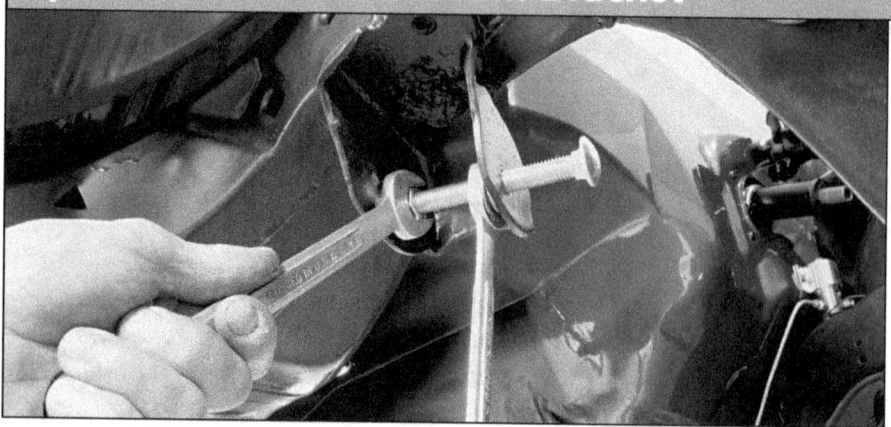

2 Begin installing the new suspension with the lower control arm. You may need to spread the frame bracket slightly to get the arm to slide into place. You can make a tool to do this out of a long carriage bolt or threaded rod, body washer, and a couple of nuts. You can also use a large adjustable wrench. As you assemble the front suspension, do not tighten the bolts until you are completely done.

CHASSIS UPDATES

Install Spring

3 Insert the spring into the frame pocket and the pocket of the lower control arm. Place a floor jack under the A-arm to help control it. On this ABC Performance front suspension with a coil-over conversion the coil-over is installed. Next, you bolt the upper A-arm onto the original frame mount. With the floor jack still under the lower A-arm, set the spindle on the lower ball joint. One person needs to raise the jack while another guides the spindle to line up with the upper ball joint. Once the spindle has been installed in the ball joint, torque down the retaining nut to the provided torque spec and insert a cotter pin.

Install Shocks

4 If you're using a coil-over front suspension, bolt the top and bottom of the coil-over in place. Note the location of the two adjustment knobs on the QA1 double-adjustable coil-overs used in this ABC Performance system. One knob adjusts the damping of compression while the other adjusts rebound. The single-adjustable coil-overs change compress and rebound with a single knob.

Torque Down Fasteners

5 With everything bolted in place, you can torque the fasteners. Every kit has slightly different specs, and you need to follow the company's directions explicitly. Systems that use all Delrin bushings can have the upper and lower control arms torqued in any position. If there is any rubber or polyurethane in the system, you need to have the suspension compressed to ride height before torqueing the fasteners. The complete ABC Performance front suspension includes adjustable upper control arms. They use threaded ends with locknuts to allow adjustments in camber and caster instead of using shims between the A-arm and the frame mount. The kit is also available with two styles of sway bars: a 1⅛-inch solid bar that is similar in design and attachment as the original, and a splined bar (shown). The splined bar allows for more adjustment and higher performance. It has flat links tucked tight against the frame rail to make room for wider wheels and tires.

CHAPTER 2

BUILDING A PERFORMANCE STEERING SYSTEM

Two aspects of building a performance Chevelle are critical to safety as well as performance: steering and brakes (covered in Chapter 5). This chapter covers upgrading your Chevelle's steering system to provide precise and reliable cornering.

One of the things that make a Chevelle so desirable to build into an all-around performance car is that the basic systems are good, and the steering system is a great example. It uses a forward-mounted recirculating ball steering box; the steering linkage uses a robust center link and idler arm configuration; and the steering column doesn't have any complicated angles in it. To build the ultimate performance steering system for your car, you don't have to reengineer anything.

With that said, there is quite a bit of room for improvement to be had with bolt-on upgrades. Many of these cars came with manual steering, which is great for keeping weight low for drag racing, but not very good for turning corners in a performance manner. The original or generic replacement steering linkage is probably worn and sloppy, and the

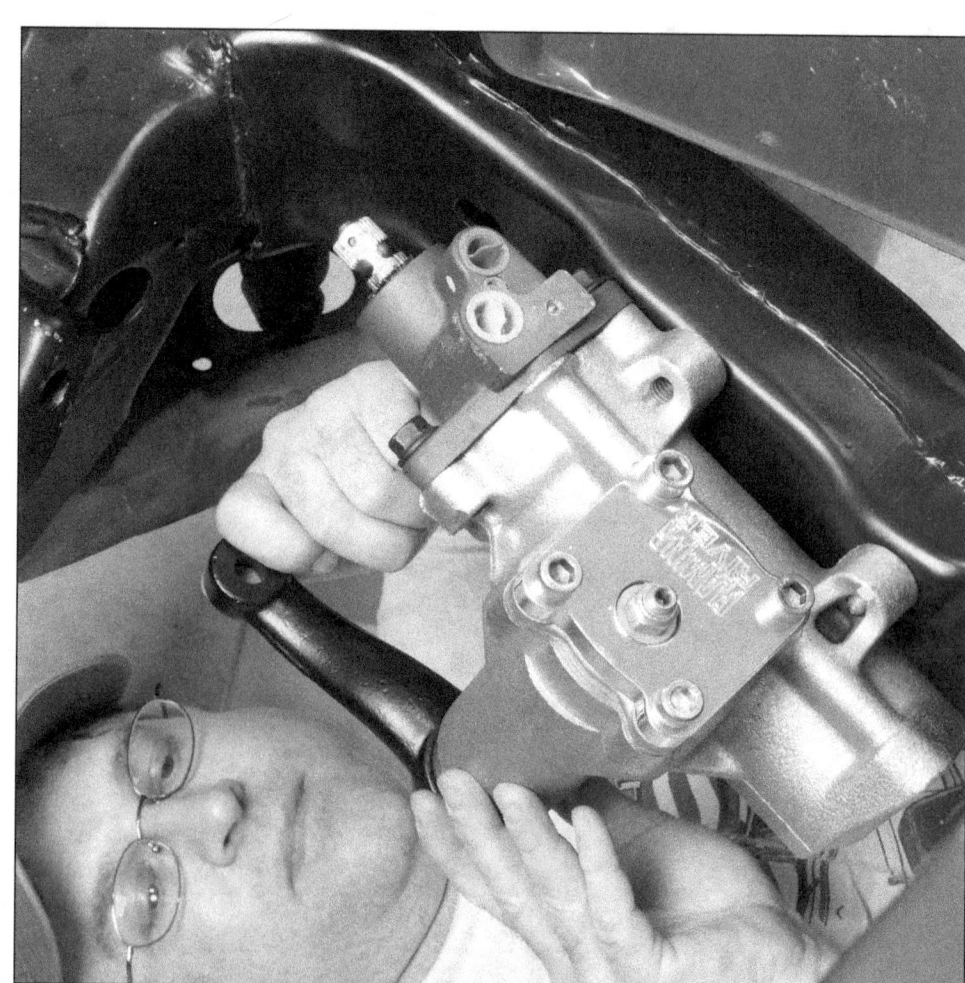

All Chevelles came with a recirculating-ball-style steering box. They also came with pretty slow ratios, because the concept of driving fast through a corner with these larger cars was still decades away. One of the best upgrades you can make is to install a new steering box with a performance ratio.

BUILDING A PERFORMANCE STEERING SYSTEM

The design of the Saginaw steering box didn't change for decades. In the past, you could go to the salvage yard and grab a box from a later performance car and bolt it onto your Chevelle. That's still an option, but that salvage yard box is so old it needs a rebuild. I recommend a new box like this one from Flaming River that eliminates the possibility of installing worn and damaged parts.

original steering columns in 1966 and earlier cars are prone to bearing failure; not to mention that it sure would be nice to have a tilt column, which was not too common in these cars.

Steering Box

The steering box is the heart of the steering system. More than any other component, it determines the performance and feel of the steering system. The original manual and power boxes used on Chevelles were made by Saginaw Steering Gear, a division of, and later a supplier to, General Motors. The same basic design was used on everything from trucks to performance cars for the better part of 70 years.

For many years, these cars were used by those with an interest in drag racing. For that purpose, an original manual steering box was the most desirable. It was lightweight and turned easily enough with narrow front tires on a typical drag-race car. Now that building a Chevelle to handle well is in vogue, completely different characteristics are required. Larger front tires require a lot more effort to steer, and trying to steer them when cornering further increases the effort. Most people also use a smaller-diameter steering wheel, which reduces the leverage, requiring still more effort. A good-quality power steering box and pump are the solution.

For the cost of finding a salvage yard box on a performance car and having it rebuilt, you can purchase a brand-new box with a fast ratio and performance valving from several companies. The Flaming River Industries steering box is an all-new piece with a cast housing and new internal components, including a rack-and-pinion valve spool for smooth and precise steering. It is available in 12:1, 14:1, and 16:1 ratios.

The ratio of the box you choose for your Chevelle is critical to how the car responds to steering inputs. The first number is how many degrees your steering wheel is turned compared to how many degrees the wheels are turned. The larger the first number, the slower the ratio, and there's a huge difference in feeling with just a two-digit difference in ratio. The original power-steering boxes were 15:1 or higher numerically, depending on the year and model. The new 12:1 boxes are extremely fast, and are ideal for autocross competition where going from full lock to full lock very quickly is a significant advantage.

That ratio may be a bit too fast, however, for higher speed racing that you might do on an open road course. The amount of steering action produced by just a little bit of steering wheel movement may create a twitchy feeling at speed, which is also undesirable for driving on the freeway. So the ratio that is right for your car depends on how you use the car. If you're only interested in autocrossing and car shows, then a 12:1 box gives you the best performance. If you also do high-speed driving, a 14:1 box is often a better choice.

Steering Linkage

A steering linkage system sits between the steering box and the wheels. Chevelles use a robust system used by General Motors on vehicles all the way up to heavy-duty trucks. The system is made up of a Pitman arm bolted to the steering box and attached to a center link connecting the left and right sides together. An

CHAPTER 2

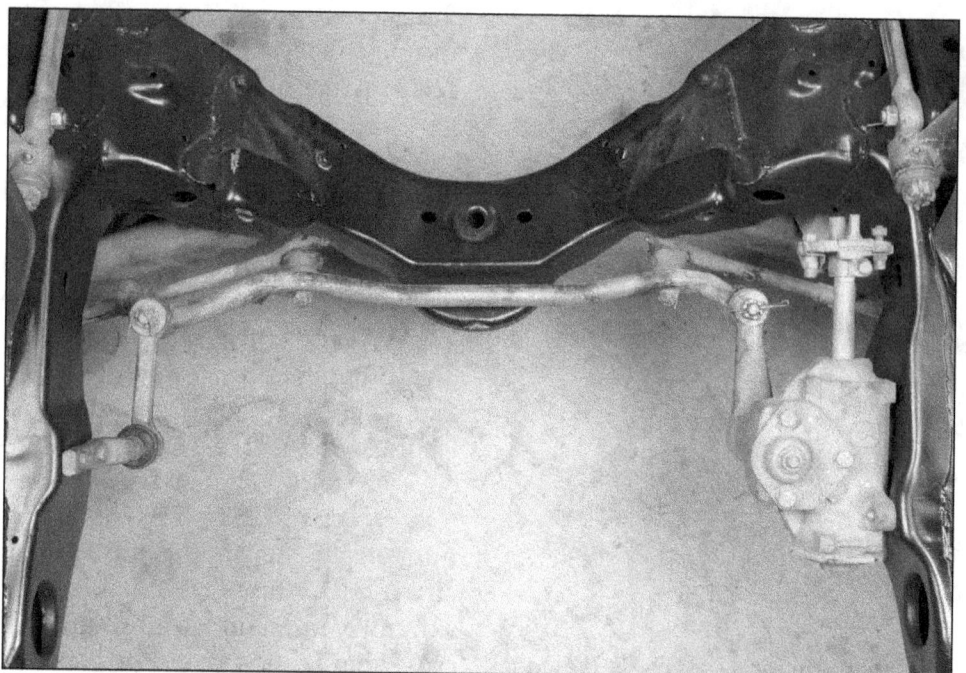

In addition to a new box, you should replace all of the steering linkage. If you start with a fresh, high-quality center link, inner and outer tie rods, and idler arm, you are in good shape. You put a lot more stress on these parts as you turn corners two to three times faster than these cars were capable of in stock form.

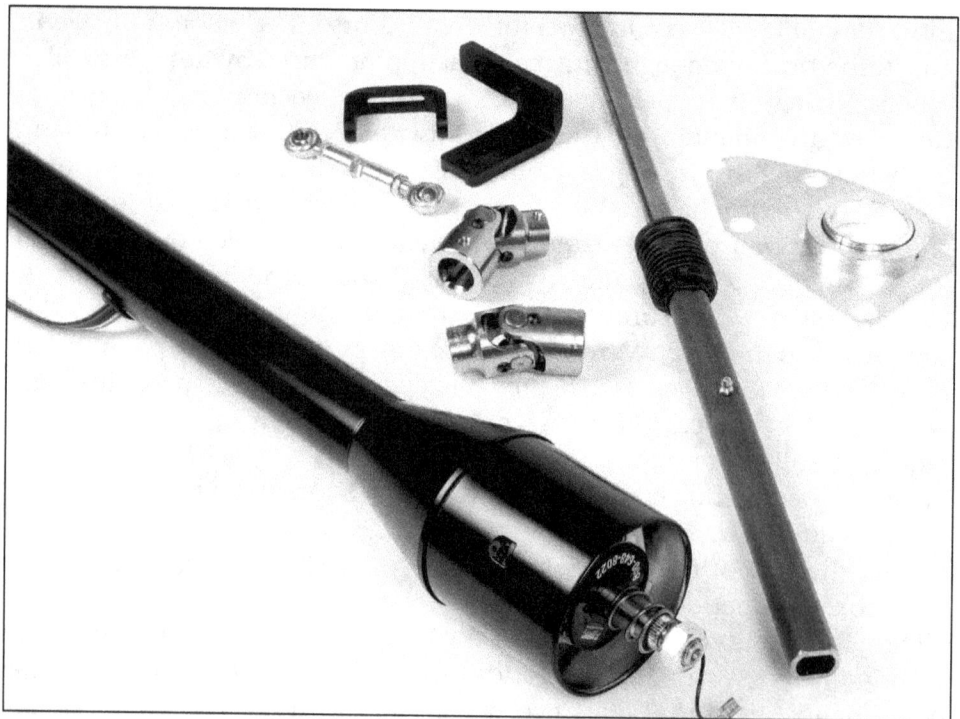

One of the most popular upgrades to the steering system is a new steering column. This is a tilt unit from Flaming River. There are a lot of options available in columns now, including direct-fit units. However, a direct-fit still requires fabricating a new steering shaft from the base of the column to the steering box.

idler arm connects the center link to the passenger-side frame rail. This and the Pitman arm are the locating points and where the leverage occurs, moving the wheels left and right as you steer. In addition, the left and right tie rods attach to the center link and also to the spindles. Each tie rod is actually made up of two tie rod ends and a threaded sleeve, which allows for toe adjustment, meaning how far the front tires point in or out relative to each other.

The center link, idler arm, and tie rod ends all have ball joints at the connection points. This allows them to solidly connect to each other, but move through various arcs as you steer from right to left. These ball joints are the primary components that wear out over time. Replacing these parts is relatively easy.

The upgrades to consider for steering linkage are good-quality replacement components and solid tie-rod adjustment sleeves. As I said, this system is very robust, and failures typically happen when a part is worn out or you hit the wall at 150 mph, at which time a broken steering linkage is the least of your concerns.

Steering Column

The upper bearing assembly in the steering column of 1966 and earlier Chevelles is prone to failure. When it fails, the steering shaft wobbles around inside the column as you steer, the turn signals don't operate properly, and sometimes the horn honks randomly as the uncontained shaft grounds the horn circuit on other metal components. In short, it's ugly. And replacing the upper bearing is a short-term fix in a performance car, as replacements don't seem to last long when there's more

Quick-Release Steering Wheel

A quick-release steering wheel allows you to remove it from the top of the steering shaft with the push of a lever. This is common in race cars because of the tight confines of a roll cage, a performance racing seat, and the proximity of the seat to the pedals and steering wheel. Basically, you have to remove the steering wheel in order to get in and out of the driver's seat. In a performance Chevelle, being able to remove the steering wheel is a bonus, or even required, for entering and exiting. The two components that usually push this need are the cage and a racing seat.

None of the racing quick-releases are for use on the street because of liability. They also don't fit a street column, as they are built to fit on small-diameter racing steering columns. So why mention them here? Because the concept is sound, and they are, in some cases, required, even on a street car.

The Grant Vehicle Security System is designed as a theft deterrent; if there's no steering wheel, it makes it more challenging for a thief to drive off with your car. The key to this is removing the steering wheel, which is the functionality desired with a quick-release. It is a little more cumbersome than the race solutions because you have to insert and turn a key before you can push the knob that releases the wheel, but that's a small trade-off for a system that fits street columns and is engineered for street use.

A variety of quick-release systems are available for racing. The concept is the same, though, with part of the release mechanism mounted on the splined end of the steering shaft and the other bolted onto the steering wheel. They either have a knob you can pull, a pin that is removed, or a collar that you lift to separate the two parts of the system and remove the wheel.

The Grant system requires the use of a Grant steering wheel adapter to fit on your steering column, and it must also be used with a Grant steering wheel. Because Grant has one of the largest lines of adapters and steering wheels, this doesn't really limit your options. So, if you feel a little cramped getting in and out of your Chevelle once you have it built, consider this slick, race-inspired option. You may also want to consider it as a theft-deterrent measure.

CHAPTER 2

A smaller-diameter steering wheel adds to a performance feel and look inside the car. The original wheels were large in diameter and small in grip; neither of which are desirable when turning corners at speed.

Steering Wheel

You might not consider the steering wheel as part of a performance steering system, but you should. It's your connection to the steering system. How it fits and feels in your hands is critical. From a mechanical standpoint, the diameter of the wheel plays an important part in your ability to steer the car quickly through corners.

Although later Chevelles used smaller-diameter steering wheels, the earlier cars came with massive wheels designed primarily to give customers sufficient leverage for turning manual steering systems. A smaller-diameter wheel doesn't actually increase the steering ratio, but it makes the steering *feel* much faster and more responsive. Your hands have to travel around the circumference of the wheel when you're steering, and a larger wheel means more distance to cover. It doesn't make much difference when you're cruising down the highway, but when you're trying to steer quickly from lock to lock in an autocross, a smaller wheel means less work and more control.

The construction of the wheel is important for fit and feel. Most original wheels were made from hard plastic, with some of the later cars having thin rubber for a slight cushion. But all of them had thin-diameter rims that didn't fit in your hand very well. For performance, you want a grip that, well, you can grip. And firmly! The specific steering wheel you choose is a matter of taste, and hopefully matches the style of your interior. There are literally hundreds of choices—but consider the diameter, grip thickness, and material so you can top off your performance steering system.

stress on the steering column shaft than it was designed to take.

These early cars also had a one-piece steering shaft. This single, solid shaft went directly from the steering wheel to the steering box, connecting with a rubber joint which absorbed vibration. Collapsible steering columns were introduced in the late 1960s. The concept here is that the steering shaft collapses in a front-end crash. This prevents the steering shaft from impaling the driver in a hard crash.

The fix for both of these shortcomings is a new steering column and collapsible shaft kit. When upgrading the column, it also makes sense to use a tilt column, making it easier to adjust the steering wheel to the perfect height for performance driving, and also making it easier to get in and out of the car. Direct-fit tilt columns are available for these cars, making the upgrade easy. In addition to a tilt column and much more robust steering-shaft bearings, the new aftermarket columns also give you more modern wiring and the addition of emergency flashers. You can also choose to move the ignition switch to the column for earlier cars, or keep it there for 1969–1972 Chevelles; and you can either retain a column shift (for an automatic transmission) or get a smooth column for a floor shift. In short, it's a great upgrade for durability, convenience, performance, and permanently cleaning up the interior if you've moved the shifter off the column and onto the floor.

If you install a new column, you have to install a new steering shaft. The new columns use a larger-diameter shaft, and you should consider a collapsible shaft for safety. Whether you opt for the collapsible version, building and installing a new shaft to connect the column to the steering box is very easy in a Chevelle.

Project 1: Quick-Ratio Steering Box Installation

Inspect Stock Steering Box

1 On this Chevelle, we're replacing a manual steering box and worn steering components to create a true performance system for the street, autocrossing, and road racetracks. The steps are very similar for all model years, although the components may look a little different. In these photos, the engine has been removed, but that is not required for the upgrades shown.

Remove Cotter Pins

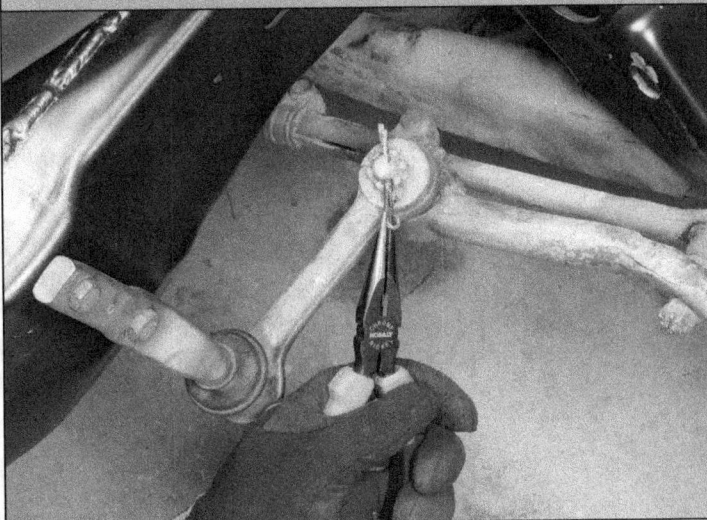

2 Remove the old components. For safety, every nut in the system has a cotter pin. Remove all of these using needle nose pliers and side cutters where needed. Loosen, but do not remove, the nuts on all of the attaching ball joints. Leave the idler arm, steering box, and Pitman arm tightly bolted in place for now.

Remove Tie-Rod Ends

3 Ball joints ensure that there is no slop in the steering system when things are bolted up tight. To release the pressure on the taper, hit the side of the mount with a metal hammer. A ball peen hammer suffices. A couple good knocks should do the job. This momentarily distorts the shape of the hole and eventually the ball-joint stud drops down in the mount.

CHAPTER 2

Remove Idler Arm and Steering Box

4 With the tie rod ends and center link removed using this technique, you can now unbolt the idler arm and steering box from the frame rails. The front steering box bolt hole may be covered by the bumper bracket. Use a 9/16-inch socket with a 6-inch extension to unbolt the steering box.

Inspect Flaming River Steering Box

5 Installing a new Flaming River Industries 14:1 steering box on this Chevelle gives great balance between fast steering and high-speed stability. These new boxes have four mounting holes, but only three are used to install the box on a Chevelle using the original holes in the frame.

Bolt Steering Box to Frame

6 Tubes welded inside the frame rail keep it from collapsing as you tighten the steering box bolts. Use a socket and ratchet to torque all 3/8-inch bolts to the frame. Use the original bolts, or purchase replacement bolts from a restoration parts supply if yours are rusty.

Torque Steering Box Bolts

7 Torque the bolts to 70 ft-lbs, and check the fasteners periodically. For race-car-like security, you can purchase bolts with drilled heads and safety-wire them in place so that they cannot back off.

Inspect Pitman Arm for Cracks

8 Manual and power steering boxes use different Pitman arms. These are keyed (one spline is wider than the others) and are shaped for specific vehicles; grabbing one off a Camaro or truck isn't going to work for your Chevelle. If you're not changing from a manual box to a power box, inspect your original Pitman arm for cracks. If you need a new one, they are available from Classic Performance Parts (CPP).

Inspect Replacement Aftermarket Steering Linkage

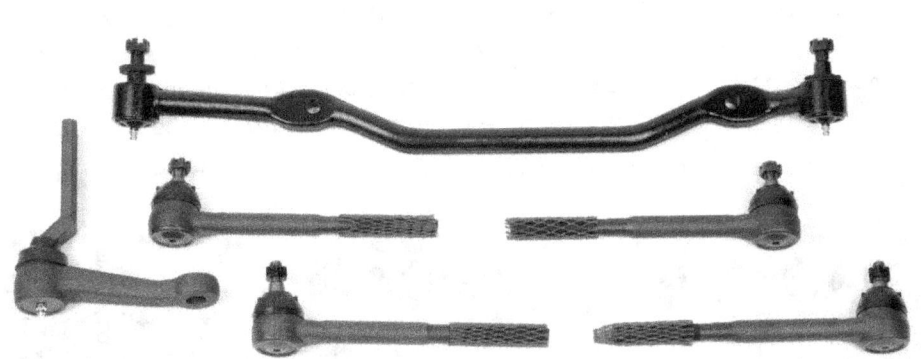

9 You can use a kit from Classic Performance Products (CPP) or Performance Suspension Technology (PST) to replace the center link, idler arm, and tie rod ends. These are all OEM-quality or better components. They come with new grease fittings (which you should install before putting the components on your car), fasteners, and cotter pins.

Install Solid Tie-rod Sleeve

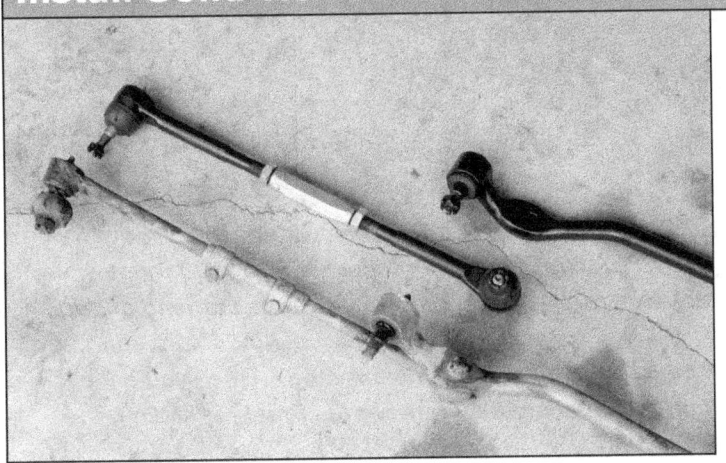

10 About the only performance upgrade available using stock replacement components, is a solid tie rod sleeve. The factory part (bottom) is a metal sleeve with clamps. They work, but they don't inspire confidence, look cool, or make adjustments easy. Aftermarket solid adjusting sleeves use locknuts on either end and have flat sides on the sleeves to easily fit a wrench over them.

Project 2: Steering Column Installation

Inspect Aftermarket Steering Column

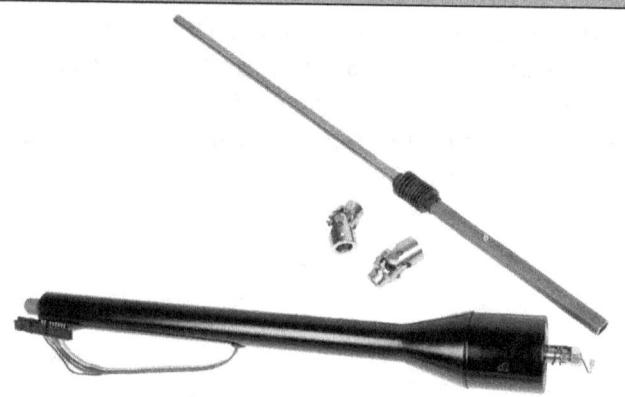

1 It may not seem like a critical part of a performance steering system, but a new aftermarket steering column can make a huge difference in the feel, durability, and safety of your steering. A new column uses later-model bearings that last longer, a larger-diameter shaft, and can be used with a collapsible shaft kit.

Inspect Firewall Mount

2 Flaming River offers a swivel floor mount for its steering columns that covers the factory hole in the firewall and provides a solid mount for the new column. The plate bolts to the firewall to cover the hole that was originally designed to let a column with a shift linkage be installed.

Install Firewall Mount

3 The firewall in this car was smoothed, which filled in three of the original holes. The existing holes need to be drilled to 5/16 inch. This allows some movement in the plate to fine-tune the location. Two set screws hold an aluminum collar around the outside of the column. When everything is in the right place, tighten the set screws to clamp the column securely.

Position Steering Column

4 Wrap the painted column with packing foam to protect it from scratches. Where you mount the column, fore and aft, is up to you. I recommend snugging the upper clamp and then sitting behind the column, working the tilt through its full range. Once you have it in a comfortable location, remove the foam and clamp the column firmly in place.

Install Steering Arm Shaft

5 With the column in place, you can now make your new steering shaft. I started with a Flaming River collapsible shaft kit, but found that I had clearance issues with the headers on my LS engine, so I used the smaller, 1-inch double-D shaft instead.

6 To get a proper shaft length measurement, install the Flaming River universal joints on the steering box and the end of the steering column. On the box, the joint slides over the splines with the set screw aligned with the machined flat section of the steering-box shaft.

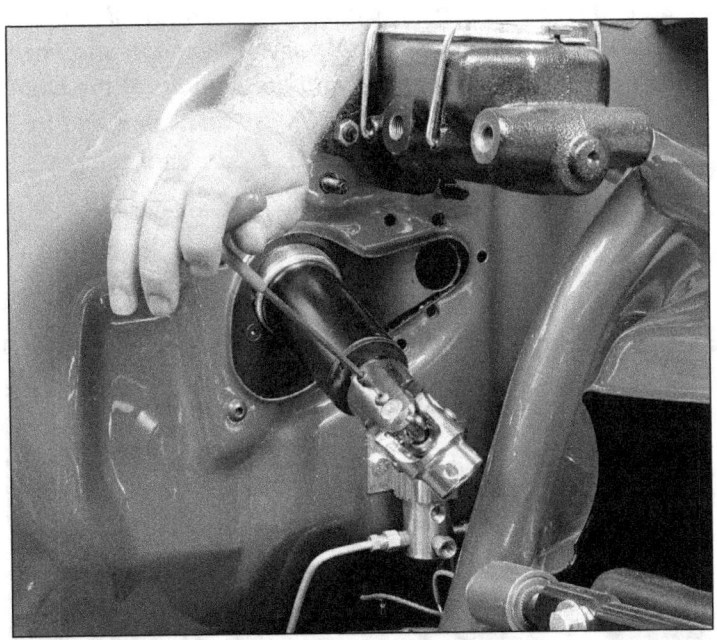

7 Hold the universal joint in place and use an Allen wrench to tighten the set screws. For now, just use the set screw; once done, use threadlocker and install the locknut. With the joints in place, measure the length for the shaft. You want the end of the shaft to be flush with the inside of the universal joint for adequate engagement.

CHAPTER 2

Install Steering Arm Shaft (Continued)

Install Turn Signal Lever

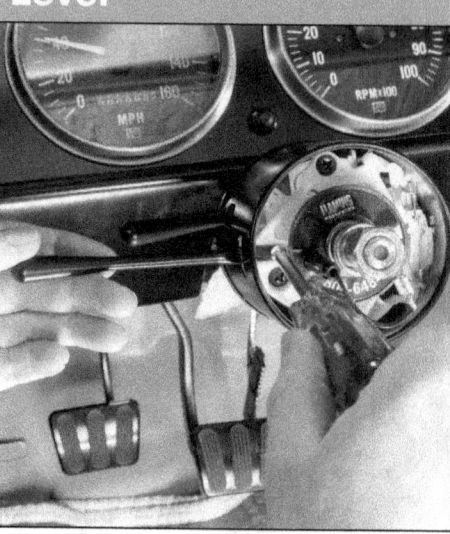

8 Once you've measured the shaft, check the measurement again, and a third time. You need to be sure it is accurate, because once it has been cut you are not able to add material back on the shaft. You can cut the shaft using various tools. I prefer a band saw because it clamps the shaft firmly in place and produces a clean cut. You can also clamp the shaft in a vise and use a reciprocating saw or a cut-off wheel. Use a file or sanding disk to clean and smooth the fresh-cut end.

9 Slide the shaft all the way into one of the universal joints. By angling the joint, you should be able to slip the shaft into the second joint. Center the shaft in the two universal joints. Make sure it is long enough and firmly engages in both joints. If the shaft is too short, order a new one and try it again.

10 To finish the top side of the column, you can install a Flaming River billet knob set painted to match the rest of the interior. You can also install an original Chevelle turn signal lever. For a factory-looking tilt lever, you can cut a reproduction turn signal lever and use a die to create threads that fit in the column. Once you cut the threads into the lever, the reproduction lever threads in.

Install Steering Wheel

11 This is a Grant steering wheel adapter and steering wheel. Use threadlocker on all of these components to guard against loosening from vibration. Permatex blue threadlocker is a good choice because you can remove it later if needed.

A Grant Performance Series steering wheel gives a simple race car look and feel. The wheel is 14¾ inches in diameter, so it's not tiny, but not so big that it's cumbersome to steer quickly. It also has a foam grip that fits well in your hand for a firm grip on the wheel as you blast through corners.

CHAPTER 3

WHEELS AND TIRES

Wheels and tires make a huge difference in the way a car looks, and they can also make a significant improvement in performance. The wheel drives most of the style, but choosing a traditional 60- or 70-aspect ratio, or a modern 30- or 35-aspect ratio for a shorter sidewall, also affects the look that the wheel and tire give the car. Together, the wheel and tire package should reinforce the image you want. After all, it's often the only radically changed external component on a classic Chevelle.

Appearance

Style is completely in the eye of the owner. There are countless styles, from retro to ultra-modern, and you can have the style you want in just about any finish too. It's also possible to use original-styled wheels, even if you want a brand-new wheel or a custom size and backspacing. Picking the right style can be aggravating, as there is no right or wrong. There are a couple of style items to consider, however. First, what will be exposed with large-diameter, open-design wheels? If you have jumbo disc brakes at all four corners, by all means, show them off with an 18-inch five-spoke wheel. But if you have stock drum brakes on the rear, think about how that will look. What else will be visible behind the wheel? If you haven't or don't plan on detailing the undercarriage, choose a wheel style that covers most of the area.

There is an endless discussion about which wheel diameter looks best on a muscle car. Traditionalists never put anything larger than a 15-inch wheel on their Chevelle. But if you want extreme performance brakes, you likely need a 17-inch or larger wheel to clear a large caliper on a big-diameter rotor. Also consider that the amount of tire that can be seen in the wheel well has more to do with how well the wheels and tires fit the car than whether the

The correct wheel and tire combination can make your Chevelle look fantastic and perform great too. The hardest part of choosing the best wheels and tires is determining exactly what fits. With the very broad variety of suspension components now available, your best bet is to measure what you have instead of trying to copy the specs from another car.

CHEVELLE PERFORMANCE PROJECTS: 1964–1972

CHAPTER 3

The design of the wheel is an important consideration. You want a style that matches the overall desired look of your car (and the wheels dictate much of it) but you also need to consider what's behind the wheels. An open wheel like this exposes much of the brake and suspension components, requiring a high level of detail on these undercarriage parts to keep the overall look of the car clean.

car wears a 15- or 18-inch wheel. In other words, the lower the car, the better the wheel and tire look. This is critical when you are building a pro-touring car with an 18- or 19-inch wheel. The short sidewall of the low-profile tires doesn't fit the muscle car proportions of a Chevelle unless you can cover part or all of the sidewall with the wheel opening lip by having the car sit ultra-low.

At the front, a very low car poses issues with steering. You likely need to find a good compromise between the optimum stance for the look you want and a ride height that allows the tire to turn without detrimental rubbing. Unlike a new-car manufacturer, hot rodders are generally okay with a little bit of tire rub as long as it doesn't destroy the tire or the car, and as long as it doesn't get much worse as the suspension moves.

At the rear, it's easier to get the look you want because the tire doesn't steer. The 1964–1965 cars have a wheel lip that hangs low, giving them a great, extra-low appearance. All of the Chevelles have a rear wheel opening lip making it possible to cover part of the tire sidewall for a pleasing appearance.

The best overall advice I can offer on choosing wheels and tires for appearance is to think about the style of car you're building and make sure the wheels are consistent with that look. A pro-touring car needs a wheel larger than 16 inches, a traditional car needs a traditional-style wheel.

Performance

When it comes to performance, however, there are right and wrong things to do, and there are tools and math to make sure you get what you need. Fitment is the first issue to master. For Chevelles, there are three groups among the models that drive the maximum tire size that fits: 1964–1965, 1966–1967, and 1968–1972. The older cars are the most restrictive in the wheel openings, with each change in body style providing a little more room for larger tires. During this eight-year run of production, drag racing was becoming extremely popular, and racers quickly learned the advantage of running wider tires on the rear of the car to provide more traction. Since the auto industry was lock-step with racers at that time, the rear wheel wells grew to accept wider tires.

Ten years ago, it would have been possible to rattle off the widest tire size for each of the three body styles, along with the wheel size and dimensions, and feel pretty confident that they would fit. That's not the case now because of so many variances in the front suspension, as well as the

Front and rear stance (vehicle ride height) plays a huge part in how the wheel and tire combination looks on a car. With this car at factory ride height, this 18-inch wheel and low-profile tire would look horrible. But with the fender opening intersecting the wheel, the car has an aggressive appearance that says, "pro touring."

increasing number of people who are switching rear axles and installing rear disc brakes. Each of these things can move the wheel mounting location; and in the front, most suspension modifications change the arc in which the wheel moves as you steer, as well as how the wheel and tire responds as the suspension compresses and rebounds.

People are building their Chevelles with much lower ride heights than ever before, which dramatically affects the maximum tire size you can fit under stock sheet metal.

And then there's the final factor, which is that a lot of people aren't leaving wheel wells stock, making room for even larger tires. That's why instead of a chart with maximum tire sizes, in the project on page 39, I review the steps on how to measure your car with your modifications and at your desired ride height.

Unlike decades ago, tire specifications are more important when building a Chevelle for high performance. If you plan on road racing your car, you very well may see speeds approaching 150 mph, which makes the speed rating of your tires a critical specification. Unfortunately, the traction rating on the tire measures good traction in a variety of weather conditions. To find tires that provide a compromise between street life and on-track traction, talk to other enthusiasts and check forums to learn what people are saying.

Owners of 1964–1965 Chevelles rejoice! The very low wheel opening at the rear makes these cars look extra low. This also makes it more difficult to get the rear tires off the car. I consider this more of a fact of life than a consideration in choosing the wheel-and-tire combination, but you may have to disconnect the shocks in order to let the rear axle droop enough to remove the largest combo that fits under the rear.

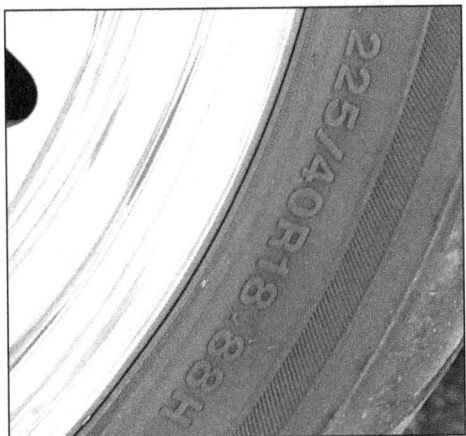

If you plan on running over 100 mph on the racetrack, you need to pay close attention to all of the information found on the sidewall. Here is what you can tell from the 255/40R18 88H spec shown on this tire. The first number is the width of the tire (255 mm). The next number is the aspect ratio or sidewall height. It is a percentage of the width. So "40" means 40 percent of 255, or 102 mm. The letter R means radial. Some tires have the speed rating with this, designated as HR or ZR. (This tire has the speed rating letter at the end, and H designates that it's rated for up to 130 mph. The other common performance speed rating is Z, which is good for 149-plus.) The last number is the wheel diameter in inches. Finally, the load index of this tire is 88, which means it's rated to hold up to 1,235 pounds (per tire).

A 15-inch wheel and tall tire sidewall on this car gives it an old-style look. You can still fit wide tires on the front and rear of the car if you retain original-diameter wheels, but you are limited in how large of a brake rotor and caliper you can fit.

Backspacing Versus Offset

Wheel measurements are given as diameter, width, and a backpacking or offset figure. Backspacing and offset are not the same measurement, and understanding the difference is key in helping you choose the right wheel for your project.

Backspacing is the measurement from the wheel mounting surface to the rear lip of the wheel. Offset is the measurement from the mounting surface of the wheel to the centerline of the wheel. The number can be positive or negative, with a positive offset meaning that the mounting face of the wheel is outboard of the centerline.

The new-car auto industry likes to talk about offset because the wheel design is done with computer modeling, where it's easy to input the suspension and sheetmetal data and then adjust the wheel offset in the model. A lot of wheel manufacturers don't like using backspacing because it measures from the outside lip of the wheel, while wheel width is measured from one bead surface to the other. So a wheel with a thick wheel lip has greater backspacing without telling you where the wheel-mounting surface is relative to the wheel's center line. This also means that two wheels can have different backspacing because of a difference in wheel lip thickness, but actually have the same offset.

However, it's a bit challenging to identify the true center of the wheel using a tape measure and straight edges, or worse, estimating how far off of the theoretical wheel center the mounting flange needs to be. And if you're off by more than 0.125 inch, you're likely to have fitment issues when trying to stuff the maximum wheel and tire package under your Chevelle. The big advantage of using the backspacing specification is that you can measure it yourself to compare the wheels you have now to what you are shopping for.

The other measurement to take note of is wheel width. The quoted spec is measured from the inside of one tire bead mount to the other. The thickness of the wheel lip affects the overall width of the wheel, which should be considered if your tire is not much wider than your wheel. This is pretty common with higher-diameter wheels and lower-profile tires. Always mount tires on a wheel width that falls within the tire manufacturer's recommendations for that tire size. This information is available on the tire company's website.

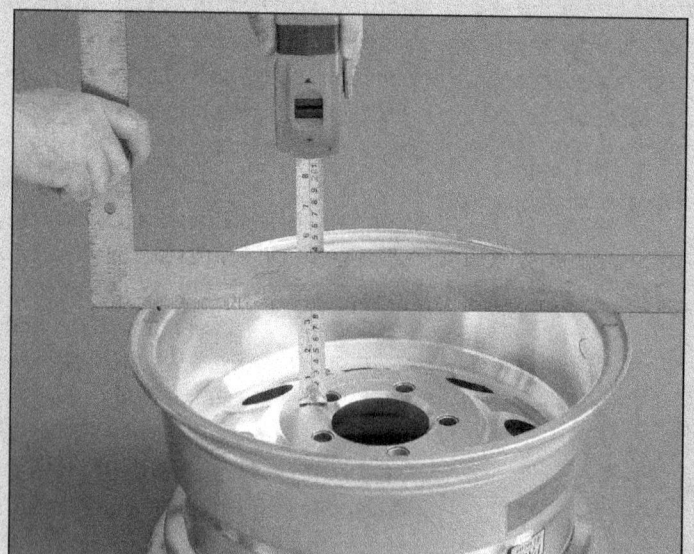

Measure the backspacing of an existing wheel by laying a metal straightedge across the outside of the wheel lip. The distance between the straightedge and the wheel-mounting flange is the backspacing.

Wheel width is measured between the inside edges of the tire-bead mount. This isn't possible with the tire mountd, but you can estimate to get a baseline of where you are starting.

Project 1: Wheel and Tire Fitment

Check Wheel Clearance

1 Choosing new wheels and tires for your Chevelle can be quite stressful. It's easy to spend more than $3,000 on the new combo, and you don't want to get it wrong. Changing from 15-inch wheels to larger-diameter wheels opens up a new set of tire dimensions to learn and understand. You also want to make sure you're getting the widest tire possible under the car for optimum performance. Make sure all four current tires have at least 30-psi air pressure, then park the car on smooth, level pavement. Steer from lock to lock and make notes of how much clearance the current wheel and tire combination has to the sheet metal, sway bar, frame rail, and so on. Also measure how high the top center of the wheel opening is off the ground.

Remove Wheels and Tires

2 Next, jack the car up and remove the wheels and tires. You need four short jackstands to return the car to original ride height. This is important so that you're sure the suspension is compressed just as it was with the tires sitting on the ground. If you don't have jackstands that are short enough, you can measure from the center of the wheel to the top center of the wheel opening and mimic this measurement, allowing the car to be higher off the ground with the wheels and tires removed. Either way, make sure the car is secure on the jackstands before doing any work on it.

Measure Wheels and Tires

3 With the wheels and tires removed, measure the overall width and diameter of the tires. Laying the tire on the floor and using a framing square as a straight edge on the sidewall helps to get an accurate width measurement. Also, measure the backspacing of the wheel (from the mounting flange to the inside wheel lip) and the overall wheel width. Using all of these measurements, along with your notes about the extra clearance you had with the wheels and tires still mounted, you can estimate the biggest wheels and tires that will fit.

Determine Wheel Dimensions and Backspacing

4 If you want to be more precise in your estimate, you can use a slick tool from Percy's High Performance called the WheelRite. This tool takes the guess work out of estimating wheel and tire fit by simulating a very wide range of wheel diameters and offsets, as well as tire sizes. It fits four- and five-lug hubs and can simulate a wheel from 15 to 30 inches in diameter. This inexpensive tool can save you a lot of money by helping you determine the correct wheel and tire dimensions the first time. The first step in setting up the tool is to adjust the wheel diameter with the set knob and sliding apparatus (A).

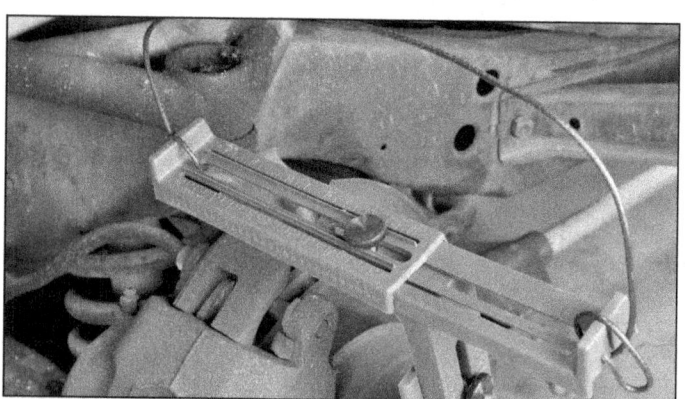

5 Use the top knob and sliders to set the wheel width and backspacing. For now, set the desired wheel width; you will adjust the tool later to find the optimum backspacing. Bolt the WheelRite to the hub using three lug nuts, tightening them snugly by hand. Make sure the tool sits on the hub flat and square. You may need to remove the brake caliper in order to rotate the tool. Bend the wire to simulate the profile of the tire. You can start with the sidewall height of the tires you removed or the ones you hope to use. You can refine this as you go, so don't worry about getting it perfect at this point.

6 Use a tape measure to verify the wheel diameter, tire diameter, wheel width, and tire width. We needed to tweak the wire to get the tire radius to 13¼ inches, which would mimic a 26½-inch-tall tire. Square-off the edges to more accurately represent the transition of the sidewalls of the tire into the flat tread section. One very important note about the WheelRite: It gives you an idea of clearance inside the wheel, but all wheels are shaped differently. You need the brake intrusion info to be sure the wheel fits over the brake caliper and rotor combo you have in mind. The more extreme the brake system, the more difficult it is to find wheels that fit.

Determine Tire Clearance

7 With WheelRite set up with your desired wheel and tire dimension, swing it in an arc and steer the car left to right. The front areas of a Chevelle that it contacts first are the center rear part of the wheel well (shown), the sway bar on the front when turned in the opposite direction, and the center top of the wheel lip if your car doesn't sit too high.

It is very important to note that the measurements must be taken with the suspension and brake package you plan on using already installed. Changing these components can move the mounting flange of the wheel, as well as change the arc that the wheel and tire move through as you steer. You also want to leave enough room to accommodate suspension compression. It's ideal to make these fitment checks with the suspension spring removed so you can compress the suspension 2 to 3 inches from ride height to simulate what happens to the tire placement when you hit a bump.

Determine Wheel Dimensions and Backspacing at Rear

8 The WheelRite process is much easier at the rear of the car where you don't have to worry about steering. You can also look for marks from the current tires rubbing the wheel well. While the factory four-link rear suspension makes the rear axle travel straight up and down with very little side-to-side play, nearly all Chevelles have different optimum backspacing from the left side to the right side. This is due to production variances, and I've seen them off by as much as 1/4 inch. Pick a tire size and wheel backspacing that leaves adequate clearance on the tighter side of your car. Also, make sure that this backspacing doesn't push the opposite side into the outer wheel opening lip.

Check Brake Caliper Clearance

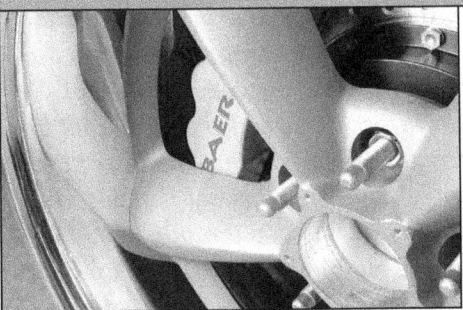

9 This car has a set of Baer 14-inch rotors and six-piston calipers, which create quite a bit of intrusion. Basically, the back part of the wheel must be pushed toward the outside edge to clear the brake caliper. Sometimes it is necessary to increase the backspacing by 1/4 inch and run a wheel spacer to provide brake caliper clearance. If you do this, get the wheel spacer from the wheel manufacturer to avoid warranty issues. Another potential clearance problem can arise with the valvestem. It's now popular to locate the valvestem on the barrel of the wheel behind the center. Big calipers can hit the valvestem, requiring a very short valvestem.

Check for Wheel Clearance

10 Before mounting the tires on your new wheels, mount the wheels on the car and raise the suspension to ride height. Check for clearance issues. At the front, move the steering lock to lock and check all of the clearances. It's easier to correct potential issues now without the tires mounted.

Get Tires Mounted and Balanced

11 Once you're satisfied that the wheels fit, and that the tires most likely will too, take them to a good tire shop to have them mounted and balanced. Be sure to quiz the shop about what tools it uses to mount the tires on the wheels, whether it guarantees the work, and what kind of weights it uses for balancing. All of the weights should be stick-on types applied behind the wheel center so they are not visible. Look for a shop that uses tools designed to avoid damaging the wheel lips.

Inspect Wheel and Tire Combination

12 This 1966 Chevelle is fitted with 265/35ZR18 BFGoodrich g-Force T/A KDW front tires on 18 x 9-inch wheels with 5¾ inches of backspacing and 1/4-inch wheel spacers. This combination works with a combination consisting of an ABC Performance suspension system, Baer six-piston calipers on 13-inch rotors, ABC Performance splined sway bar. These tires and wheels work at this ride height, but may not work with other components or at a lower height.

Verify Ride Height

13 I can't stress enough the impact that ride height has on the tire size that will fit under stock sheet metal and on the appearance of the car. The height of this car looks great, and the wheel lips are right at the top of the wheel openings. This gives the car a very low, aggressive stance. However, this is as far as the front tire can turn before hitting the top of the wheel opening. This car is fitted with QA1 coil-overs, so the ride height was increased one inch by using spanner wrenches to raise the lower spring perch on the coil-over body. The performance and the ability to adjust ride height have made coil-over and air-ride suspensions very popular on pro touring cars.

CHAPTER 4

BUILDING A PERFORMANCE REAR AXLE

All of the horsepower in the world won't be very enjoyable if you cannot put it to the ground. Part of that equation is the suspension (see Chapter 1), but the other part is the rear axle. A proper axle assembly for a high-performance Chevelle has the right components to deliver nearly equal power to both rear tires and is strong enough to do so time and time again without a mechanical failure.

Both of these are tall orders, especially as the ability to make gobs of horsepower and torque has become easier and easier. The idea of making 700 hp with a naturally aspirated engine is completely reasonable. Factor nitrous or a supercharger into the equation, and you can easily knock on the 1,000-hp door. There are quite a few items that further complicate the rear-axle solution: more traction, greater lateral forces, and increased braking power.

A modernized high-performance Chevelle often has considerably more engine power than it had originally. That's a lot more twisting force being applied to the rear axle. Today's tire width (and contact patch) can be triple that of the original tires, and performance rubber compounds offer significantly more traction. The traction coefficient of the compound combined with the increased contact patch can be as much as 100 times greater than when these Chevelles sat on new-car dealer lots. Aftermarket suspension systems have also greatly increased the traction, planting the tires on the ground rather than allowing wheel hop or uncontrollable tire spin.

It's also possible to take your Chevelle around corners better than engineers of the 1960s ever thought possible. That places an entirely new

Thanks to a variety of bolt-in replacement rear axles, upgrading an original Chevelle axle is an easy swap. Companies now offer brand-new 12-bolt axles that benefit from the latest, strongest components, as well as Ford 9-inch axles with suspension mount brackets made specifically for a Chevelle.

type of stress on the rear axle: lateral loads. When you turn hard into a corner, in addition to a twisting force driven by the engine, the weight of the vehicle is applied laterally against the wheels and tires. This translates into force trying to bend the axle shafts and axle housings, stressing all of the attachment points of the axle assembly. This force is exponentially larger than what the original axle assemblies were designed to handle.

Finally, there is significantly more braking power. Most of these cars had four-wheel drum brakes, which provide only a percentage of the stopping power of today's 12-, 13-, and 14-inch rotor disc brake systems. Every time you nail the brakes, the axle has to manage rotational force that is, again, exponentially greater than what the original design could generate.

Upgrades to Your Original Axle

With only a handful of factory Chevelles manufactured with a 12-bolt rear axle, most came with a 10-bolt rear end. These 10-bolts had an 8.2-inch ring gear and 28-spline axle shafts. And the newest one is more than 40 years old. That's the definition of weak and worn. However, you can greatly improve the strength and durability with either a 10- or 12-bolt.

I don't recommend building a 10-bolt for a very high-performance Chevelle, but there are several upgrades you can make for use in a driver that you're not going to abuse. In fact, I had a reliable 10-bolt under my Chevelle behind a 410-hp engine and Muncie 4-speed for 15 years, but the car was basically a daily driver and made a few trips to the racetrack.

The differential is the heart of rear axle. This is an Eaton Truetrac, which uses helical gears to transfer power through the axle assembly. The concept of a street differential is to allow some differentiation in wheel speed between the two tires when going around a corner, but provide equal—or near equal—power to both tires under acceleration. (Photo Courtesy Eaton)

These upgrades also apply to building a 12-bolt to handle moderate power and abuse. If you have a 12-bolt, though, it probably has value to a restorer as an original Chevelle high-performance rear axle. If you really want to build your car to perform to today's standards, you may want to sell your original axle and purchase an aftermarket 12-bolt or 9-inch, both of which are stronger than the original 12-bolt.

The key components in a 10- or 12-bolt that should be upgraded for strength and performance are the differential and the axle shafts.

Differential Choices

The best differential offered from the factory was a limited-slip Posi-Traction. This is a clutch-type differential that delivers torque to both rear tires up to a point when the clutches slip. This design allows for smooth driving around corners when you need that slippage, and moderate performance. You can install a brand-new Posi, which is still made by Eaton.

There are several alternatives that have a greater bias for performance, though, and the most popular are helical-gear types, such as the Detroit Truetrac, which is also made by Eaton. Instead of clutches, this differential uses helical gears to send power to both tires, but still provide differentiation around corners. This type is preferred with cars that are expected to perform well on an autocross course and drag strip, but not create any negative driving characteristics on the street. It delivers the power smoothly, without ratcheting or harsh catch-and-release mechanisms.

The latest helical-gear differential for muscle cars is the Wavetrac. It is similar to a Truetrac in that it uses the helical gears to provide smooth differentiation. It's different because it has a wave-shaped design in the center of the differential applying force against the two side gears when one tire approaches zero traction. This causes the Wavetrac to send nearly equal power to both tires, even if one of them is completely off the ground

Baer Full-Float Rear Axle Conversion

The rear axle under your Chevelle has to manage more forces in more directions than ever before. We expect our cars to handle well, stop better, and accelerate faster than a new Corvette. At some point, however, you reach the limits of the original design of certain components. In the rear axle, an example of this is the load-bearing axle shafts when pushed to the boundaries of their handling capabilities.

The axle shafts support the weight of the vehicle, transferring that weight to the axle housing through bearings located in the ends of the housing. When you apply significant lateral loads during cornering, the weight of the vehicle works against the traction of the tire, and the axle shaft deflects. The better your car handles, the more force created, and the more the axle shaft bends. This fatigues the axle shafts over time, but you find other issues first.

Because of the axle shaft deflection, the bearings and seals in the ends of the axle housing wear faster. It can also cause misalignment between the brake rotor (which is mounted on the axle shaft) and the caliper (which is mounted on the housing). Deflection of only 0.010 inch at the axle shaft can be as much as 0.100 inch at the tip of a 12- or 13-inch rotor. In extreme cases, the rotor can push the pad into the caliper, displacing brake fluid within the system. This can make the brake pedal unpredictable and may even require pumping to move fluid back into the caliper.

The conversion process involves cutting the ends off your existing axle housing and welding on new ends supplied with the kit. You can maintain the overall width of the axle so you don't need wheels with different backspacing. The Baer axle ends contain two large bearings (per side) to carry the weight of the vehicle and manage lateral forces. The brakes and hub install on a new spindle. New axle shafts are required, which have splines on both ends. The outer splines engage a 4130 chrome-moly drive flange, which is how power is transferred from the axle shafts through the hub and to the wheels.

In addition to strength, the Baer Tracker also improves handling by keeping the tires flat on the ground; and it improves brake quality through predictable and consistent brake-pedal height. The kit has a fully integrated parking brake assembly, and a wheel index of 2.410 inches to work with late-model wheels. Centering rings are available for use with wheels having a larger index diameter.

The Baer Tracker is a full-float conversion kit. For decades, heavy-duty pickup trucks have come from the factory with full-float axle assemblies to increase the load-carrying capacity of the vehicle. A full-float axle design separates the work. The axle housing carries the entire load while the axle shafts only spin the tires. In a performance car application, the Baer Tracker uses this same full-float design to eliminate axle shaft deflection during cornering. The kit comes with everything that you need to convert a 10-bolt, 12-bolt, or Ford 9-inch, and use a Baer brake system or another manufacturer's disc brake system.

during hard cornering. The Wavetrac uses 9310 steel gears in a case-hardened billet steel body.

There are also several automatic and selectable lockers. However, these operate as open differentials until they are locked. When locked, there is zero differentiation. These are very good for drag racing, but not well-suited for all-around performance Chevelles.

Axle Shafts

There are two factors to consider when choosing new axle shafts. The first is size. You hear people talk about spline count, and I've already referred to axle shafts by this measure. The spline count tells you the diameter of the shaft. A 30-spline shaft is larger than a 28, and a 33 is larger than a 30. Assuming the material is the same, the larger the diameter, the stronger the axle shaft.

CHAPTER 4

How to Choose Your Gear Ratio

With most performance Chevelles being built with overdrive transmissions, you can toss everything you used to know about choosing a gear ratio out the window. Not only does the overdrive gear ratio allow you to run a numerically higher axle gear ratio, but the first gear ratio of the transmission may also be bigger, which affects your launch. And if you are thinking about autocrossing your Chevelle, you need to look at speeds and engine RPM in every gear to make sure you pick a rear axle gear ratio that gives you performance when you need it.

There are a variety of gear-ratio calculators online and you need to find one that allows you to input the transmission gear ratios as well as the tire diameter, vehicle speed (MPH), and rear axle ratio. You also need to know what the power band of your engine looks like so you can choose a gear ratio that allows you to accelerate out of corners but minimize shifting on autocross courses.

For example, I worked through several scenarios with a Tremec 6-speed and 515-hp Chevrolet Performance LS3 crate engine, and 26-inch-tall rear tires. Traditional thinking for a street-and-strip car would have put me around a 3.55:1 or 3.73:1 gear ratio. Using an online calculator, considering speeds in every gear, and looking at the published torque and horsepower graph for this engine, I determined that I couldn't go lower than 4.10:1 rear gears because the engine would be lugging under 70 mph in sixth gear. In fact, the power output chart for the engine doesn't go below 2,000 rpm, so even a 4.10:1 gear may actually be too low. I paid special attention to

The gear ratio determines how many times the driveshaft makes a rotation compared to the number of rotations of the rear tires. This is accomplished by changing the number of teeth on the pinion gear and the ring gear. The gears are matched to each other, so in order to change gear ratios, you need to change the ring and pinion gear set.

the MPH and RPM of each combination in second and third gear to find a combo that would minimize shifting on an autocross course.

For the way this particular car will be used, I decided on a 4.30:1 rear gear ratio. This gave the car 1,945 rpm cruising at 70 mph and an RPM range between 2,300 and 6,000 for speeds from 20 to 50 mph for autocross racing. Prior to overdrive transmissions, this would have been unheard of in a true street car.

Axle Spline Count	Shaft Diameter (inches)
28	1.20
30	1.29
33	1.41
35	1.50
Information courtesy of Eaton	

The axle shaft spline count needs to match the number of splines on the side gears inside the differential. If you have a 12-bolt with 33-spline axles, you can't just step up to 35-spline axle shafts. You have to change the axle shafts and the differential. If you're doing a complete axle rebuild and will be using a new differential and new axle shafts, go with the largest spline count you can get, which is typically 35.

The other consideration when choosing axle shafts is material. There are many mixtures of steel alloys used to make aftermarket axle shafts. Some of the strongest materials manage twisting loads exceptionally well but don't tolerate impacts, such as potholes, without the risk of breaking. The best advice is to select an alloy that fits your intended use of the vehicle. Typically, a street/strip axle shaft is made from a good, all-around alloy that holds up to the shock impacts of street use as well as the twisting forces of moderate racing.

BUILDING A PERFORMANCE REAR AXLE

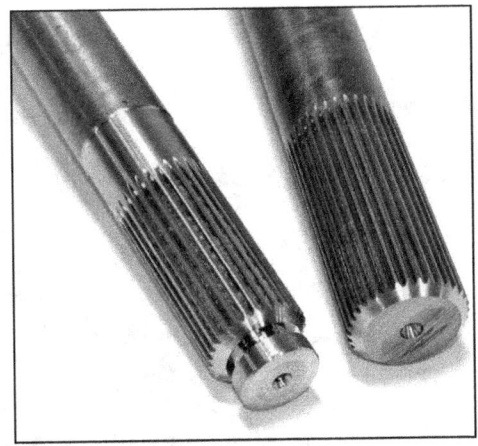

The axle shafts are important pieces of the rear end to upgrade. If you put serious power under the hood, 35-spline axle shafts virtually eliminate the chance of breaking an axle. The axle on the left is for a 12-bolt, and it uses a C-clip to be retained in the assembly. The axle on the right is for a 9-inch, which uses a backing plate at the end of the axle to hold the axle in the housing.

Complete Aftermarket Housings

For the strongest possible rear axle assembly, use a complete aftermarket housing. This gives you a brand-new housing, and the axle tubes and center section are typically thicker and stronger than the originals. Also, with a new housing you know it hasn't been bent at some time during its 40 years of use.

There are quite a few companies offering 12-bolt and Ford 9-inch housings that have the suspension mounts, spring pads, and shock mounts in the proper location, so you can bolt the housing right into your 1964–1972 Chevelle without any modifications.

Whether a 12-bolt or a 9-inch is best for you depends on your intended use. Generally, the 9-inch is considered stronger because of its larger-diameter ring gear, pinion-gear mount, and the engagement between the ring and pinion gears. The biggest difference between the two axle housings is in the basic design. The 9-inch uses a drop-out center section to mount the differential and gear set. This makes it easy to change if you want a different setup for various racetracks, or if you find you don't like the specific differential or gear ratio that you started with. Some also argue that the mounting of the differential in this third member is a stronger design.

The 12-bolt is a Salisbury design, and the cast center section holding the differential and gears is an integral part of the housing. To change the gear ratio or differential, you have to set up the entire axle housing. With either style of aftermarket rear axle, you have a significantly stronger housing than the original.

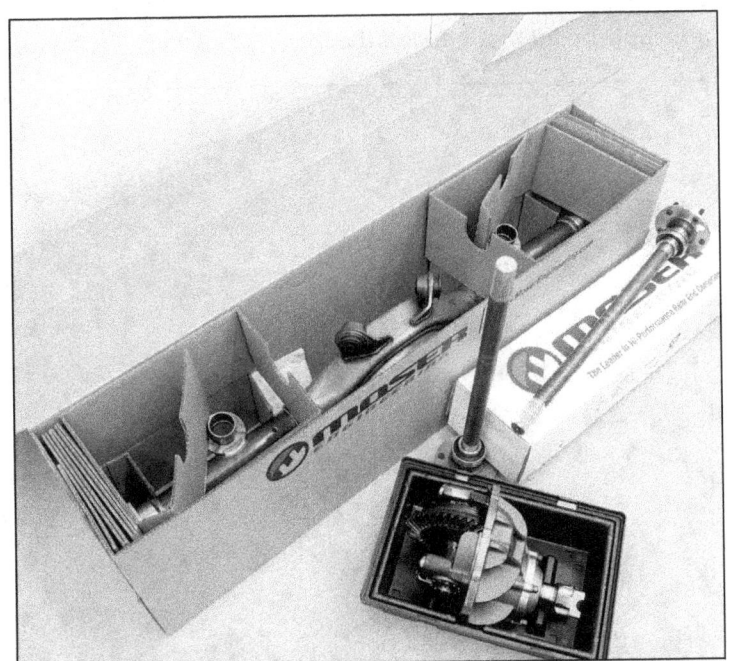

This is the easiest and perhaps the best way to upgrade the rear axle in your Chevelle: install an all-new housing with high-performance axle shafts, differential, and gear set. This Moser Engineering 9-inch fits 1964–1972 Chevelles. The company also offers a MusclePak, which comes completely assembled.

Moser and several other aftermarket companies offer brand-new 12-bolt and 9-inch axle assemblies. Moser casts its own 12-bolt center sections. This one is for a leaf-spring application, but the company also offers one with the upper suspension mounts for A-Bodies.

If you choose a Moser 9-inch, the center section is welded from heavy-gauge metal. Popular options for the housings are an oil-fill bung welded on the rear of the housing and a drain plug installed in the bottom. This makes changing fluid much easier.

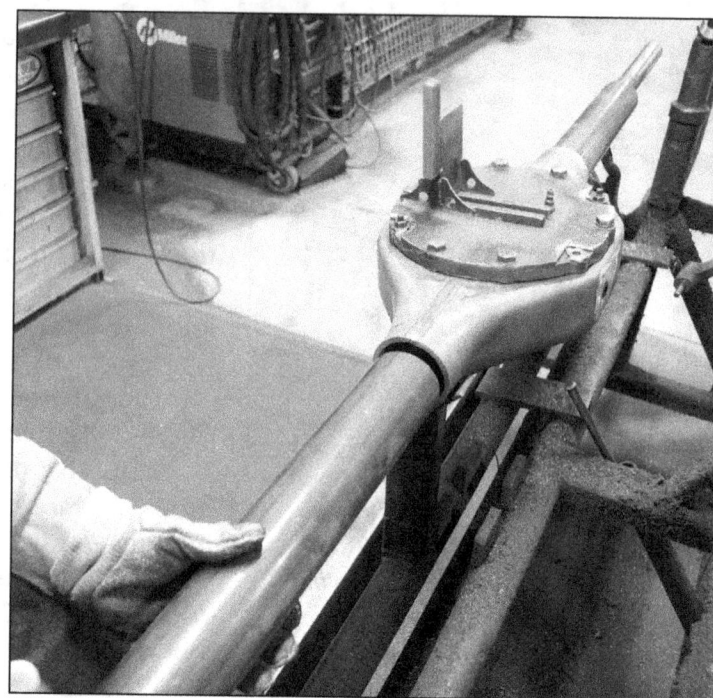

Moser fabricated its own jig to precisely locate the suspension mounting points on its 9-inch housings. Another jig is bolted where the center section would go, and then the axle tubes are inserted into the housing. Steel tubes engage the center-section jig to mimic axle shafts and precisely position the axle tubes.

The axle tubes are then welded to the center section. Moser also welds the axle tubes on the inside of the 9-inch housing. Everything is held in place for perfectly straight axle housings and correct angles for the axle ends and suspension mounts.

Moser manufactures upper shock suspension mount brackets and installs new bushings prior to the mount being welded onto the housing.

Most brake companies make systems that bolt to a variety of axle ends. Choose ends that are popular, in case you want to change brakes later. The large Ford ends, also called Torino ends, are one of the most common.

The lower suspension mounts and spring perches on the Moser axle look different than the stockers, but Moser locates everything in the right place. The entire axle assembly is a bolt-in and usually takes only a couple of hours to install in the car.

The venerable Eaton Posi-Traction differential is the standard for muscle cars. It uses spring packs and clutches to distribute power to both tires, but allows differentiation (slippage) for cornering. It's a good all-around differential, but not the best for higher-performance cars in which greater traction in all conditions is desired. (Photo Courtesy Eaton)

The Wavetrac is a helical-gear differential distributed in the United States through Moser. It features case-hardened billet-steel body construction and all ARP fasteners. The helical-gear differentials, such as this one and the Truetrac from Eaton, are the preferred differentials for all-around performance Chevelles.

CHAPTER 4

One of the performance features of the Wavetrac is a wave cut in the side gear and center part of the differential. When the axles begin to turn at different speeds, the ramps on the wave gears slide against each other, pushing them apart and applying additional pressure. This continues to drive both tires, even if one is completely off the ground.

Another Wavetrac performance feature is a carbon-fiber friction material mounted under the helical gears in the differential housing. This provides a resistance to spinning, increasing the torque bias. The bias can be tuned by changing this friction material.

Project 1: Setting Up a Ford 9-inch Differential

Press Bearings onto Differential

1 The team at Moser showed how they set up a Ford 9-inch differential. The first step in assembling the differential is to press the carrier bearings onto the differential. Use a hydraulic press to press the bearing into the differential case. Moser does as much or as little of the assembly work as the customer wants.

Install Ring Gear

2 Heating the ring gear on a hot plate makes it easier to slide onto the differential. The heat expands the ring gear slightly. Install the ring-gear bolts (available in a ring-gear installation kit from Moser) with Loctite Red threadlocker. Torque the ring-seam bolts in a star pattern to 85 ft-lbs.

BUILDING A PERFORMANCE REAR AXLE

Remove 12-Point Bolts

3 With all of the ring-gear bolts in place, you can remove these two small, 12-point bolts. These hold the two halves of the Wavetrac differential together during shipping, but serve no purpose once you torque the ring-gear bolts in place.

Set Pinion Depth

4 The pinion depth on a Ford 9-inch is adjusted with shims behind the bearing support. This makes it a bit easier to adjust the pinion depth compared to a Salisbury axle design, which uses a crush sleeve to set resistance, and shims under the nose of the pinion for pinion depth.

Note Pinion Gear Support

5 On a 9-inch differential, the rear of the pinion gear is held in the third member. The pinion tries to climb the ring gear during acceleration. The design of a 9-inch has a significant strength advantage, because the pinion is supported on both ends.

Install Differential in Housing

6 The differential bolts into the housing with two large caps. In a Salisbury axle assembly, the gear mesh is adjusted with washers on either side of the differential. A 9-inch has spanners on either side that allow you to adjust the position of the carrier without removing it. Tighten the main bearing cap fasteners to 85 ft-lbs.

CHAPTER 4

Set Backlash

7 With the pinion gear and the carrier installed, there are two critical measurements to check: backlash and mesh pattern. Backlash is how much the gears rock back and forth between engagement. The ring and pinion gear manufacturer determines acceptable backlash, which is printed in the setup instructions.

Check Mesh Pattern

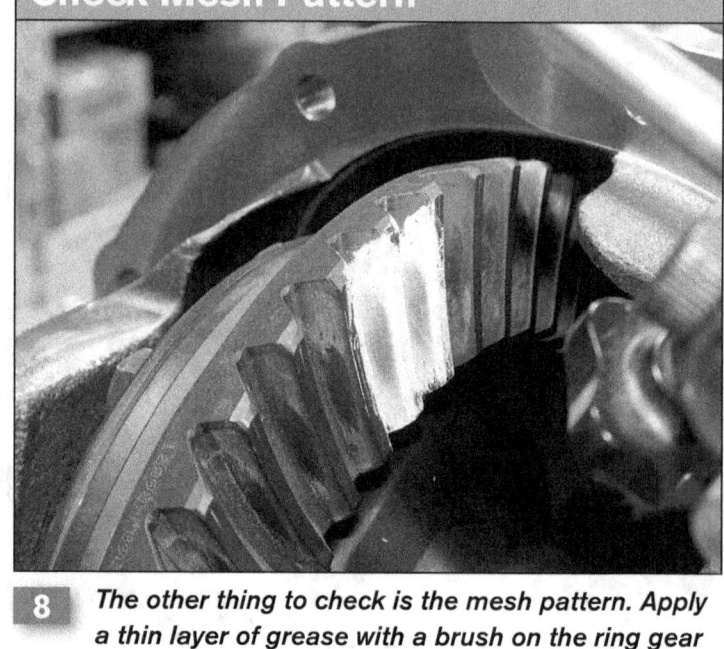

8 The other thing to check is the mesh pattern. Apply a thin layer of grease with a brush on the ring gear teeth and rotate the pinion as if the car was driving forward. A pattern like the one shown is ideal. The teeth are meshing in the middle part of the ring gear without being too close to any edge. There are adjusters on the side of the differential to affect the gear mesh.

The complete third-member assembly is ready to bolt into the 9-inch housing. At the pinion flange, you have several choices. The original U-joint in your Chevelle was most likely a 1310. A 1330 has a wider cross-bar construction and larger caps, which is considered a good performance option. There is also a 1350, which has the same cross-bar width as the 1330 and slightly larger caps, making it an extremely strong U-joint.

If you're building an all-new axle, go for the biggest axle shafts that fit with your differential. In this case, the Wavetrac for the 9-inch is available in 35-spline. Moser forges these 35-spline axle shafts, which are induction heat-treated to optimize torsional strength, and Magnafluxed. These axles are specifically designed to endure the stress of racing and street use.

CHAPTER 5

BRAKE UPGRADES

Just 10 years ago, building a performance Chevelle for most people meant focusing only on going fast in a straight line. You don't have to go too fast, however, to realize that a performance braking system is a wise upgrade.

Many Chevelles came from the factory with front disc brakes, which work pretty well in mild-performance applications. In fact, the easy upgrade for earlier all-drum brake Chevelles was to simply grab the spindle, hub, and brake assembly off the front of one of these later cars. Those early cars, however, came with what is now a very archaic system that most would consider extremely inadequate, even for street driving. They had a single-reservoir master cylinder; if you lost pressure anywhere in the system, you lost all braking ability. If you've ever driven a vehicle with four-wheel drums, you know that they are adequate for one stop from 60 or 70 mph, but they heat up and become nearly worthless after a few hard stops. It's definitely not a performance setup.

Luckily, there are more brake upgrade kits available for Chevelles than there were brake variations over the entire 1964–1972 run of these cars. Everything from very mild bolt-ons to wild systems that rival that of a current ZR1 Corvette are available. Naturally, the costs of these systems vary widely, so a careful evaluation of what you really need and what else will be affected is a wise place to start.

When doing a brake upgrade, make sure all of the parts in the system work together. And I don't just mean that they physically fit together. It's extremely important that your front

The game has changed considerably for performance brakes over the past decade. You can now buy a bolt-on kit that allows you to put world-class brakes on your Chevelle. Naturally there are trade-offs, but there are now more options than ever before.

CHAPTER 5

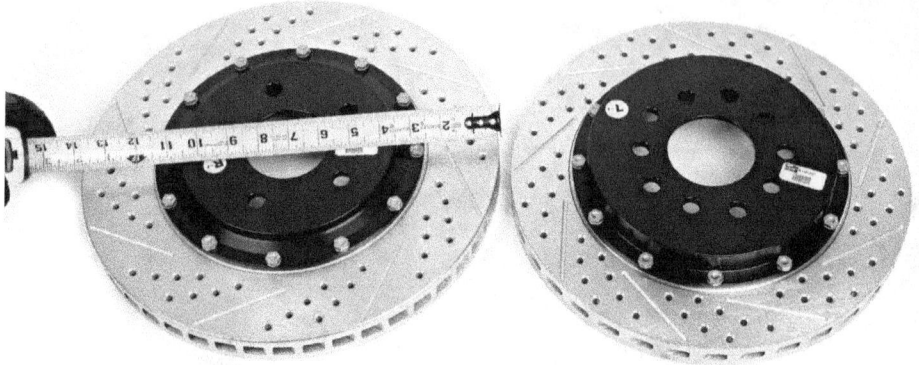

Rotor size is how most people describe and compare a disc brake package. And that's an important measurement, as it determines much of the performance of a disc brake system. Rotors that are 11 and 12 inches in diameter are nice street systems, while 13-inch and larger brakes are required for competition-level performance.

and rear brake systems complement each other. It's also critical that your master cylinder be matched to provide the volume and pressure needed to make use of the new brakes at the wheels.

Performance Factors

The front brakes provide the bulk of a vehicle's stopping power, so that is where most people concentrate their efforts. If you are building a Chevelle primarily for street driving and want good brake performance without competition-level performance, then a decent disc-brake upgrade up front with stock rear drums can be adequate. However, the brake system does need to be reasonably balanced. If you install 14-inch rotors and six-piston calipers on the front, you need to upgrade the rear to be in the same league.

Clamping Force

When it comes to disc brakes, stopping power is defined by swept area, leverage, and clamping force. Of these, clamping force is the hardest to determine. It is affected by the master cylinder bore and volume, whether the system is boosted (power brakes) or not, caliper volume, number of pistons, size of pistons, brake-line diameter, pedal ratio, and a few other factors. When shopping for a disc brake upgrade, the only indicator of clamping power you can garner is the number of pistons and piston diameter. For the rest of it, the factors are dependent on other components on your car.

Swept Area

The other elements that determine a system's braking power are something you can compare. Swept area is a factor of rotor diameter and pad height. If you visualize the path that the pads cover on the rotor as the rotor spins, that is the swept area. You can also use this formula to determine your swept area:

$Swept\ Area = A1 - A2$
Where:
$A1 = (3.1416 \times D1^2) \div 4$
$A2 = (3.1416 \times D2^2) \div 4$
And:
D1 = the diameter of the outside circle created by your brake pads
D2 = the diameter of the inside circle created by your brake pads

The swept area of a new disc brake system should be a published specification available from the manufacturer.

Pad Position

The third factor in braking performance is how far the pads are mounted from the rotor centerline. The farther away they are, the greater the leverage of the pads and caliper and the better they are at stopping the vehicle. This is why rotor diameter is so important. Naturally, a larger-diameter rotor may require a larger-diameter wheel, which may or may not play into your plans.

Generally, a 12-inch rotor is the absolute largest that fits in a 15-inch wheel, and some of these require a 16-inch wheel for proper caliper clearance. When you have more than 12 inches in rotor diameter, you need to get the brake intrusion template from the manufacturer and make sure that the wheels you have, or the wheels you want, will clear the rotors.

One of the biggest trade-offs you face with the larger brake packages is wheel diameter. There is a limit to how much brake rotor and caliper you can fit in a 15- or even a 16-inch wheel. And the largest brakes, such as the Baer 14-inch rotor, six-piston caliper system shown here, require specific wheel designs. This dictates your wheel diameter and, in some cases, which wheel companies you can choose from.

BRAKE UPGRADES

As well as matching the rear brakes to the front, the master cylinder also needs to be matched to the overall brake system. A four-wheel disc system requires a different master cylinder than a disc/drum system. Most disc brake kits are available with a master cylinder sized for that system.

Proportioning Valve

If you make a size change in rotors or calipers, you definitely want to install a new proportioning valve. A lot of kits come with a distribution block that provides pre-determined proportioning, but I prefer an adjustable valve so I can dial in the front-to-rear brake bias for the car. No two performance Chevelles have the exact same front-to-rear weight distribution or weight transfer during braking. To optimize the brake bias, you have to be able to adjust it. This is also very handy if you plan on taking your car on the track, as you can dial the car in for that specific track and how the car is performing that day.

Master Cylinder

The other brake component to consider upgrading is the master cylinder. If you are changing the architecture of the system (from disc/drum to disc/disc, for example), you need to change the master accordingly. Often the the manufacturer of your rotors and calipers have a matched

If you will be drag racing the car, install a roll control system. This is an electric solenoid that mounts in the front brake line to lock the front brakes, allowing you to do a burnout without working against the rear brakes. They are inexpensive, easy to wire, and easy to install between the master cylinder and the junction block that splits the front brake line left to right.

When considering a brake upgrade for your Chevelle, select a system for the level of performance you desire and how you use the car. If you have drums at all four corners and are not looking for ultimate performance, an 11-inch front disc brake upgrade makes a huge improvement without breaking the bank. However, if you want to drive your car hard at the autocross and road courses, and want to raise the eyebrows of new Corvette owners, consider some of the great 13- and 14-inch, six-piston kits that are available. The best part is that they bolt on! For this Chevelle project, I'm installing a 14-inch, six-piston Baer Pro+ system on the front and a 13-inch version of the same system on the rear. The rear has an internal parking brake assembly with a mini-set of brake shoes that sit inside the hub part of the rotor.

Bending Brake Lines

There are quite a few options for your brake lines when upgrading your Chevelle. If the system is all original, it's a good idea to change lines. If the car sat for any period during its life, the lines can have sludge in them. And the lines themselves can rust as moisture builds up in the brake fluid. Inline Tube makes a reproduction hard line that lets you re-plumb your entire car with stainless steel for a very reasonable price. It also offers universal kits that already have 45-degree double flare ends on the hard line, and street rod kits with AN fittings and bulkhead fittings, making it easier to hide the majority of the brake lines in the frame rails. You can also plumb your brake lines from scratch, as shown here.

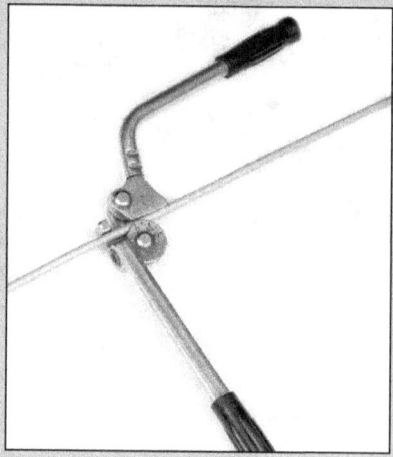

To create custom routing for your brake lines, the best method is to buy straight tubing and bend it yourself. You can purchase straight sticks of brake line tubing from most auto parts stores or from companies such as Inline Tube. When bending tubing, the most important thing is to use a good quality tubing bender. Many have dies that accept multiple sizes of line.

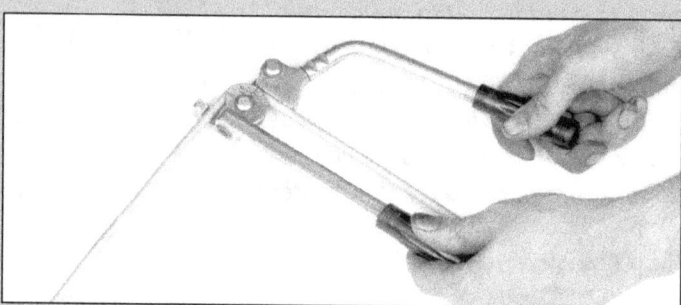

Using the proper tool keeps the line from flattening out or kinking as you bend it. You can make the bends any angle needed, up to 180 degrees, with a bender like this. In most cases, you can map out the desired brake line with measurements and a protractor before bending the actual line. If you're more of a visual person, you can use a coat hanger to create a template.

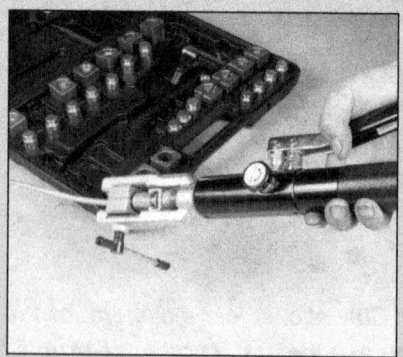

Straight tubing comes with flared ends, but you usually need to cut the tubing to create a custom line that fits your car perfectly. At any cut, flare the end. This can be a challenging and frustrating exercise. Use a manual flaring tool that holds the end of the line and uses a plunger that you thread down by hand to expand the line into a flared end. The Snap-on tool (shown) is a hand-operated pneumatic tool. This tool can also bend stainless-steel lines, which are very hard to do with a manual tool because the line is hard and brittle.

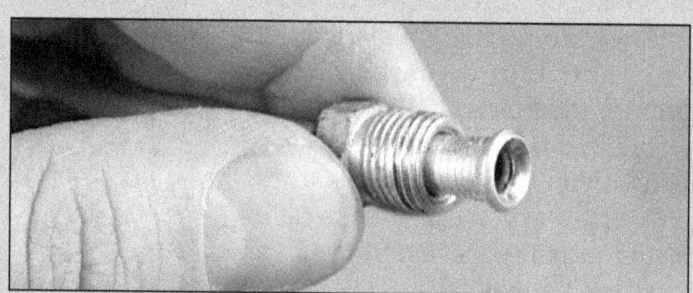

Flares of different degrees are used for different purposes. A 45-degree flare is the standard for brake lines, and this is what most flaring tools create. A double flare bends the top of the tube over slightly, and the flare is made from two layers of tubing, making it less prone to cracking and providing a better seal. Brake lines should have double-flare ends. The Snap-on tool also has the capability of creating 37-degree flares, which are used for AN lines.

BRAKE UPGRADES

Power or Manual Brakes

Nearly everyone building a performance Chevelle with big brakes opts for power brakes. While many simply want a light pedal feel, when you move up to giant calipers, it's hard to produce the pressure needed without a power booster and using the stock pedal and brake pushrod.

The brake pedal ratio is the distance between the pivot point of your brake pedal and the end of the pedal (where you put your foot), divided by the distance from the pivot point to where the brake pushrod connects to the pedal. The greater this ratio, the more pressure is created in the brake system for the amount of effort you apply to the pedal.

Chevelles have a very low pedal ratio of approximately 4:1. Without a power booster, you have to apply massive pressure to create the approximately 1,200 psi needed to effectively operate a four-wheel disc brake system. Even within power boosters, there is quite a bit of variation. The smaller diaphragm boosters are popular because they look nicer and take up less space under the hood. A single-diaphragm 7-inch booster, though, can produce 10 percent less psi in the system than a dual-diaphragm design of the same size.

However, some cars' engines don't produce enough vacuum to operate a power booster, and some people just don't want the clutter on the firewall or the reduced feedback through the brake pedal that comes with a power-assist system. Very few purpose-built race cars have a power booster. But because of the poor pedal ratio in the Chevelle brake pedal assembly, you get the best results from a manual system by either not going too crazy with the size of the brake calipers or by replacing the pedal-and-master-cylinder arrangement for a race-style unit, like those offered by Tilton Engineering. The latter requires quite a bit of custom fabrication under the dash to make the new pedal assembly fit, but it provides the best manual-brake performance.

This 1970 Chevelle has a factory-style brake booster and a master cylinder designed to be used with disc brakes on the front and drums on the rear. This is one of the largest power diaphragms available, and the system provides extremely high pressure in the brake system. It's critical that you use a master cylinder matched to your new brake setup.

master cylinder. Some builders like to use late-model GM master cylinders, which generally have a metal bore and plastic reservoir. These do match the volume and bore diameter requirements of many of the larger brake systems, but they require metric-to-SAE adapters for the brake lines. By sticking with an aftermarket master cylinder, you can use one that performs well and has SAE threads for the brake lines.

CPP even makes a master cylinder that retains the muscle car look while providing the volume and diameter that works with most big brake systems; and it offers brake line ports on both sides of the master, letting you choose whether the brake lines run to the left or right of the master.

One of the nice things about a GM master cylinder, and an aftermarket one for these applications, is that the bolt pattern to attach it to the firewall and the brake pedal shaft hasn't changed. You can bolt a master cylinder meant for a 1970 Corvette or 1976 GM truck right onto a 1964 Chevelle firewall.

Roll Control Solenoid

If you plan on drag racing, installing a roll control solenoid is a good idea. This splices into the front brake line and holds pressure to the front when activated. It keeps the front brakes locked when you release the pedal and lets the rear spin freely. When you let off the switch, the front brakes release.

CHAPTER 5

Project 1: High-Performance Brake System Installation

Inspect New Disc Brake Kit

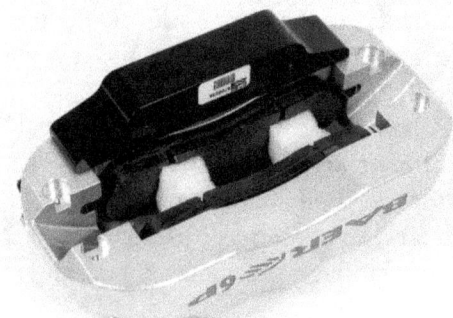

1 The Baer rear kit comes with a park bracket, which replaces your drum brake backing plate. Baer makes quite a few park brackets to fit the factory axles, as well as the popular axle swap and aftermarket ends. For example, the Moser 9-inch axle in this car has early Ford large bearings. Measure the outside diameter of your axle bearing and the distance (height and width) between the backing plate bolts to make sure you order the correct park bracket. Before installing the park bracket, remove the parking brake shoe and the attaching hardware.

Disassemble Parking Brake

2 This Moser axle is brand new and has never had any brakes mounted on it. Assuming that you're starting with drum brakes, you need to remove the drum brake assemblies and backing plates from the axle. On a Ford axle, a retaining plate bolts to the axle flange. This holds the axle in place; a GM axle uses C-clips in the middle of the differential.

Install Parking Brake Hardware

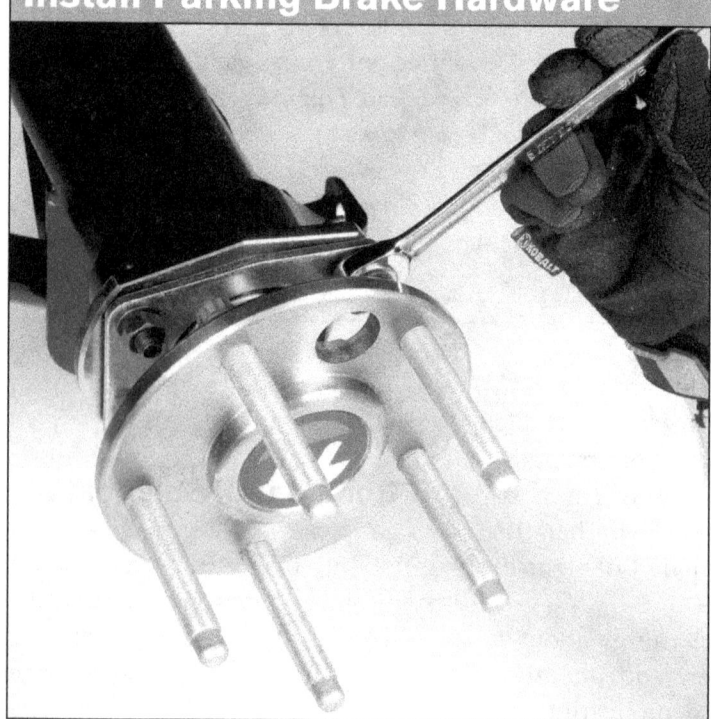
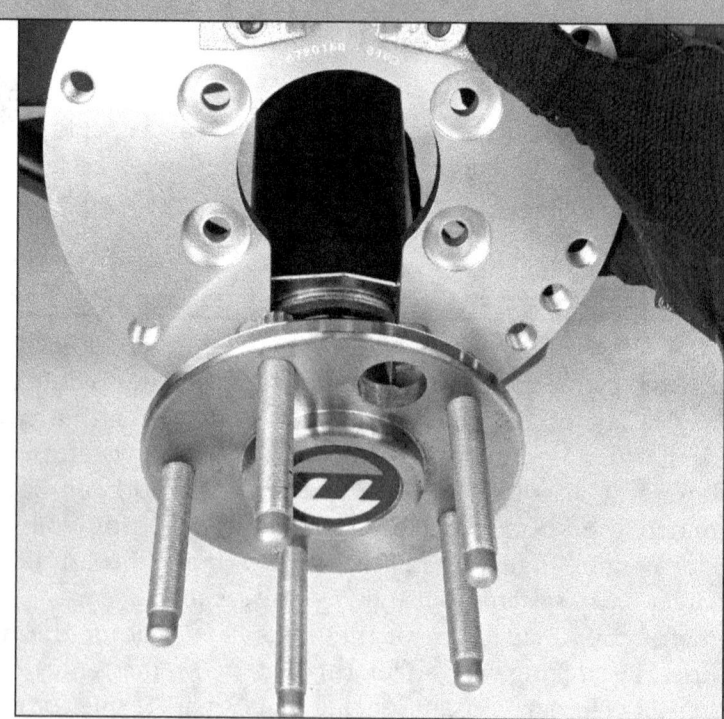

3 The parking brake bracket slips over the axle shaft with the parking brake lever facing the center of the car and the recessed holes for attaching bolts to the axle end facing outward. Mounting these with the parking brake levers on top of the axle keeps things clean looking from underneath as possible. You can also swap the park brackets side to side and mount them with the parking brake levers on the bottom of the axle, if you prefer.

BRAKE UPGRADES

Install Parking Brake Bracket

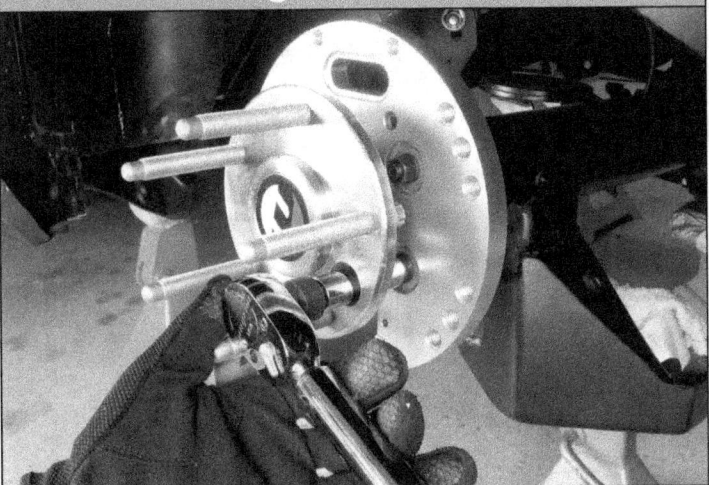

4 Use the original backing plate T-bolts to bolt the parking bracket bracket in place. Your axle flange should have an access hole in it that allows you to fit a socket and torque wrench on the nuts; rotate the axle to torque the bolts in a crisscross pattern. For 3/8-inch T-bolts, torque them to 45 ft-lbs. If you will be using the parking brake, install the shoe over the actuator. Baer makes a parking brake cable system that attaches to the factory Chevelle cable coming from the parking brake pedal.

Install Rotor over Wheel Studs

6 Use three lug nuts to snug the rotor onto the axle. The lug nuts on this car have a shoulder that is supposed to face inward, so they were installed backward to hold the rotor in place, which is pretty typical. This was done so it doesn't ruin the shoulders of the bolts. Make sure that you put the rotor on the correct side of the car; the "L" sticker tells you that this rotor belongs on the driver's side of the car. This ensures that the grooves in the rotor are angled the correct way.

Install Caliper Brackets

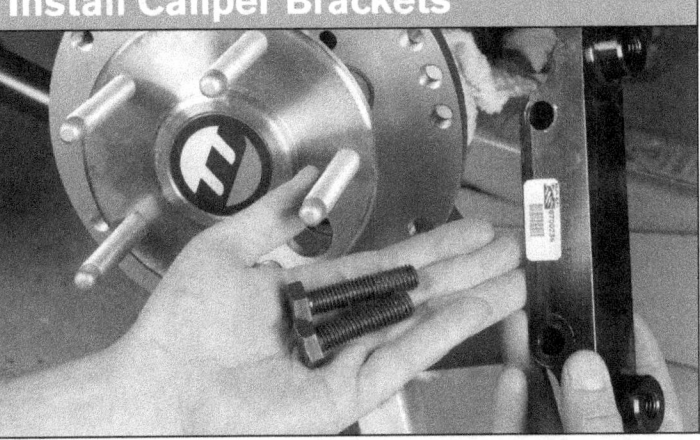

5 Baer supplies two sets of caliper bracket bolts; one pair comes with Vibra-Tite threadlocker applied, and one comes without it. Use the bolts without the threadlocker for the first mockup, because you will most likely need to take them back off, insert shims from the selection provided, and try it again. Install the bolts with threadlocker once you have the shim pack completely figured out and are ready to install the caliper bracket for the last time. The caliper mount bracket bolts to the back of the parking brake bracket. One side is complete tapered and does not rest flat against the rotor without the wheel installed. It's tapered to fit inside the tapered cup of the wheel.

Install Calipers

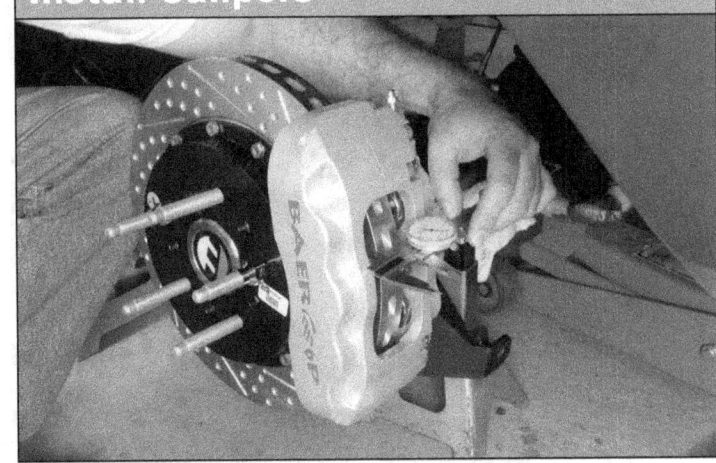

7 This is the only difficult part of installing the brakes, and it isn't that hard. With the rotor tightened onto the axle, slip the caliper over the rotor and tighten it onto the bracket. Using dial calipers, measure the gap from the rotor to the caliper body at the top inside, top outside, bottom inside, and bottom outside. Record all four of these numbers.

CHAPTER 5

Determine Shims Required

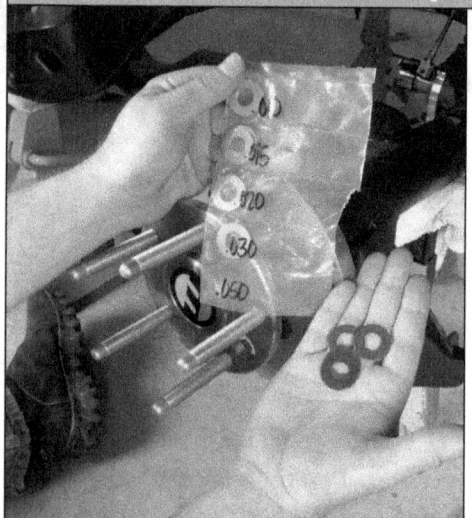

8 Subtract the top inside number from the top outside number, and then divide that number by two. This is how big of a shim you need to install between the caliper bracket and the park brake bracket at the top bolt. Do the same with the measurement from the bottom of the caliper to determine the shim needed there. Baer supplies a good selection of precise shims with the kit.

9 Install the shims between the park bracket and the caliper bracket and check the measurements again. You want to get these gaps as close to equal as possible, and ideally within .005 inch to minimize brake noise. Once you have it correct, replace the caliper bracket bolts with Vibra-Tite-coated bolts and torque them to 85 ft-lbs.

Install Brake Pads and Calipers

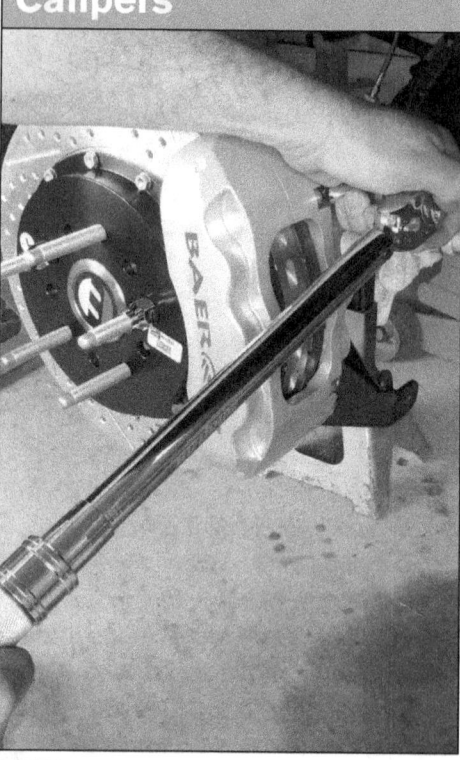

10 Install the pads in the calipers, and then bolt the calipers onto the brackets. These bolts should be torqued to 75 ft-lbs.

Install Banjo Bolt and Brake Lines

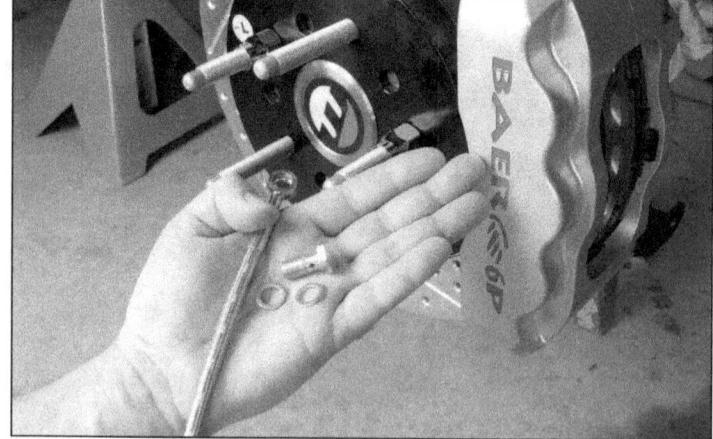

11 The kit comes with a banjo bolt, two copper washers, and a flexible brake line. Place one copper washer on each side of the banjo fitting on the steel-braided line and insert the banjo bolt. Once the line is positioned the way you want it on the axle, tighten the banjo bolt to 15 to 20 ft-lbs.

Install Front Caliper Bracket

12 Baer makes various caliper brackets and rotors for the popular front suspension upgrades. If the OEM spindle and hub are not compatible with aftermarket brake parts, Baer provides new billet aluminum hubs to install with its rotors. You need to repeat the mock-up, measuring, and shimming routine you performed on the rear to install the front.

Set Spindle Nut

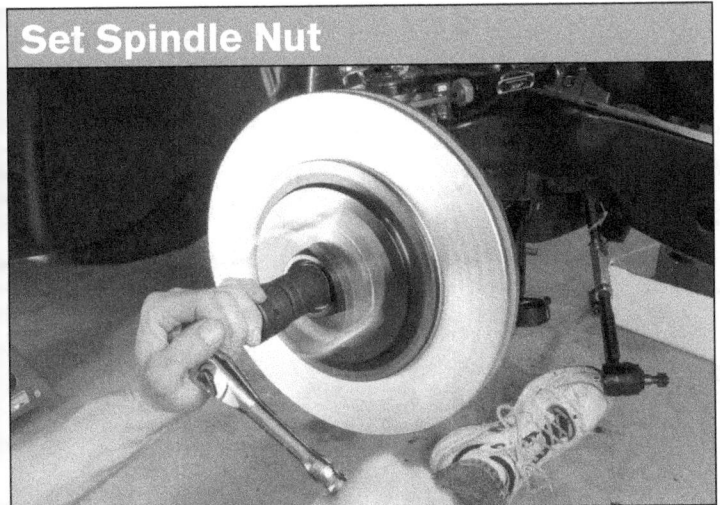

13 To properly set the spindle nut, bolt the rotor to the spindle with three lug nuts, tighten the spindle nut to about 10 ft-lbs, and spin the hub, seating the bearings. Loosen the nut and repeat this procedure once more. Next, loosen the nut, and then snug it by hand. Spin the rotor and slowly tighten the nut using a ratchet and socket until there is a very light drag placed on the spinning rotor and hub assembly. Install the cotter pin and dust cap.

Torque Caliper Bolts

14 Once you have shimmed the caliper bracket, tighten the three 1/2-inch bolts to 110 ft-lbs, the two caliper bracket bolts to 85 ft-lbs, and the caliper mounting bolts to 75 ft-lbs. The front brakes also come with banjo bolts, copper washers, and braided-steel brake lines. Route the brake lines carefully so that they do not bind or get caught in suspension components as you steer and drive the car.

Determine Location for Proportioning Valve

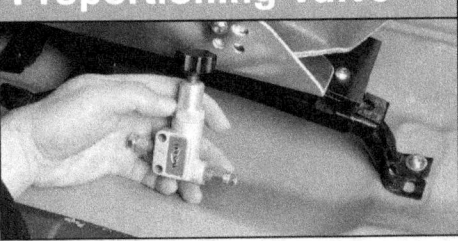

15 Installing a Baer adjustable proportioning valve lets you dial in the front-to-rear brake bias, effectively turning the braking power at the rear up or down to match the driving conditions. This valve can be spliced into the rear brake line anywhere along the chassis. Some people mount it under the master cylinder. For a street car, once you tune the brake system, you probably never need to adjust it again. However, if your car will see a lot of very different types of racing, you can mount it with the knob within reach of the driver while he or she is belted in.

Mount Rear Brake Line

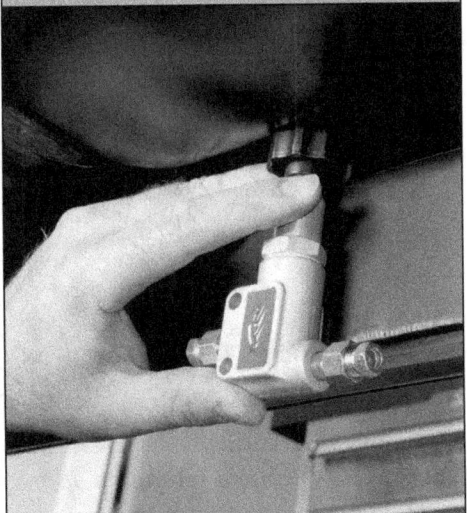

16 The rear line runs along the driver-side frame rail. This frame has been boxed for rigidity using an ABC Performance Frame Boxing Kit. This provides a solid surface to run the brake line on and to mount the proportioning valve where it can poke through the floor just outboard of the driver's seat.

Mount Brake Proportioning Valve

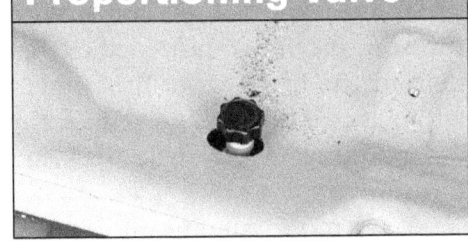

17 Mark the location and use a 1½-inch hole saw to drill a hole in the floor. Before drilling, make sure you have a grommet that fills this hole and fits tightly around the neck of the brake proportioning valve. The grommet seals around the proportioning valve as it enters the interior of the car, keeping dirt and water out while you're driving. Once you cut this access hole, you can determine the valve's mounting height and mark the position to drill and tap holes in the frame. The Baer proportioning valve comes with the necessary fittings to plumb it into the brake line.

CHAPTER 6

ENGINE UPGRADES

This book is dedicated to helping you create a well-rounded performance Chevelle, paying attention to everything from brakes to suspension to fuel system, and even the interior. That's because a modern muscle car needs to be able to perform in all of these areas far better than what was previously expected. It's too easy to throw money at go-fast goodies that help in the horsepower department without considering the rest of the car, resulting in a vehicle that isn't much fun to drive.

The most significant engine upgrade (engine swaps) is covered in Chapter 7. But there are quite a few ways you can improve the performance of your existing engine. The key to making good decisions on what to upgrade is to take careful inventory of what you currently have, and consider how you want to use the car. Today, finding a Chevelle that's completely stock under the hood is pretty rare. The original engines have usually been replaced, and there may be a hodge-podge of performance parts in place. Before you start making more changes, you need to know exactly what you have.

There is no shortage of engine upgrades, and many of them do not require a total engine buildup. If you have a solid-running small-block or big-block engine in your Chevelle, you can upgrade everything from the ignition system to the cylinder heads.

If you currently have a relatively stock V-8 that runs well, there is a lot of potential to increase the power without pulling the engine out and doing a complete build-up. The key is making sure all of the components you ultimately install are matched to each other. Make sure they are intended to work in the same engine speed range, and for approximately the same power output. There are hundreds of dyno-proven

ENGINE UPGRADES

A GM HEI ignition system, such as this one from Performance Distributors, is a great way to install an electronic ignition system in your Chevelle. If you upgrade from a contact-points-type distributor to an HEI system, you need a new set of spark plug wires because the boot at the distributor is different.

combinations for small- and big-block Chevrolet engines. Pick one that mimics your short-block (displacement, piston type, etc.) and copy the combo.

There is a process to upgrades that usually yields the best results. Following this order gives you results that reward you for your efforts as you go, and prepares the car to best use the next upgrade.

Ignition System

While later GM cars came with a dependable HEI ignition system, all of the 1964–1972 Chevelles came with a contact points-type ignition system that is problematic at best. Upgrading to an electronic ignition system makes the system more reliable. Depending on the condition of the system you're replacing, you may see a performance and fuel economy improvement.

There are quite a few options when it comes to upgrading to an electronic ignition system. One option is to simply change to an HEI distributor. There is enough room at the firewall for the larger distributor and the coil-in-cap configuration.

Another option is to convert the contact points distributor to an electronic module from Pertronix or MSD. These bolt in place of the contact points mechanism, retaining your original distributor. You can reuse your cap, rotor, and plug wires, as long as they are in good condition. Naturally, using a high-output coil and a quality set of plug wires is also a good upgrade when addressing the ignition system.

Exhaust System

If no other parts or systems are failing or questionable, turn your attention to the exhaust system. If your car has exhaust manifolds, a set of headers and true dual exhaust make a noticeable performance difference, even with an all-stock engine. Chapter 10 covers this topic in detail.

Intake System

The next stage of upgrades should focus on the air and fuel intake. There

Installing a set of headers makes a performance difference you can feel every time you accelerate. The size of the header tube should be matched to the size of your engine and horsepower level, as should the rest of the exhaust system.

CHAPTER 6

This Dart single-plane intake is perfect for a 500-plus-hp small-block, but doesn't work well on a low-horsepower engine. Make sure you match the components in your engine so they work together.

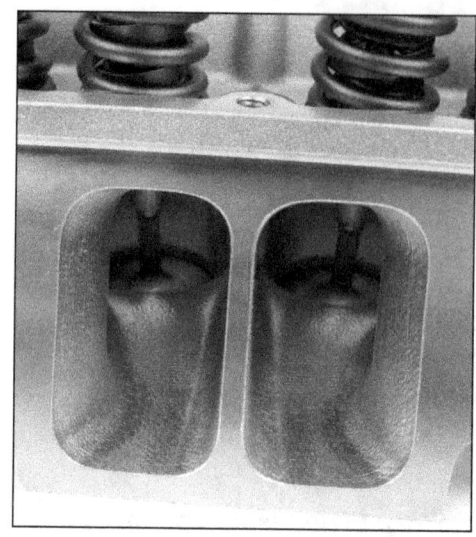

Cylinder heads can make a dramatic difference in engine power. These are CNC-ported Dart heads, which flow amazingly well. Dart offers a full range of cylinder heads for small- and big-block Chevrolet engines that work well on engines ranging from stock to ultra-high horsepower.

are a few choices to make at this stage, such as whether to stay with a carburetor or go with fuel injection. Converting to fuel injection is so popular now that a project is included in this chapter showing you what's involved. You also need to know how wild you'll get with this engine in the future so you can size the carburetor or fuel injection properly.

For example, if you're planning on changing the cylinder heads and camshaft later, a carbureted high-rise dual-plane intake may be a good choice that is drivable now and still works well with later upgrades. If you make too big a jump, however, you can actually decrease performance and really hurt drivability, neither of which make you feel good about your purchases. If you're planning a radical change, you're better off stockpiling the parts and changing the intake, carb, heads, and cam all at once.

Cylinder Head and Camshaft

Whether you change cylinder heads or the camshaft next varies according to what you have. Much of the same work is involved, so many people change both at once.

Another reason for doing both at once is that the valvesprings need to be matched to your camshaft. If you put aftermarket heads on a stock engine with springs set up for a more aggressive cam, you may damage your stock camshaft.

It's also much easier to change valvesprings with the cylinder heads removed from the engine.

Picking the right cylinder head and cam combination is an intense science and, in fact, there are several books available to help guide you through this process. The secret to success is getting the combination of port size, compression ratio, cam timing, and intake type correct so that all of the engine parts complement one another.

Camshaft selection is difficult because there are so many choices. Since the cam controls the timing of the valve actuation, it plays a critical part in how your engine runs, how much power it makes, and how drivable the engine is. It's usually best to order a matched set of valvesprings and lifters with the camshaft.

CHEVELLE PERFORMANCE PROJECTS: 1964–1972

Project 1: Performance Ignition System Installation

Select New Ignition System

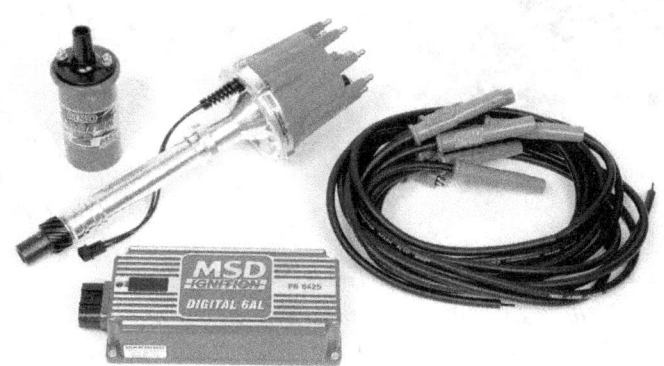

1 An ignition upgrade can fix a lot of problems in a Chevelle. These cars all came with contact-points-type distributors, which require maintenance and are not the best for performance. We're going to look at the installation of a complete MSD ignition system, including a drop-in billet distributor, Digital 6AL ignition, Blaster 2 coil, and 8.5-mm plug wires. The MSD billet distributor retains a small-diameter cap and small spark plug boot at the cap. You can install the Digital 6AL box with just about any distributor and coil.

Disconnect Battery

2 As with any electric component, a spark during installation can damage the component, causing frustration when you finish and the engine doesn't run. Disconnect the negative battery cable, so that touching the wrench to something metal while loosening the clamp does not result in a spark. Once the negative is disconnected, it's not necessary to remove the positive battery cable.

Inspect MSD Digital 6AL

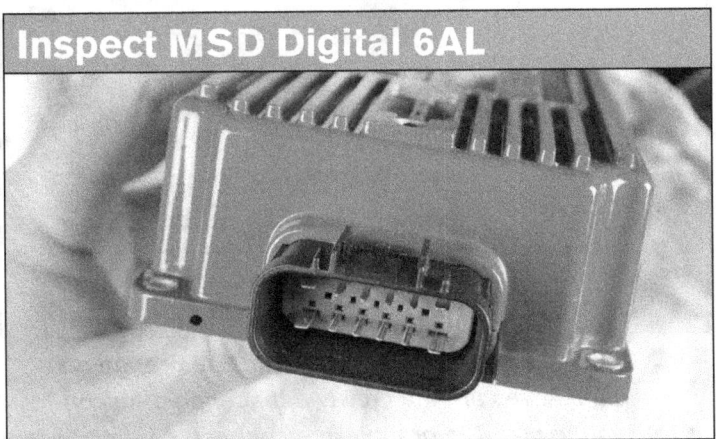

3 The distributor is a straight-forward drop-in installation, the same as any other distributor. The 6AL installation may be intimidating if you haven't installed one before. The current family of MSD ignition boxes uses a single plug at the box to connect the wiring harness. This lets them use the same box for multiple applications by changing the supplied harness. It makes the installation easier, as you can mount the box, route the harness, and then connect the two of them together. This also makes damage to the box less likely if the wires are pulled on.

Inspect Ignition Harness

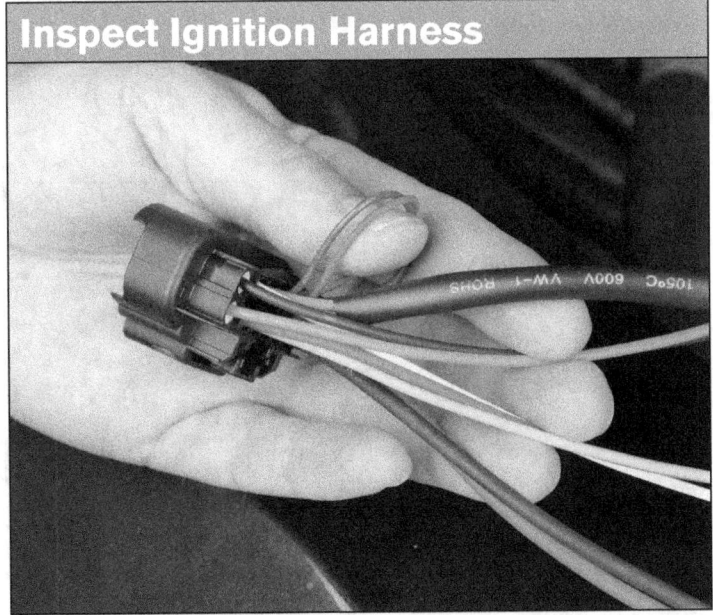

4 The harness has all of the wires needed for installation. On non-Digital 6A boxes, you had to extend the tachometer wire and route it to the box, but the tach lead is now included in the harness of the new box. You must connect the tachometer to the ignition box, even if you are not changing the distributor or coil. The red and blue loops are how you select four or six cylinders, which is not necessary when building a performance Chevelle.

CHAPTER 6

Mount Ignition Box

5 Finding a place to mount the ignition box is the hardest part. You can mount it in the engine compartment as long as it is not too close to headers or other high-heat sources. You also want the ignition box to get fresh air, so it should not be mounted in a glove box or some other enclosure. Make sure that the wires reach their destination with the desired box location. The most common choices are on the firewall (shown) or high on one of the inner fenderwells. An alternative is to mount it under the dash, but this requires extra effort to pass the wiring through the firewall. Rubber mounts are supplied to absorb vibration.

Install Positive and Negative Leads

6 Primary positive and negative leads must be mounted directly to the battery. If your car has a trunk-mounted battery, you need to install a power distribution block underhood. Don't use the alternator for this as it can create problems. Also, make sure you have a very good chassis ground throughout the entire car if you have a trunk-mounted battery. The most common problem with electrical components is not properly connecting the power and ground leads to clean, reliable sources.

Connect Ignition Wire to Ballast Resister

7 All of these cars came with ballast resisters, which decreased the voltage to the ignition system. You bypass this with the new MSD ignition system. If you install an HEI system or some other electronic ignition system, you need to bypass this as well. Connect the smaller red wire in the MSD harness to the wire that provides power to the ballast resister. Disconnect both wires, hook the battery up, turn the key to ignition position, and check to see which wire has power.

Connect Wires to Ignition Coil

8 When using an MSD Digital 6AL, the orange and black wires are the only two that should be connected to the coil. The orange wire connects to the positive side of the coil, and the black wire goes to the negative side. The only other wire that may have been there was the tach lead on the negative side, which should now be connected to the gray wire in the MSD harness. Any other wires must be relocated to other power sources. Connect the last wires to the ignition trigger. If you are using an MSD distributor designed for an MSD ignition box, there is a harness plug with violet and green wires. This plugs directly to the distributor. Any other type of distributor is connected using the single white wire.

ENGINE UPGRADES

Adjust Rev Limiter

9 The difference between the MSD Digital 6A and the 6AL is the integrated soft-touch rev limiter. You can adjust the engine speed limit in 100-rpm steps by popping off the black cover on the face of the box and turning the sealed rotary switches with a small flat-blade screwdriver. The rev limiter drops spark to individual cylinders for a load-free limit that is easier on the engine. The ignition box also has an LED that flashes with each trigger signal. It is solid red when the engine is running at higher speeds, and also when the box has power but the engine is not running.

Project 2: Fuel-Injection System Installation

Select EFI System

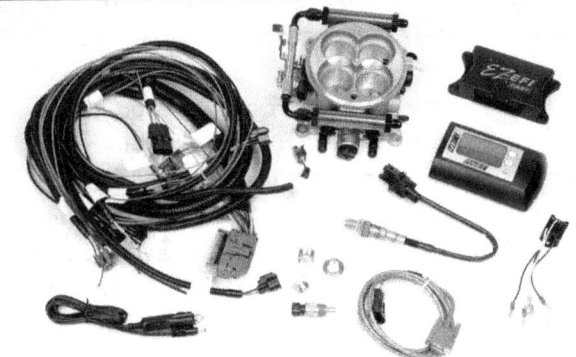

1 Another popular engine upgrade is converting your Chevelle's intake from a carburetor to fuel injection. Most of the EFI kits are pretty easy to install, but they look intimidating because of the massive wiring harness, the ECU, and required fuel-system upgrades. The FAST EZ-EFI self-tuning system aims to make the conversion as easy as possible, and makes the tuning of the fuel injection system child's play.

Inspect FAST EZ-EFI System

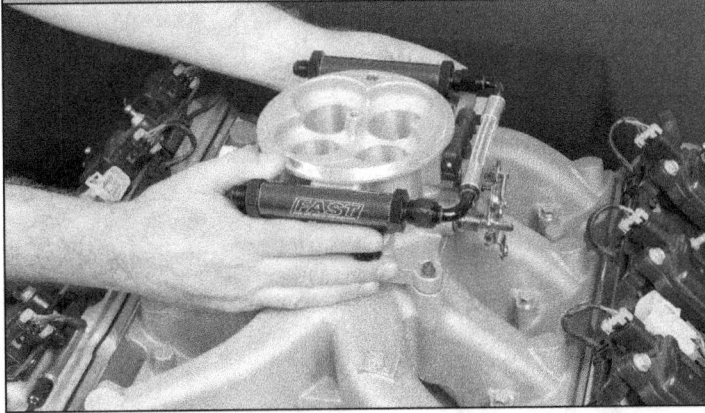

2 The FAST EZ-EFI system uses a throttle body instead of a port-injection system. Four fuel injectors are mounted in the base of the throttle body, so the entire mechanical part of the fuel injection system simply bolts on in place of the common square-flange Holley carburetor. A throttle-body system doesn't provide as many advantages as a more-complicated port-injection system, but it eliminates fuel slosh in a carb during cornering and hard braking, and increases efficiency.

Choose Fuel Pump Kit

3 Optional fuel pumps and fuel line kits are also available from FAST, and come with just about everything you need. I say "just about," because you need about 6 more feet of fuel line to complete the return line in a Chevelle. The FAST fuel pump and regulator ensure that all of the parts are matched and meant to perform together, and the wiring harness has the proper plugs to simply connect to the fuel pump and snap into the main FAST EZ-EFI wiring harness for an easy installation. The system is designed to be regulated to 43 psi.

Inspect Cushion and Clamps

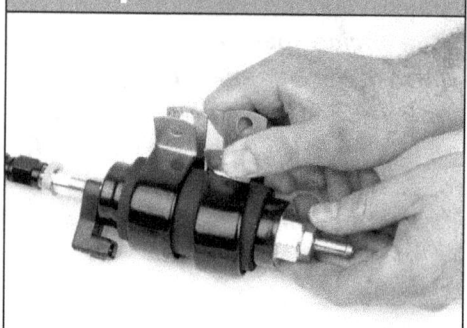

4 A cushion and clamps are provided with the fuel pump kit, making it easy to mount. These pumps push fuel very well, but are not that good at pulling it, so they should be mounted as close to the fuel tank as possible. The kit comes with a fuel filter that is meant to be installed between the fuel pump and the throttle body. You should either retain the sock on the fuel pickup tube or install a pre-filter between the tank and the pump to catch larger pieces of debris that might damage the pump.

Mount Fuel Pump to Trunk Floor

5 Bolt the pump to the raised section of the trunk floor directly in front of the fuel tank. Use 3/8-inch bolts to secure the clamps directly to the floor. The vibration is minimal while the pump is running and the engine is off, and you cannot hear the pump at all once the engine is running. If you have a very quiet car, you could further cushion the mount of the fuel pump, or consider using an in-tank pump.

Install Hoses

6 The FAST fuel line kit uses push-fit -6 AN hose and hose ends. Regardless of the type of AN hose you use, route it from the rear of the car to the throttle body. Thread the hose end onto the fuel rail and cut the hose to length. It's best to leave an extra inch or two, but you don't want too much extra. The push-fit hose can be cut with heavy-duty cutters (shown). Most braided line needs to be cut with an air-powered cut-off wheel. To assemble a push-fit hose, hold the hose firmly and push the barbed fitting into the hose. This is extremely difficult, even if you use the recommended lubricant.

Inspect Hose Options

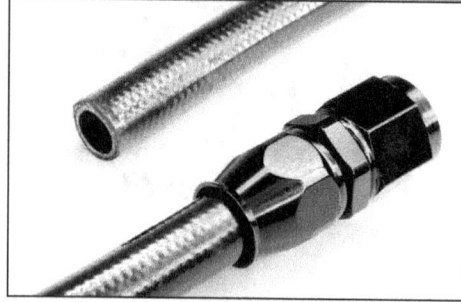

7 An alternative fuel line is a new product designed specifically for issues with today's fuel. TechAFX Black-Wrap AN hose features a polytetrafluoroethylene (PTFE) conductive-core inner liner that is made to resist the deterioration and seepage that is possible with standard rubber-lined hose and some other forms of braided-steel lines. BlackWrap has a black polyester outer covering applied over braided stainless steel to create an impact-resistant hose. TechAFX PTFE AN hoses are also conductive-core, which means they have a carbon lining that dissipates the static electricity generated by fuel moving through PTFE hose. (Photo Courtesy TechAFX)

Mount ECM Under Hood

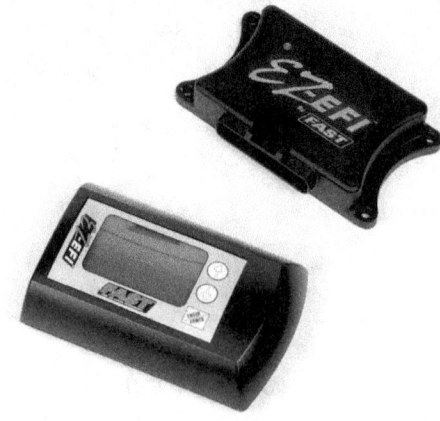

8 The ECM for the system is only a few inches wide, making it easy to mount. It should be located away from high-heat sources, but it can be mounted underhood. You can also mount it inside the car, under the dash. You want it somewhere you can easily access it though, as the handheld controller plugs into the controller harness near the ECM. Also, before you drill holes to locate the ECM, make sure the harness reaches all the necessary sensors and connections on the engine.

ENGINE UPGRADES

Plug Wiring Harness into Throttle Body

9 Almost all connections in the wiring harness plug into the throttle body. Each fuel injector has its own electrical connection; there are two facing the front of the engine and two facing the rear. Another connection is the air-temperature sensor. At the rear bottom of the throttle body is the idle air motor. The last connection at the throttle body is the MAP sensor, located on the driver's side.

Mount Temperature and Oxygen Sensor

10 The only two sensors the FAST EZ-EFI system uses that aren't located on the throttle body are the temperature sensor and the oxygen sensor. The temperature sensor should be installed in a cylinder head. For the oxygen sensor, a weld-in bung and plug are included with the kit. A 3/4-inch hole needs to be drilled in the header collector, and the bung welded in place. The plug is provided so you can do this in advance and drive the car without the oxygen sensor installed. It is a heated sensor, and having it installed but not operating while the engine is running can damage it.

Connect Throttle Cable

11 The remaining wires to connect are the primary positive and negative wires, which should be routed directly to the battery, the white signal lead to the negative side of the coil, and the tach connection to supply a signal to your tachometer. Finally, you can hook up the throttle cable. The throttle body accepts a Holley-style linkage or cable. This is a Lokar cable, mount, and throttle return spring bracket, which mounts securely. Check it for mechanical wide-open throttle with the gas pedal all the way down, and adjust it if needed.

Set Initial Calibration

12 The FAST EZ-EFI system is self tuning, so it doesn't require a software engineering degree to set it up. Instead, it calibrates itself. Often, the most difficult part of installing an EFI system is properly calibrating it for engine and operating environment. The FAST system asks you a series of questions when you first power it up, such as engine size and idle speed, and then it has you calibrate the throttle position sensor. Then you're ready to start the engine. You can tune the fuel map after you drive the car to see what is necessary. The system also learns as you drive, automatically adjusting the fuel delivery to stay on the target air/fuel ratio.

CHAPTER 7

ENGINE SWAPS

When you're thinking of building a performance Chevelle, one fact is undeniable: you need more power than the stock Chevelle came with. Even the engine that set the muscle car world on its ear—the venerable and almost myth-like LS6—is outdated for what most people want in their modern Chevelle.

An engine swap doesn't necessarily mean changing to something totally different under your hood. If you have a small-block car, you can now build a 427-ci version of the old mouse motor that makes more than 600 hp and runs on pump gas without any power adders. Factor in a supercharger or turbo, and things can get really crazy. And if you have a big-block, the sky is the limit.

Even swapping out a small-block for a big-block isn't terribly challenging, since these cars were available with both originally. People have been swapping back and forth since 1964, so there is a plethora of parts and knowledge on exchanging a mouse for a rat and vice versa. You can have either small-block or big-block in all-aluminum, short-deck, tall-deck, strokers, and just about anything else you can dream up. I don't want to oversimplify these swaps, but frankly, there's a ton of really good information already available on how to do this.

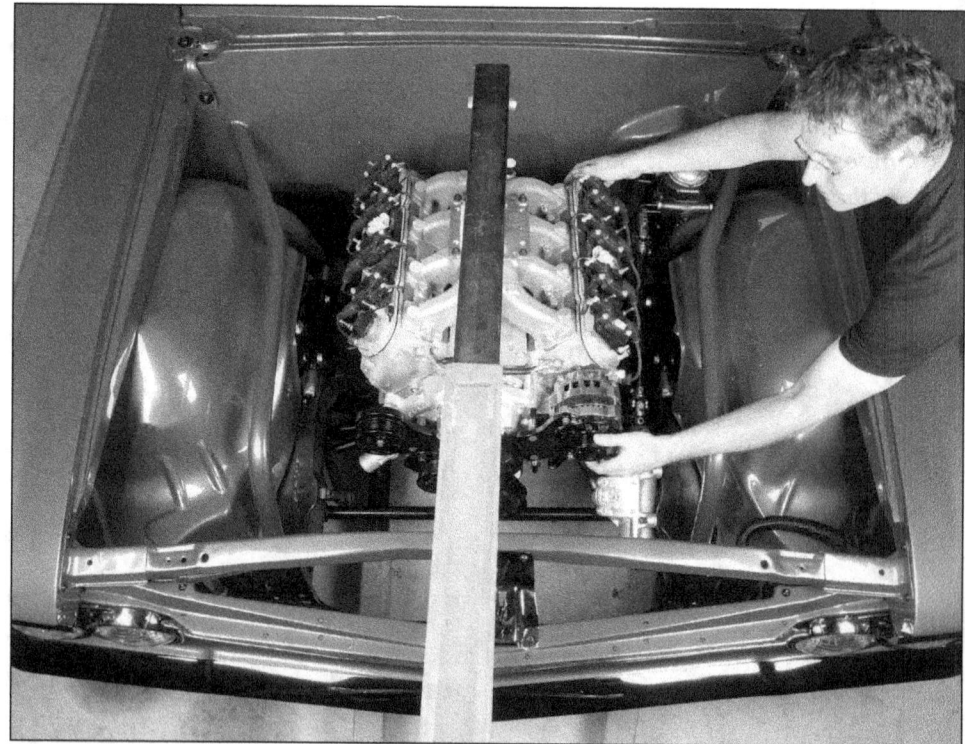

Building a completely modern performance Chevelle almost certainly requires an engine swap. Today, it's hard to find a Chevelle with a useable original engine. Even if you do, most of them were small-displacement versions of what's possible to build today.

Gen I vs LS

The engine swap detailed in this chapter is the most commonly talked-about and the least understood by the

ENGINE SWAPS

The LS family of engines is the one of the most popular swaps, providing an engine with great power for its displacement, high efficiency, and the option of going all-aluminum. However, they do not simply bolt in, and you need to change or adapt just about everything that attaches to the engine when installing one in your Chevelle.

majority of Chevelle owners today. I'm talking about replacing your Gen I small-block or big-block with an LS engine. If you look at the top-performing Chevelles at national events, it's hard to find one without some version of an LS engine between the vintage fenders. And by the looks of automotive magazines, you'd swear there isn't a Gen I engine used in these cars anymore. I'd like to be the first to tell you that isn't true.

And here's another myth I'm happy to set straight: An LS swap is neither easy nor inexpensive. To help with perspective before you decide you need an LS, consider that a Toyota Tundra V-8 has as much in common with your Gen I small-block as an LS engine. Blasphemy, you say? Let me explain.

The Simplicity Factor

It's a common misconception that *all* Chevy engines are easy to swap and have a ton of commonality among variants. That's probably because since 1955, with the introduction of the first small-block Chevrolet V-8 engine, all small-block Chevy engines retained the critical specs. Those include the head-bolt spacing, the accessory bolt-hole locations on the block, the bellhousing bolt pattern, and so on. The commonality became ingrained in performance builders to the point where most took it for granted. It nearly caused pandemonium when the one-piece crank seal was introduced, changing the crank, seal, and flywheel/flexplate centering register. These are now all referred to as Gen I small-blocks.

The Commonality Factor

The introduction of the LS design in 1997 ushered in a new era of Chevrolet engines. It shares nearly nothing with the Gen I. The exhaust ports are in a different location and the bolt pattern is different, absolutely none of the old accessory brackets bolt on, the water pump is completely different, the bellhousing bolt pattern is different, and the external dimensions are different.

To add to the challenge, all LS engines offered in production vehicles were fuel-injected, which means no factory carbureted intake manifolds and no mechanical ignition distribution system—it's all computer-controlled.

LS-Series Benefits

So, why the emphatic acceptance of an engine that requires the learning curve of a performance BMW or Mercedes engine? It is due in part to the fact that it is a Chevrolet V-8, and also because it is still a pushrod engine.

One of the biggest arguments for the LS engine design, though, is that the valve location and port design in the cylinder heads is fantastic for making power. This wasn't possible in the Gen I design, even in highly modified cylinder heads requiring unique intake manifolds and relocated exhaust ports. The LS arrangement solved a great many problems in moving the air/fuel mixture from the intake manifold into the cylinders with great efficiency. This cylinder head design also smoothes out more radical camshaft profiles which can be used without the choppy idle and decreased low-end torque that you would expect.

CHAPTER 7

These engines have cylinder heads designed to make efficient power. With a multi-port injection and computer-controlled ignition timing, an LS engine in front of an overdrive transmission is capable of producing over 500 hp and achieving more than 20 mpg.

Most people hear about $500 salvage yard LS1s and dream about easy 750-hp combos. The first step in an LS swap is to very carefully research what's available and what it takes to make the power you want in your Chevelle. Often, a brand-new Chevrolet Performance crate engine is the best route to getting very good power for your dollar.

Another reason the engine is popular is that it has been mass-produced for more than a decade, placing literally millions of them on the road. They are also, to this day, the most powerful mass-produced engines General Motors has ever produced.

The bottom line is that the LS engine family is growing in popularity for engine swaps, and is definitely favored among the top car builders. This has led to a growing availability of parts to make installing one in your Chevelle a little easier than dropping in the aforementioned Toyota Tundra V-8. But this swap is far from a drop-in, bolt-on exercise. In addition to some custom work, you have a lot of choices to make. That starts with which LS engine to use.

Engine Sources

Over the years, the engine has been available in all-iron, all-aluminum, and iron-block-with-aluminum-cylinder-heads versions. The displacement has varied from Vortec 4.8-liters (295 ci) to LS7 7.3 liters (427 ci), and power has ranged from 270 hp to 638. And the engines have been used in everything from pickup trucks to Corvettes.

Choosing your engine comes down to what is most important to you and how you use your car. And, naturally, your budget is a factor. An all-aluminum version has an advantage for all types of racing, reducing the front weight of your Chevelle more than 100 pounds. These engines are typically more expensive, but are also usually higher performance in stock form.

Another factor to consider is whether you'd be happy with the stock power. If not, you likely need to replace the crank, rods, and pistons to create a durable engine. It's quite easy to spec out a $10,000 LS engine to make 500 hp or more.

Crate Engine

Which brings us to brand-new LS engines from the Chevrolet Performance bin of crate engines. When we went to press with this book, Chevrolet Performance offered nearly a dozen versions of the LS engine as complete crate engines, plus a few race versions. They range from an economical LS327 (which is an iron-block 5.3-liter (327 ci) minus intake, exhaust, and accessories) all the way up to the LS9 supercharged 6.2-liter (376 ci) found in the 2012 ZR1 making 638 hp.

If you're looking for a drop-in LS engine that's brand new, this is a

ENGINE SWAPS

LS Engine at a Glance

There's a whole alphabet soup involved in the codes used for the various models of LS engines, and not all of them contain "LS" in the name, such as the 4.8-liter Vortec and the L92. This chart provides the specifications of the most popular LS engines.

Engine	Size (ci)	Size (Liters)	Block Material	Power (hp)	Ft-lbs	Year and Model
LS1	346	5.7	Aluminum	305-350	335-375	1998-2002 F-Body, 1997-2004 Corvette, 2004 GTO
LS2	364	6.0	Aluminum	400	400	2005-2007 Corvette; 2005-2006 SSR, GTO; 2006-2007 CTS-V; 2006-2009 Trailblazer SS
LS3/L99	376	6.2	Aluminum	400-430	410-428	2008-2012 Corvette, G8; 2010 Camaro; 2007-2012 Escalade, Tahoe, Silverado, Yukon, Sierra, Hummer H2
LS6	346	5.7	Aluminum	385-405	385-400	2001-2004 Corvette Z06, 2004-2005 CTS-V
LS7	427	7.0	Aluminum	505	470	2006-2012 Corvette Z06
LS9	376	6.2	Aluminum	638	604	2009-2012 Corvette ZR1
LSA	376	6.2	Aluminum	556	551	2009-2012 CTS-V
LQ4/LQ9	364	6.0	Iron	300-347	360-380	1999-2004 Silverado, Suburban, Yukon, Hummer H2; 2002-2006 Escalade; 2003-2007 Silverado SS, Sierra
LY6	364	6.0	Iron	352	382	2007 Silverado, Sierra, Suburban, Yukon
L76	364	6.0	Aluminum	361-366	376-385	2007-2012 Silverado, Sierra, Suburban, Yukon, Avalanche, G8
LR4	293	4.8	Iron or Aluminum	270-295	285-305	1999-2012 Silverado, Tahoe, Yukon, Sierra
LM4LM7/ L33/L59	325	5.3	Iron or Aluminum	285-320	325-340	1999-2012 mid- and full-size trucks, SUVs

great way to go. No rebuilding, no used engine parts. But you still have quite a bit of homework to do before it's bolted into your car and purring like a kitten.

Used Engine

On the used-engine front, you often hear about someone finding a complete LS engine for just a few hundred dollars. That might be tempting, but realize that these are usually 100,000-plus-mile engines that require rebuilding, and the displacement is seldom more than 5.7 liters (350 ci). One of the most sought after salvage yard engines is an L92/L99 6.0-liter engine out of a Denali or Escalade. These are all-aluminum. You can toss a carb and headers on one and make 430 hp and still have a 650-rpm idle without changing any internal engine parts.

Budget Requirements

The LS7 may be one of the most desirable candidates for swapping. It's the largest in displacement and the highest in naturally aspirated power output from the factory. It's all-aluminum, and it's pretty cool to have a 427-ci engine in your classic Chevelle. There's usually a "however," and the however in this case is that it came from General Motors

CHAPTER 7

This isn't your father's small-block Chevy. When performing a swap, there are a few basics about the LS engine that are helpful to understand. Even if you aren't building one from the crank up, knowing some of the key variances from Gen I small-blocks help you adapt the engine for your Chevelle. First, there is no coolant routed through the intake manifold. Instead of a thermostat housing at the top center of the intake, coolant enters and exits the block only through the water pump. The thermostat housing is built into the water pump, and there are no ports in the intake for the temperature sensor. This also creates the need for a steam line in many factory applications.

Production LS blocks have only 10 head bolts per side, a problem that plagued Ford engines for decades. This is fine at production cylinder pressure levels, but if you want to make serious power, you fight head gasket problems. Aftermarket blocks, such as this LSX block from Chevrolet Performance, have additional bosses for head bolts. This is a great choice if you are thinking about adding a supercharger or a turbo and pushing beyond 750 hp.

On the LS, the oil pump is at the front of the engine. It bolts to the block around the snout of the crank. The key in the crank drives the pump. This means several things for retrofits. First, the oil pump sump needs to run from the back of the engine (rear sump) all the way to the front. This is problematic for 1964–1967 Chevelles because of oil pan-to-crossmember clearance. Second, there is no way to spin the oil pump without spinning the crank to pre-lube the engine before you start it for the first time. There are pre-lube devices available that basically tap into the oil system externally.

with a dry-sump oil system, and the oil pan requires significant surgery to your Chevelle crossmember for proper fitment. The unique crank makes it difficult to change to a wet-sump oiling system. I've seen a couple Chevelles with the LS7, but there was a lot of custom fabrication involved.

The biggest number to keep in mind is how much the various engine-swap components cost. It's not uncommon to spend $4,000 on parts just to put an LS into your Chevelle.

While this may be one of the most-talked-about swaps today, before committing to an LS engine, ask yourself why you want one and determine how much it really costs. Replacing a 400-hp Gen I small-block with a 400-hp LS is an expensive venture for the benefit of being able to tell people your Chevelle has an LS engine in it. On the other hand, if you have no engine in your Chevelle, or are already planning on upgrading the headers, accessories, transmission, and so on, the LS should definitely be on your consideration list.

Sensor Tutorial

An LS engine, whether you buy it used or brand new, has a lot of sensors that may not be familiar to you. Every production LS engine has computer-controlled fuel injection and ignition timing. Even the Chevrolet Performance carbureted version comes with all of the production sensors installed in the block, and you need to tap into most of them to make your engine run properly.

Most LS engines have a coolant sensor in the driver-side cylinder head at the front of the engine. This one sends data to the ECM that's used to operate the original temperature gauge and supply data to the fuel injection. If you run fuel injection, leave this one in place. In the other cylinder head at the rear is a plug that you can unthread and replace with a sending unit for an electric temperature gauge.

At the rear of the block is a sending unit for oil pressure. In almost all cases, you need to remove this and install an adapter to run a traditional sending unit for an oil pressure gauge. Auto Meter makes a 1/8-inch NPT to M16x1.5 adapter (part number 2268) specifically for this purpose, and it works with most electric sending units the adaptor will also accept a fitting for a mechanical oil-pressure hose.

The camshaft sensor connection is found near the damper on the front of the engine. This is one of two sensors used by the ECM to control the spark. Even if you use an aftermarket or stand-alone ignition controller, it still needs to connect to the camshaft sensor as well as the crank sensor.

The crank sensor is near the rear of the engine, and it can be in one of two places. On earlier engines, it is located on top of the lifter valley, near the oil-pressure sensor (shown here). On later engines, it is on the passenger side of the block, behind the starter (see photo below).

The crank sensor is hidden behind the starter on later engines (A). You want to make this connection before installing the starter motor. The other sensor in this photo (B) is the knock sensor. Factory ECMs use this, but many aftermarket controllers do not.

CHAPTER 7

Project 1: LS Engine Installation

Prepare for Installation

1 There's quite a bit of prep to do before you're ready to hoist your LS engine over your fenders for the first time. The very first thing you should do is buy yourself a good set of metric tools. That's right, metric. Everything on these engines is metric. Start with a good kit, like this one from Kobalt, which comes with sockets, wrenches, and Allen wrenches. You also should have a set of six-point sockets, ratcheting wrenches, and Allen socket drivers.

Choose Adapter Plates

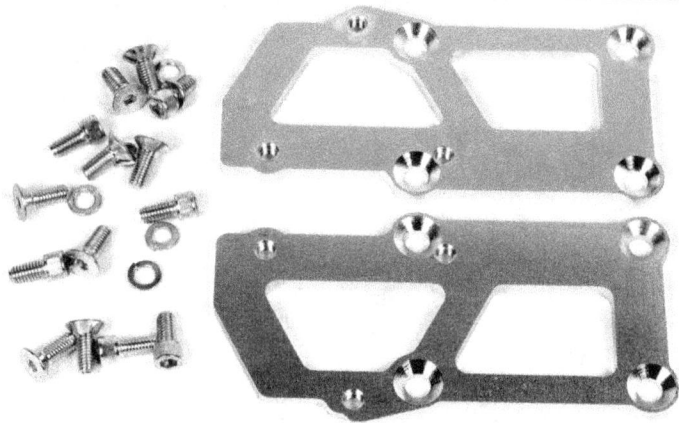

2 LS engines use a totally different style of engine mount compared to older Chevys. Several companies offer adapter plates that bolt to the sides of the block and accept a traditional engine mount for a simple solution. However, all of these adapters place the engine in a slightly different location, fore and aft, in the chassis. The headers and oil pan may come in contact with the body or subframe. My recommendation is to get the engine mount adapters, headers, and oil pan from the same company, which means you have to consider all of the components when selecting one. The billet aluminum adapters shown are from Hooker, which also makes full-length 1¾-inch primary tube headers and oil pans. Three versions of the adapters are available: one positions the bellhousing flange at the stock location, another moves it forward, and a third moves it backward. Keeping the engine at stock location or moving it rearward is best for fitment of the headers and oil pan, as well as weight balance.

Install Adapter Plates

3 This Trans Dapt engine mount adapter is installed on an LS3 engine. It requires a bit of grinding to clear a boss on the engine. Use Moroso solid engine mounts that are 1/4 inch taller than factory to help with oil pan clearance in an early Chevelle. The engine in the 1964–1967 Chevelles sits more than 1 inch closer to the engine crossmember and steering linkage than the engine in the 1968–1972 cars. This creates a challenge with oil pan clearance, and moving the engine up slightly with these engine mounts helps. Moroso also offers stock-height solid mounts. I prefer solid engine mounts because nothing moves as the engine revs. They do transfer more vibration to the chassis and, ultimately, the driver and passengers. Polyurethane mounts from Energy Suspension are an option for better control and durability than rubber, and better vibration isolation than solid mounts.

Select Headers

4 The exhaust manifolds on some high-performance stock LS engines provide decent flow. But most of them do not fit in the chassis of a Chevelle very well. The best solution is a set of headers made specifically for an LS engine that's going into a Chevelle. Hedman Headers makes mid-length and full-length headers designed to fit with Trans Dapt engine adapter plates. They have 1¾-inch primary tubes and 3-inch collectors. Hooker makes full-length headers designed to work with its engine adapter plates. You can also have custom headers made. This is usually more expensive and requires access to a talented fabricator, but it normally results in the best-fitting headers.

Fit Headers

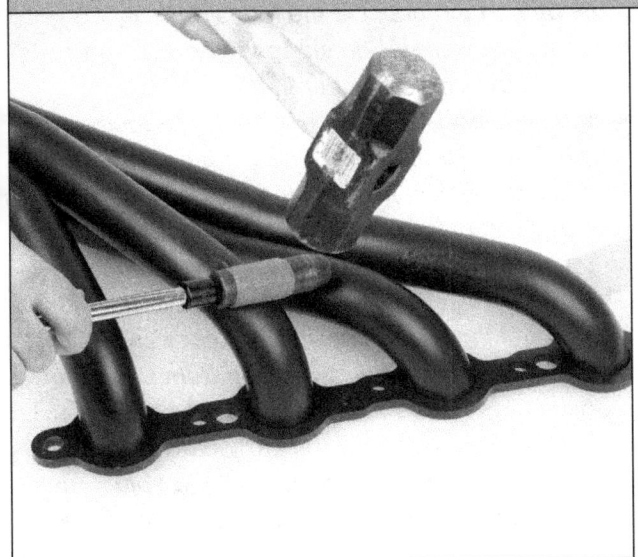

5 I used Hooker black ceramic-coated 1¾-inch primary tube headers with 3-inch collectors for installing a Chevrolet Performance 515-hp LS3 into a 1966 Chevelle. The headers were the best-fitting set I've installed on a Chevelle out of the box. However, I did have to massage them with a hammer in a couple of places because of our specific situation. First, the number five tube hit our steering shaft. I had previously converted the car's steering shaft and were running a Borgeson 1-inch double-D shaft. This may or may not be an issue with the stock steering shaft on 1964–1967 cars, but I suspect it will be really close if not touching. It should not be a problem on the 1968–1972 Chevelles. To create a smooth dimple for clearance, wrap an impact socket with several layers of masking tape, place it on the tube at the correct area, and hit it with a hammer. Lay the port flange of the header flat on the ground to keep from bending it.

Weld Temperature Sensor Bungs onto Headers

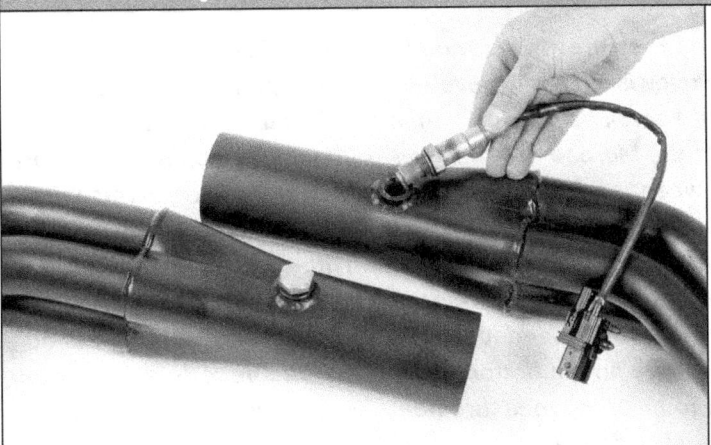

6 Most of the headers available for LS swaps come with oxygen sensor bungs welded into the collectors. If you're using shorty headers, weld these bungs into the exhaust tubing approximately where the exhaust meets the flat section of the floorboards. If you're using an aftermarket fuel-injection system or controller for the factory hardware, it most likely comes with weld-in bungs. If not, you can purchase them from most aftermarket fuel-injection companies.

Oil Pan Options

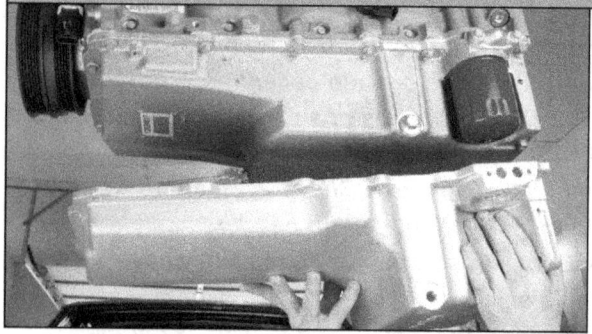

7 The oil pan for an LS engine is one area that highlights the difference between 1964–1967 Chevelles and the later 1968–1972 cars. Because the crossmember, inner tie rods, and center link are closer to the oil pan on the early cars, finding an oil pan that fits is extra challenging, and most oil pans designed for Chevelles fit the later cars better than the early ones. Many of the most desirable LS engines come in Corvettes, trucks, or other applications that use an oil pan that don't fit in any Chevelle. The sump generally comes too far forward, and the front section hangs down too low for crossmember and steering linkage clearance. Some people opt to cut, plate, and box the crossmember and convert to rack-and-pinion steering. If you go this route, make sure the manufacturer of the rack-and-pinion system assures you that its system fits your plan. Every oil pan comes with an oil pump pickup tube specific to the pan.

Inspect Oil Pan Options

8 Here are some oil pan options. On the left is a Holley LS conversion pan for Chevelles. The sump is generous and sits about the same height as the crossmember in the car.

The pan in the middle is an F-car pan, used on LS1-equipped Camaros and Firebirds in the 1990s. If your LS engine is moved as far back as possible in the chassis, this fits, but barely. It also makes getting the engine in and out extremely difficult because of the tight fit of the oil pan on the crossmember and the engine against the firewall. Street & Performance sells a modified version of this pan that reduces the sump, making it a better fit in the chassis.

The pan on the right is a muscle car swap pan from Chevrolet Performance. The shape of the pan solves some issues, but the extra-deep sump hangs more than 1 inch below the crossmember in an early Chevelle. It also contacts the crossmember and steering linkage on the early cars. Milodon makes sheet-metal oil pans for LS swaps. A lot of people use these without any trouble, but the factory cast-aluminum pan is a structural part of the engine, providing strength on the bottom end. Reports vary as to how well these fit the early cars, although they do seem to fit the 1968–1972 cars well.

Modify Pan for Clearance

9 The Holley oil pan requires fewer modifications to fit an early car than the others. Also, Holley is currently developing a new pan that should address these issues, as well as provide baffling in the sump for road and autocross racing. Use the Moroso 1/4-inch-tall solid engine mounts and insert 0.150-inch shims between the engine mounts and adapter plates to raise the engine another 1/3 inch in the chassis. This is sufficient to create a tiny gap between the Holley oil pan and the crossmember. With solid engine mounts, you don't have settling or movement, so a tiny gap is enough. The fix for inner tie rod clearance is much more involved. With the engine in the car, mark the sides of the pan with the amount of room needed. Then raise the engine just high enough to be able to fully steer lock to lock, and trace the arc of the linkage on the bottom of the pan. The tie rods deflect when the car is cornering hard, so you need to add about 3/16 inch to all of the measurements. The result is that two windows need to be cut into the cast-aluminum oil pan by using an air-powered cut-off wheel and a reciprocating saw.

ENGINE SWAPS

Fit Pickup Tube to Oil Pan

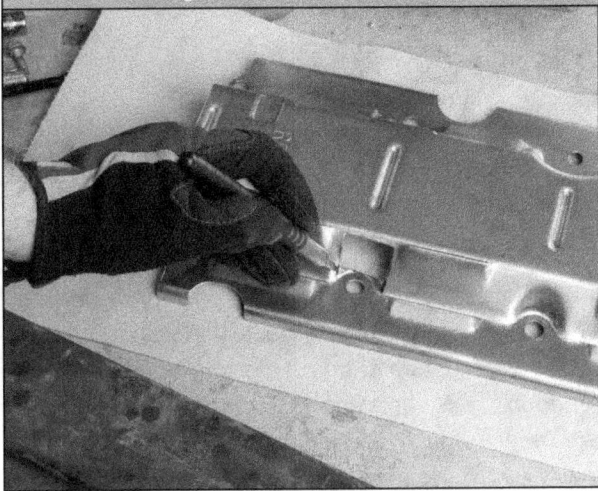

10 If the oil pan you plan to use comes with a pickup tube running along the opposite side of the engine than the one you're removing, or it connects to a different mounting location, you need to modify the windage tray. For example, the LS3 came in a Corvette and had the pickup tube on the driver's side of the engine. The Holley pan (and most LS oil pans) has the pickup tube on the passenger's side. You need to mock-up the placement of the tube under the engine and mark where it interferes with the windage tray. Typically, you need to cut away material near the mounting stud, and you may also need to trim the mount on the new oil pickup tube. Do so carefully, however. You do not want the pickup tube mount to break, allowing the tube to fall, potentially suctioning itself against the bottom of the pan and starving the engine of oil.

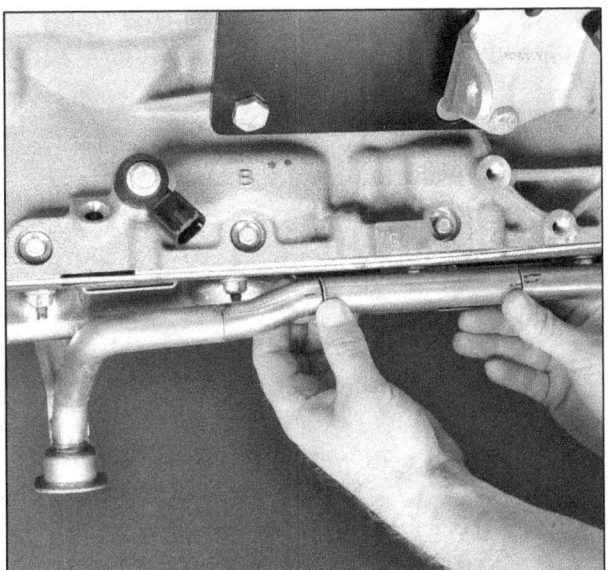

11 In early Chevelles, you need to reduce the depth of the oil pan where the pickup tube runs. This means cutting and welding the tube so it is as tight against the bottom of the engine as possible. This modification requires extreme care, because even a pinhole in the welds allows the oil pump to suck air, aerating the oil being pushed into the engine. That's bad. You can order an F-car pickup tube from General Motors, which starts out fairly tight against the engine, and start cutting. You need it to be even higher than the original F-car tube, so make the first cut at the first bend in the tube as it connects to the pump. Then cut and weld a section to get the clearance you want and position the pickup exactly where Holley designed it in the oil pump. Hand-file the cut pieces and TIG-weld them for clean and controlled welds. Then pressure-test the tube by plugging the ends, applying air pressure through one of the plugs, and running soapy water over the tube to check for air leaks.

Install Oil Trap Door in Pan

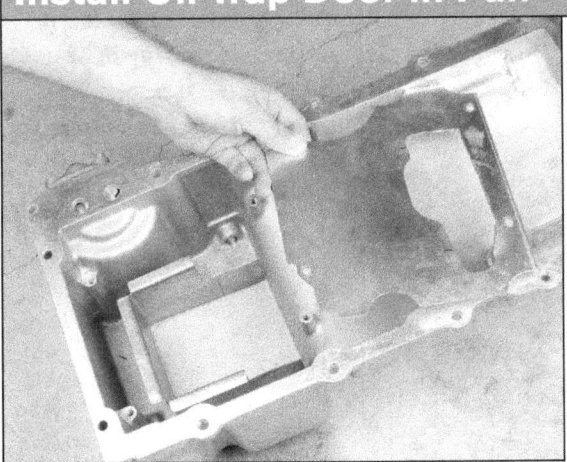

12 You can build a trap-door system in the sump area of the Holley oil pan for better oil control during hard cornering. The idea is to create a box around the oil pump pickup. By using trap doors to make it easy for oil to enter the area, but hard to exit during cornering, this reduces the chance of momentary oil starvation during high lateral G maneuvers. The Holley pan comes with the baffle shown, which bolts to the pan to further reduce windage. ABC Performance custom fabricated the metal insert located in the sump area of the pan. This cuts the horizontal surface area of the sump section by about 40 percent. Rivet this piece to the original bolt-in baffle. Both pieces need to be trimmed to fit the oil pump pickup tube, which means mocking up all of it on the engine, trimming, and repeating as needed.

Install Oil Trap Door in Pan (Continued)

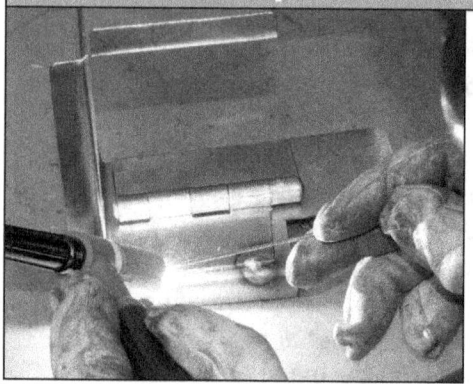
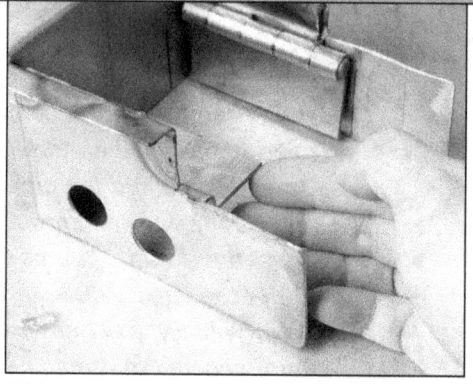
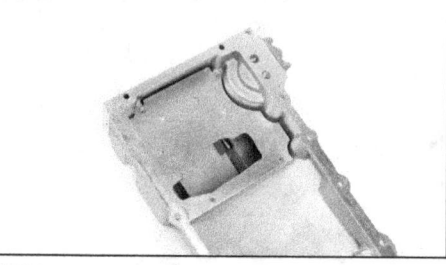

13 Most hinges are designed to screw onto a building's door and have holes cut in them. It may take a bit of searching local hardware stores to find some without holes. You also want steel so you can weld them in place. Before they are welded in, cut them to fit around the clearance openings for the pickup tube. After cutting them, make sure that they still swing freely. Used a TIG or MIG to weld them in place.

14 Once the hinges are welded in, drill 3/4-inch holes where they are covered with the hinges down. These don't have to seal. The idea is just to slow the oil and keep it close to the pickup tube. The hinges don't fully open when installed, because they will contact the pickup tube. But they open enough to let oil enter the area when turning one direction and close to restrict oil movement in the other direction.

15 Attach the trap-door system to the baffle. Set the system in place and bolt the baffle to the pan. Measure the location of the oil pump pickup when installed, and position the trap-door system accordingly. Mark the position of the system on the baffle and then remove everything. Clamp the system to the baffle and drill several 1/8-inch holes through both pieces. Use rivets to attach them. Next thoroughly clean the entire assembly. For the final installation, use Blue Loctite on the four bolts that hold the baffle to the oil pan.

Inspect Finished Oil Pan

16 This is the finished, modified Holley pan prepped to fit an early Chevelle chassis. I had ABC Performance bend and TIG-weld aluminum sections into the windows I cut out for inner tie rod clearance. This is tricky welding, as you are joining sheet aluminum to a cast aluminum pan. And oil has a way of seeping through the tiniest pores. The oil pan is a significant challenge for owners of early Chevelles wishing to do an LS swap.

Project 2: Water Pump and Front Accessories Installation

Select Front Accessories Drive System

1 Most desirable LS engines do not come with a front accessory drive system that fits in a Chevelle, or at least they don't look very nice. Most of the Chevrolet Performance crate engines come with a water pump and damper, but nothing else. In either case, you need an accessory drive system designed to mount the accessories you want and fit it into the Chevelle chassis. There are several companies offering kits, including Billet Specialties, DSE, and March Performance, Inc. They typically come with the accessories (power steering pump, air conditioning compressor, and alternator) because the variance in what could be used might lead to fitment issues with the brackets. Including the accessories with the kits ensures that they fit in the brackets and don't cause interference problems.

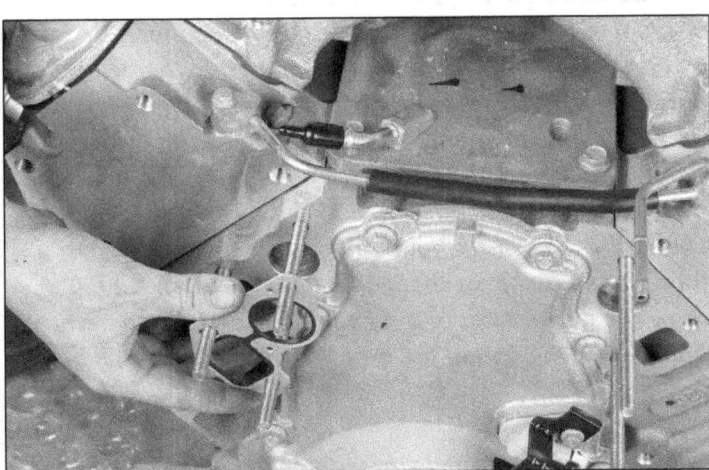

2 General Motors used quite a few different water pumps, depending on what vehicle the LS was installed in and what accessories it had. Because the water pump has most of the accessory mount bolt holes in it, most aftermarket companies provide a new water pump with their kit. Some also provide a new damper for similar reasons. I installed a Billet Specialties Tru Trac accessory drive system with power steering and alternator (no air conditioning) on this car. If your engine has any accessories on it, remove these, as well as the water pump.

Install Water Pump

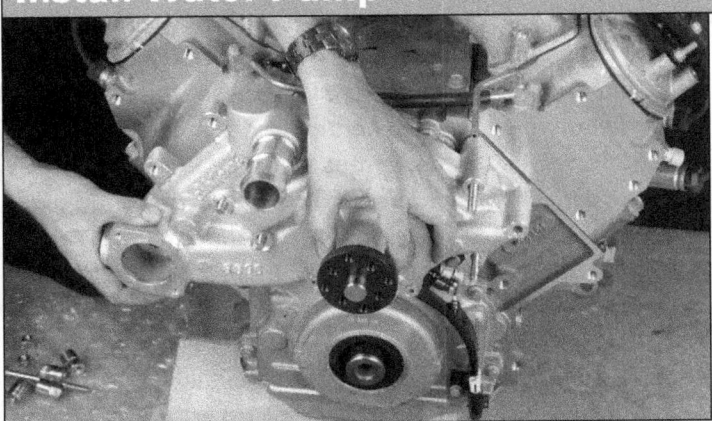

3 The Billet Specialties accessory drive system comes with an Edelbrock aluminum water pump. Pay attention to where the various fasteners, studs, and spacers are supposed to install. Also, use anti-seize on any fasteners installed into aluminum. Bolt the water pump to the block. The Edelbrock water pump moved the upper radiator supply hose from the driver's side to the passenger's side of the engine. This is the more common placement on an LS engine, placing the inlet and outlet on the same side of the engine. (This one is on the driver's side because it was a Corvette engine.)

Install Accessory Brackets

4 With the new water pump in place, you can start bolting on the accessory brackets. Most accessory drive kits come in polished aluminum finish. This kit's parts are powder-coated black. Most of the brackets are dual-purpose. This one mounts the alternator and is the top bracket for the power steering pump. The pump provided with the Billet Specialties Tru Trac is a remote reservoir style, but does not include a reservoir. You can use an original-style remote reservoir found on most late-model vehicles or order an optional billet aluminum reservoir from Billet Specialties. In either case, you need to remotely mount the reservoir, such as to the radiator core support right next to the radiator.

Install Harmonic Damper

5 The Billet Specialties system includes an ATI damper because different dampers of various thicknesses were used by the factory, and this new damper eliminates that variance. However, there is no woodruff key in the crankshaft to align the damper. Using a flashlight, you can see the slot farther back for the key that drives the oil pump. ATI sells a kit that lets you pin the damper to the crank to keep it from spinning on the snout of the crank. This is advisable for all LS engines and should be considered required on any engine making more than 500 hp, or that you intend to rev above 6,000 rpm. The kit consists of a locating device (shown here bolted over the end of the crank), two drill bits, drill guides, and a pin.

6 Once the crank is drilled and you've cleaned all of the metal shavings away, install the new ATI damper. The damper has a very tight tolerance to the crankshaft's outside diameter. If you align it perfectly, and there is absolutely no damage to the outside crank surface, the damper slips right on. Otherwise, you need to use an installation tool to pull the damper onto the crank. The Billet Specialties system comes with a brand-new GM damper bolt. Before you use the new bolt, install the old one and torque it to 240 ft-lbs, and then remove it. This seats the damper completely without stretching the new bolt. Then install your new bolt and tighten it to 37 ft-lbs. Finally, turn the bolt an additional 280 degrees (mark a reference point on the engine so you know when you reach this). It is most likely necessary to work in two increments of 140 degrees instead of trying to tighten the bolt with one almost full rotation of the ratchet.

Inspect Accessories

7 This is what the setup looks like when complete. The pulley came already installed on the new PowerMaster alternator from Billet Specialties. You can choose either a 105-amp alternator or one that makes 140 amps. The pulley on the lower passenger's side is an idler pulley. This is spring-loaded and applies tension on the serpentine belt. In the Billet Specialties system, this is a unique part. Some other kits use a GM idler pulley, so you can get a replacement just about anywhere. The pulley that's high on the passenger's side is where the air-conditioning compressor goes. If you do not have air conditioning, it's just a dummy pulley to make the serpentine belt route properly.

Project 3: Engine Installation

Install Engine in Chassis

1 It pays to do your homework in advance and prep the engine as much as possible before lifting it over the sheet metal. You will probably still have to put it in and take it out a couple of times, but this is better than a dozen times. With the radiator out of the car, there is plenty of room to drop the engine into the engine bay with the front accessory drive and complete clutch assembly bolted on. It gets tight if you also have the bellhousing bolted in place. However, if you are using engine mount adapter plates that place the engine farther back in the chassis against the firewall, the upper driver-side bellhousing bolt is extremely hard to get to once the engine is in place, so installing the bellhousing first is a good idea.

Some people like to bolt the engine and transmission together and use a tilting engine lift to swing it all in at once. If you don't want to risk damage to the painted firewall or core support, install the bellhousing and transmission later. It is a very good idea, however, to bolt the transmission to the engine on the ground before installing the engine to trial-fit everything. If you don't do this you may end up lifting the heavy transmission into place several times under the car to get things sorted out.

Select Wiring Harness for Engine

2 Once the engine is bolted to the frame for the last time, you can start wiring it. If you have retained the factory fuel-injection system, you have a few choices for an engine controller and wiring. You can modify the factory wiring if you grabbed it with the donor engine. There are forums that describe how to do this, but I don't think it's the best option. There are lots of sensors and variables used in a factory setting that aren't needed and may not exist in a retrofit, creating the potential for a frustrating experience chasing engine codes. Going this route also eliminates the opportunity to tune the engine for performance rather than for emissions; the factory system must balance both, often at the detriment of performance. There are several aftermarket ECUs designed for retrofits. These come with a wiring harness that plugs into the factory engine sensors and connects to the original fuel injectors. Most control the ignition spark as well.

Shown here is a Holley HP system, which allows you to use a laptop to modify the fuel and spark maps to fine-tune the engine. You can also purchase an optional handheld controller, which allows you to make broad changes to the fuel and spark without a laptop. This kit literally takes just a few hours to install (mounting the ECU and routing the wires are the hardest parts if your exhaust already has a bung for the oxygen sensor).

Install Drive-by-Wire Throttle System

3 If you use the factory fuel injection, there is another obstacle. Almost all of these engines, and certainly the desirable versions, came with a drive-by-wire throttle. That means there is no throttle cable, and no provision to add one. You can purchase a drive-by-wire throttle pedal from Chevrolet Performance or Lokar. The advantage of this is that you do not need a cable or linkage protruding through the firewall. Some owners do not want to rely on a fully electronic drive-by-wire throttle, and therefore opt for mechanical throttle linkage. If you use a FAST EFI crate/transplant kit, a new cable-operated throttle body is included.

Install Starter

4 If you have a higher-horsepower factory LS engine or a built-up one, you want a starter with more cranking power than that of a factory unit. MSD makes this starter as part of its Advanced Power System (APS) line. Its core features are a 3-hp electric motor and 4.4:1 gear set. Internally, it has a very high quality assembly, including a balanced armature, and it is guided by two ball bearings for smooth engagement. A key advantage is that the billet mount can be clocked in different positions to fit in tight applications, which you have with headers in a Chevelle chassis. To fit the MSD starter, flatten the inside of two header tubes approximately 3/16 inch using the technique shown earlier. The starter comes with shims, which may be necessary for perfect alignment on the flexplate or flywheel, but this application didn't require any. In most cases, you need to install the starter and passenger-side header at the same time.

Inspect Chevy LS3 Carbureted Intake System

The Chevrolet Performance LS3 engine comes with a carbureted intake manifold. I like the look of a traditional 4-barrel carb under the hood of a muscle car, but wanted the advantages of fuel injection, so I installed a FAST EZ-EFI system. This uses a throttle body designed for a Holley 4-barrel that bolts to the mounting flange. Four injectors are located in the base of the throttle body, so all of the mechanical fuel injection is in one bolt-on part. This is not as efficient as a multi-port system, but the simplicity has many advantages including computer-controlled fuel injection. This system uses an easy-to-read-and-use handheld controller. This is a universal system, not designed specifically for an LS engine, so a separate ignition control system is required. The FAST EZ-EFI system comes with everything pictured here. The only additional items you need are a fuel pump, fuel filter, pressure regulator, a fuel line to run a primary feed line, and a return line from the throttle body. A kit with all of these components is also available from FAST (see Chapter 6).

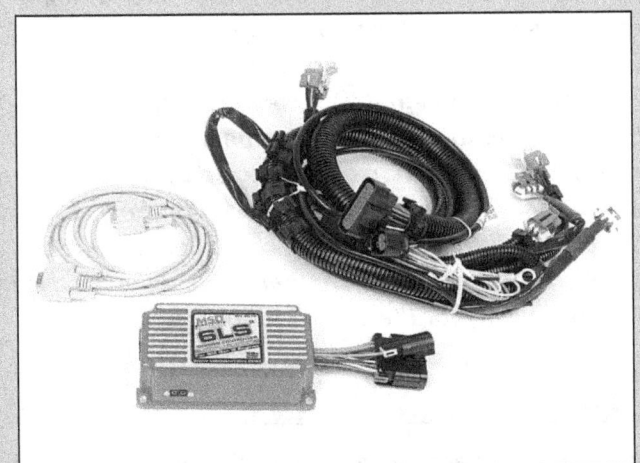

Although most aftermarket EFI systems for the LS also control the ignition system, some do not. If you are using one that does not, a carburetor, or a system like the FAST EZ-EFI that was not specifically designed for an LS, you need a stand-alone ignition controller. This MSD 6LS plugs into the factory crank and cam sensors for trigger points and attaches to the mini harnesses on each bank of coils. The box comes with several chips that have baseline ignition curves. You change the chips by removing and installing them into a port on the side of the box. Using a laptop, you can tailor any of these curves to your liking. With a laptop you can also customize the two-step rev limiter, vacuum advance curve, a step retard, and a custom boost retard map.

Select Radiator

5 Technically, you don't need a new radiator. However, for a clean installation devoid of funky adapters and ugly hose routing, a new radiator, such as this Flex-a-Fit aluminum radiator from Flex-a-lite, is in order. Plus, you are probably stepping up in power, which means you should increase the cooling capacity as well. The inlet and outlet should both be on the passenger's side of the radiator for an LS swap. This makes the radiator a dual-pass (the coolant enters on the passenger's side, flows to the driver's side, down to the lower half of the radiator, and back to the passenger's side before returning to the engine) providing more cooling. The inlet and outlet should both be 1½ inches in diameter.

Fit Steam Tube or Install Block-off Plates

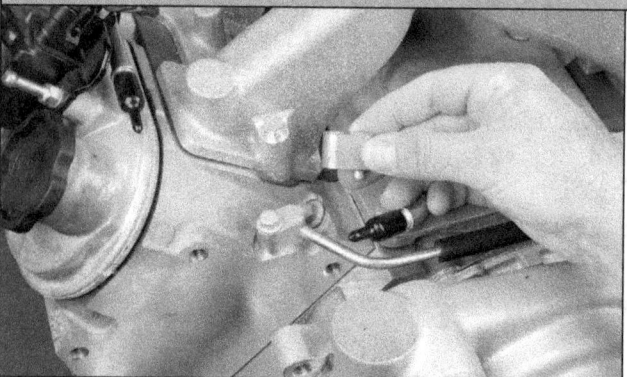

6 Coolant does not flow through the intake manifold on an LS engine. This means that coolant in the engine is higher than the water outlet connected to the radiator. LS engines have a steam crossover tube at the front of the block connecting the coolant passages in the cylinder heads. This allows air trapped in the system to escape and be routed back into the cooling system. There are several ways you can deal with this steam tube. You can drill and tap the flat surface of the water pump and connect the steam tube to it. You can also have a fitting installed in the radiator and route the steam tube to the radiator with the upper radiator hose. If you choose to remove the steam tube and install GM block-off plates. If you block the passages, you need to remove the plugs when you first fill the radiator with coolant or water and allow all of the air to escape the system. When only water or coolant flows out of these holes, insert and tighten the plugs.

Install Recommended Thermostat

7 If you're using a salvage-yard engine or a crate engine from Chevrolet Performance, it has a thermostat with a higher opening temperature than you probably want. The "88C" stamped in this thermostat tells you that it is rated to open at 88 degrees C (190 degrees F). That's not too bad, but some are even higher. If you run fuel injection, I suggest that you ask the controller manufacturer what temperature thermostat it recommends. The manufacturer's fuel and timing maps are affected by the operating temperature of the vehicle. Typically, a thermostat between 160 and 180 degrees F works well with aftermarket controllers and helps keep the temperature of the engine lower, especially at highway speeds. Higher-temperature thermostats are used from the factory to help the engines meet emissions standards, but are not necessary for the engine to run properly.

Select and Install Radiator Hoses

8 You need to find radiator hoses that fit the custom engine and radiator combination. The exact hoses you need depend on what combination of water pump your LS engine has, where the engine has been located according to what engine mount adapters you used, and what custom radiator you have. With that many variables, it's impossible to provide part numbers for hoses that fit. The best thing to do is to bend a coat hanger or TIG welding rod to the shape you need for the upper and lower radiator hoses. Cut it to length and then visit a parts store. If you ordered a custom radiator with a 1½-inch inlet and outlet, the hoses need to be a consistent diameter. If you didn't, then you also need to note the radiator hose diameter needed on each end. There are hundreds of preformed radiator hoses; if your parts store has a good selection, you will be able to find ones that fits. You may need to do a little trimming for length to fit perfectly.

Install Oil Vapor Catch Tank

9 Most LS engines have one vent tube on each valve cover and another one on the lifter valley plate. This allows oil vapor and pressure from inside the engine to be released. From the factory, this pressure—and specifically the oil vapor—has to be captured and managed for emissions reasons. In a performance application, you want to make sure that the pressure is allowed to escape, and you want to capture the oil vapor to keep things clean under the hood. The easiest way to do this, if you're running the factory valve covers, is to plumb the lines to a vapor catch can that mounts on the firewall or the radiator core support. There are several aluminum versions as well plastic ones. Essentially, the pressure pushes the oil vapor into the canister, which is designed to let the pressure pass through and release into the atmosphere, but extracts the oil and lets it collect inside the canister. You need to empty the canister periodically, and most have a drain petcock built in to make this easy.

Inspect Finished Installation

10 This is what my LS engine installation looks like when it is finished. In contrast to the LS engine's original form, which kept all of the modern, high-tech induction and exposed ignition coils, the finished product shows the under-the-hood appearance I wanted, retaining the muscle car heritage of an older Chevelle. This is one reason to opt for an LS engine with a single 4-barrel intake converted with the FAST EZ-EFI fuel injection rather than a port-injected system. The coils are hidden under coil covers from Holley. These are plastic covers that snap onto studs threaded into the stock GM valve covers. They are supposed to mimic a big-block valve cover appearance. The air cleaner is a 14-inch, spun-aluminum assembly with a 1-inch dropped base and a 14 x 3-inch K&N air filter. I painted the air cleaner and the plastic Holley coil covers with Mercedes silver paint. Even with shimming the engine upward and using the 1/4-inch-tall Moroso engine mounts, I was left with nearly 1/2 inch of clearance between the stock steel flat hood and the top of the air cleaner. This is the classic muscle car look, with the modern performance and efficiency of a fuel-injected, computer-controlled LS engine under the hood.

CHAPTER 8

PERFORMANCE FUEL SYSTEM

You may think about upgrading your carburetor or converting to electronic fuel injection, but most people don't give much thought to the rest of the fuel system. As you push the performance boundaries of your Chevelle, you eventually reach a point where you must upgrade the entire fuel system.

The fuel system is made up of the fuel tank, fuel line from the tank to the engine, fuel filter, and fuel pump. Each of these components has its limitations, and all of the stock components were designed with some pretty limited performance expectations in mind. At best, the original big-block cars had larger steel fuel lines to deliver a higher volume of fuel. With the other upgrades you're making to your car, you need to manage the force created by turning corners at speed, improved braking, and possibly accommodate fuel injection. This chapter covers everything in the fuel system leading up to the carburetor or fuel injection system.

Upgrading your car's fuel system is not the sexiest part of building a performance Chevelle. But if you overlook the details of doing this correctly, you neither look nor feel good struggling with performance and drivability issues. The fuel system has to be designed for how you plan to use the car and to match the needs of the engine and induction system.

Fuel Tank

If your fuel tank is in good condition, you don't necessarily need to replace it. An original or replacement tank works fine in all but extreme performance applications. Once you reach certain speeds, or in certain types of racing, a fuel cell is required for safety in a crash. Many aftermarket fuel tanks also include baffling to keep fuel near the pickup tube as

PERFORMANCE FUEL SYSTEM

Most racing sanctioning bodies allow you to use the stock fuel tank for all except the highest performance classes. Many people, however, choose a fuel cell because of the advantages in fuel control and safety. (Photo Courtesy Jaz Products)

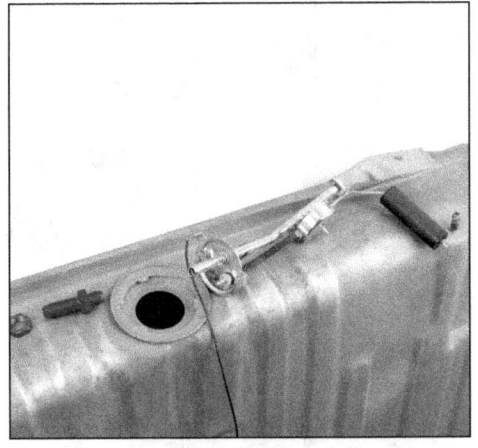

If you do retain the stock fuel tank, you should have your original cleaned or replace it with a brand-new one. This eliminates the chance of clogging fuel filters with rust and other debris that may be present in an old tank.

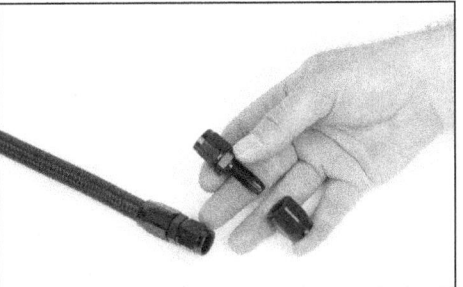

Modern fuel is hard on rubber products, causing seepage and eventually failure. An original Chevelle system used rubber to connect the steel line at the front and rear of the car. Almost all braided-steel line has a rubber lining. TechAFX BlackWrap features a polytetrafluoroethylene (PTFE) conductive-core inner liner made to resist deterioration.

you accelerate, turn, and brake. This is especially critical with fuel injection, because you don't have the float bowls of a carburetor to act as a reserve. Any time the pickup tube isn't covered with fuel, you suck air through the fuel system and feel a momentary loss of power.

The simple way to mount a fuel cell is to bolt it to the inside of the trunk floor and vent it to the outside. The drawbacks are a loss of trunk space and the need to open the trunk lid every time you refuel. The alternative isn't a whole lot better, which consists of cutting a hole in the floor and recessing the fuel cell through the floor. This lowers the fuel cell for better center of gravity, but doesn't remove the drawbacks. This also requires custom fabrication to attach the fuel cell to the frame rails.

If you use a factory or replacement fuel tank, you want to inspect, and in most cases, change the pickup tube and fuel-sending unit assembly. The six-cylinder and many of the V-8 cars came with 5/16-inch fuel lines, which are too restrictive for a modern V-8. You can purchase a stock-replacement assembly with a 3/8-inch pickup tube and new fuel-sending unit for the fuel gauge.

A 3/8-inch fuel line is roughly equivalent to a -8 AN line, and is capable of supplying the volume of fuel needed to feed up to approximately 600 hp. Once you're above that level, you need to consider a fuel cell with -10 or -12 outlets, internal fuel control, and the whole nine yards.

Fuel Line

The type and size of fuel line you use from the tank to the front of the car is very important. Race cars use braided hose because it is quick and relatively easy to plumb. The connections thread together, and leaks are very rare. It is essentially a rubber hose with braided steel around the outside to protect it from abrasion and to increase the burst-strength rating. Some hoses have additional layers, such as a Teflon insert or higher-strength exterior wrap. You can cut the hose to length and assemble it to create a custom-length hose that looks great. There are a couple of drawbacks, however. In a racing application, the fuel line is replaced entirely every two to three years, and sometimes every year in a pro application. This is because this type of hose deteriorates over time, especially when used with an aggressive chemical such as gasoline. There is no way to check a line, either, which is why race teams just replace them.

Another issue is that fuel today is much more aggressive. Using regular braided steel almost surely results in a constant raw fuel smell while the car sits in the garage. The fuel is actually seeping through rubber lining the traditional braided-steel lines. It doesn't allow enough to escape to result in a liquid leak, but you smell the fumes. TechAFX has developed a conductive PTFE braided-steel line that is designed specifically for today's fuel, which has many more additives than were used just a decade ago.

For a street car, I don't typically expect to replace items like a fuel line every few years. The other

CHAPTER 8

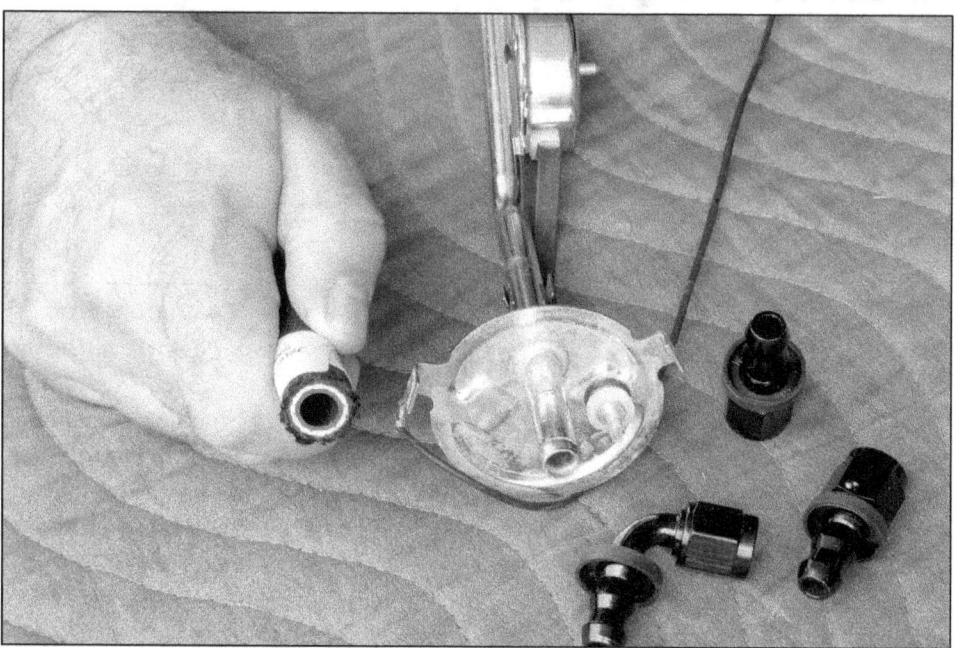

When designing the fuel system and choosing specific products, you need to make sure that the inside diameter of the hose and fittings maintain a minimum size. If you have determined that you need at least 3/8 inch, then you want to ensure that there are no restrictions smaller than that in the entire system.

drawback to braided steel is the expense. With fittings, it can easily cost $600 to make a supply and return fuel line. The alternative is to purchase and bend your own hard line. You need a tubing bender and a flaring kit. If you're talented with these tools, you can make a beautiful fuel line that performs for years. You can also purchase pre-bent lines from Inline Tube. They can make a fuel line in the exact shape of the original, and can upsize the line to feed engines that are hungrier than your Chevelle's original stock engine.

Deciding what size fuel line to use can be a challenge. This is partly because there is no foolproof formula. Every engine is a little different, and how you use the car makes a big difference. A professional drag race car engine must get the fuel it needs for 10 to 13 seconds without any variance. A road race car engine needs fuel delivery for a much longer time, but usually not at wide-open throttle for the whole time. Much of this rests on the shoulders of the fuel pump, but if the fuel line is the wrong size or otherwise too restrictive, the fuel pump can't get all the fuel to the engine.

Another issue to consider is that the fuel line is only as good as the smallest restriction in the system. If you have a 1/2-inch fuel line, but the fuel pickup tube or a fitting somewhere in the system is only 3/8-inch in diameter, you won't be able to flow the volume that you would if the whole system was 1/2-inch. Check the inlets and outlets of all fuel pumps and filters that you are considering using, and the size of the fuel tank pickup tube. This is another reason why race cars use fuel cells or custom fuel tanks where the fuel line at the tank can start at -10 or -12 and remain that size all the way to the regulator at the engine.

Generally speaking, there is no reason to use fuel line with an inside diameter smaller than 3/8 inch, and this size is usually sufficient up to 600 hp, depending on your fuel pump and the way you use your car. For an engine making 600 hp, a 1/2-inch line is more appropriate. If you expect ultimate performance on the track, or have more power than that, you need to move up in fuel line size.

You also want to limit 90-degree bends. Each tight bend like this reduces the fuel flow and can make a 1/2-inch fuel line only capable of delivering the volume of a straight stretch of 3/8-inch line. This is when careful routing pays off.

AN Hose Diameters

Here is a list of the AN fuel line sizes and the corresponding internal diameter of the hose.

AN Hose Size	Internal Diameter (inches)
-4	0.188
-6	0.313
-8	0.406
-10	0.500
-12	0.625
-16	0.820

Fuel Filter

Fuel filters should be a top priority on any performance car. They protect the expensive carburetor or fuel injection from debris that, at the very least, causes drivability issues

PERFORMANCE FUEL SYSTEM

Even if you have a brand-new fuel tank, you want high-quality fuel filters to protect your expensive carburetor or fuel injection. System 1 makes several sizes of filters that you can disassemble and clean, and you can also replace the element as needed. These are available with barbed fittings or with AN fittings (shown).

and, at the extreme, can damage engine components.

As you might imagine, there are fuel filters designed specifically for high-performance applications. This is important, as the fuel filter can be a significant restriction to fuel pressure and volume, neither of which is desirable. But you also want the filter to catch anything that could cause a clog or damage the fuel system. A filter's ability to screen out debris is expressed in microns. One micron is equal to 1 millionth of a meter, or 1 thousandth of a millimeter. For a carbureted application, a filter rated at 30 to 60 microns is a good choice. Fuel-injection systems have smaller orifices at the engine that can be more problematic, and a fuel filter rated at about 10 microns is preferred, but check with the manufacturer of your fuel-injection system.

If you're running an electric fuel pump, it's a good idea to run a pre filter before the pump to protect it. This should be less restrictive than

The fuel pump must be matched to the requirements of the carburetor or fuel injection. This Holley pump is designed to supply fuel to a very-high-flow carburetor. Most high-performance fuel pumps require a regulator mounted close to the carb or fuel injection, and a return line that sends excess fuel back to the tank.

your primary filter, around 100 microns. That way it does not pose a higher-than-necessary restriction for the pump to pull fuel through. Most electric pumps are not as good at pulling fuel as they are at pushing it, which is why they should be mounted as close to the fuel tank as possible, or even in it.

Fuel Pump

Notice that I talk about fuel pumps last. These are a crucial part of the fuel system, and the one that people often purchase first. As you can see by everything else I've talked about first, the fuel pump is only as good as the rest of the fuel system you build. You have loads of choices when it comes to fuel pumps for carbureted engines.

A mechanical fuel pump is a viable option up to about 500 hp. High-volume units can provide the fuel your engine needs. The key advantages of mechanical fuel pumps are that they are quiet and don't require wiring. Decades ago, they were more reliable than electric pumps, but electric pumps are now every bit as reliable.

Electric pumps come in all sizes and shapes. You need to find an electric pump with a flow rating and fuel pressure rating that meets the requirements of your engine. There are several internal designs. The traditional Holley red and blue pumps are a vane style. These are less susceptible to damage from contaminants, but are louder. Some people say these are not good for street use, but I have used them in continuous-duty applications, including cross-country drives, without any problems.

Another electric fuel pump design is the geroter style. These are quieter and rated for continuous duty. They also generally have more consistency in output volume and pressure. The drawbacks are cost and vulnerability to debris, so a good pre-filter is required.

For fuel injection, the pumps are almost always a geroter design. Some are designed to be mounted in the tank where they are quieter and cooled by being immersed in fuel. Others are made to mount outside the tank, but still very close to it. These pumps produce the 40 to 80 psi that fuel-injection systems

Assembling Braided-Steel Line

The ease and speed of braided-steel hose makes this type of line one of the most popular for fuel and other liquids in a performance vehicle. If you haven't worked with braided-steel hose before, it looks intimidating, but following simple steps will result in a leak-free hose.

Always use hose ends from the same company that made the hose. Also, most hose companies make various types of hose, which may require special hose ends. Variations in inside and outside hose diameters can cause assembly problems or leaks if they are mismatched.

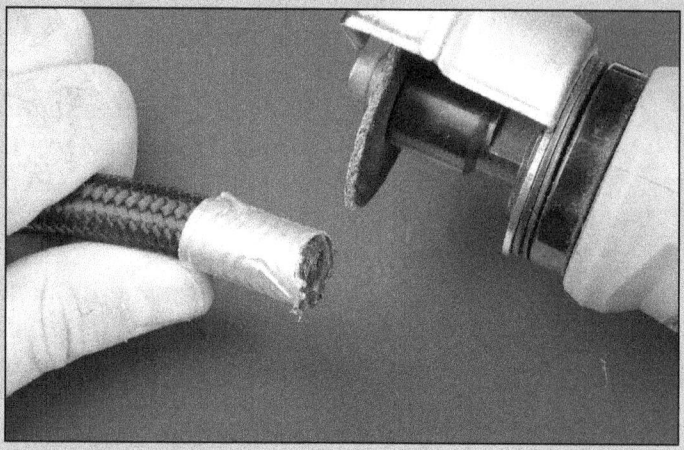

1 *Find the desired length for the hose. Wrap the hose tightly with duct tape where you want to cut it. Hold the hose in a vise and use a cut-off wheel to make a clean cut through the braided steel and inner rubber hose. Make sure the cut is clean and straight. The duct tape helps prevent fraying of the outer wrap.*

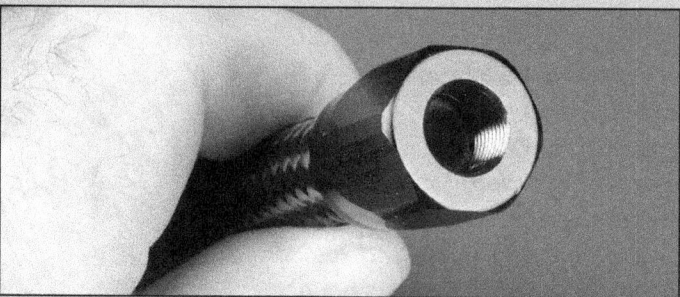

2 *Remove the duct tape and use compressed air to blow debris from the hose. Next, push the collar onto the hose. Be careful that the braided material stays inside the collar and doesn't push down as you insert it. Twisting the collar as you install it usually helps. Look inside the collar and push it down until the hose butts against the stop visible inside the collar.*

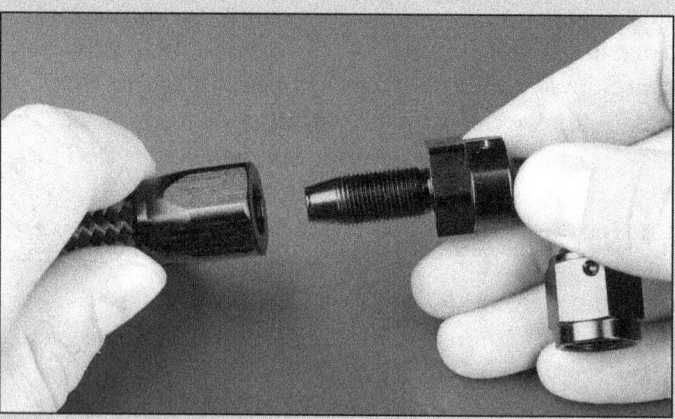

3 *Use a bit of engine oil or lubricant specified by the hose-end manufacturer to slip the nipple inside of the collar and thread it together. It's usually easiest to start threading the two pieces together holding the components in your hands, and then move to a vise for final assembly.*

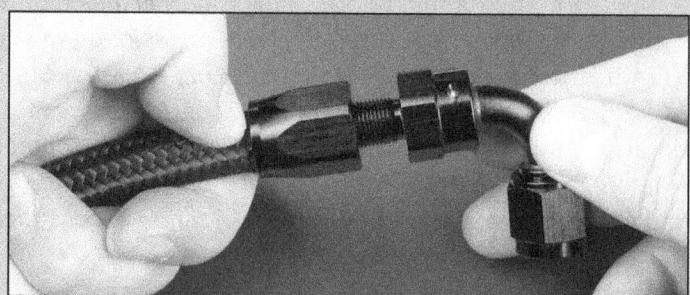

4 *As you thread the nipple into the collar, the hose pushes out of the collar slightly. Mark the hose with a pen or piece of tape so you are able to tell if it's more than 1/8 inch, which is all that is acceptable. I show the assembly here in my hands for photographic purposes, but threading the assembly together is much easier if you hold the collar in a vise. You can use aluminum AN wrenches to keep from marking the hose-end fittings, or wrap the jaws of your vise and adjustable wrench with painter's masking tape. Thread the two pieces of the hose end together until there is a gap of approximately 1/16 inch left between them.*

PERFORMANCE FUEL SYSTEM

require. Lower-pressure versions of inline pumps like this can also be used in carbureted applications.

With most performance electric pumps, a regulator is required at the engine. In fact, many of the pumps are sold with the regulator, or the manufacturer recommends a regulator that works well with the pump. Regulators adjust the fuel pressure to whatever the carburetor or fuel-injection system requires. Some fuel pumps can tolerate a deadhead arrangement with no return line from the regulator to relieve the excess pressure. Most, however, require a return line to let the excess fuel return from the regulator to the gas tank.

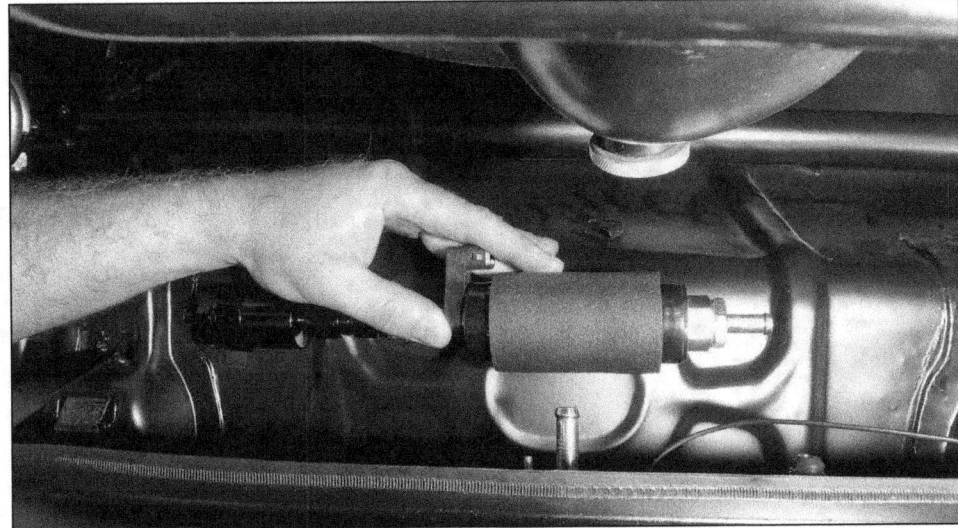

The easiest way to add a high-pressure pump for a fuel injection system is to use an inline pump mounted as close to the fuel tank as possible. You can also use an in-tank pump, but these are more difficult to set up. Some aftermarket fuel tanks are available with a pump already mounted.

Project 1: Fuel Line Installation

Drill Hole for Bulkhead Fitting

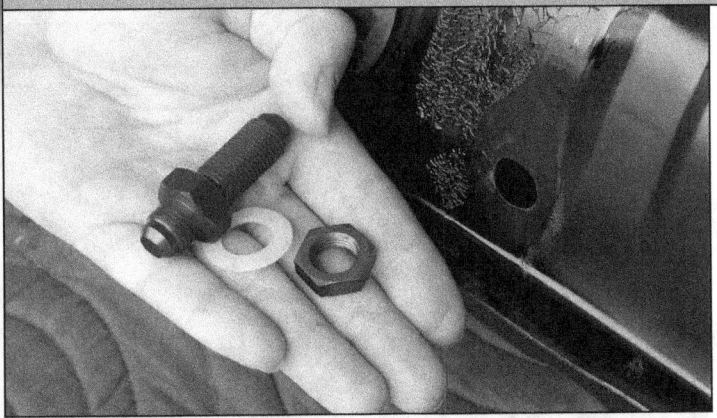

1 *Installing a return line for fuel injection or higher-performance carbureted applications is not difficult, even in a stock fuel tank. You need a bulkhead fitting for whatever type of fuel line you're using; in this case, a -8 AN fitting. The bulkhead fitting has a nut and nylon washer to seal the fitting against the wall of the fuel tank. Before drilling the gas tank, flush it with water to remove any gasoline or gas vapor. Measure the diameter of the threads and drill a hole in the tank that provides just enough clearance, and no extra. Use a magnet on a string to fish out the metal shavings left after drilling.*

Install Nut and Washer for Bulkhead Fitting

2 *To get the washer and nut on the bulkhead fitting, insert a long screwdriver through the hole and slide the washer and nut over the end of the screwdriver. Then, back out the screwdriver while pushing the nut and washer against the inside of the fuel tank with your finger, reaching through the sending-unit hole. Note that you want the return hole as high in the fuel tank as possible so it can return fuel without having to push against fuel sitting in the tank. This tank is sitting upside down on the floor.*

Install Bulkhead Fitting

3 While holding the washer and nut firmly against the inside of the fuel tank, start threading the bulkhead fitting into the nut. If you're using aluminum AN fittings like this, stop if the threads don't engage perfectly. Aluminum galls easily, and forcing it only ruins the fitting. Slip a wrench inside the tank and hold the nut firmly to tighten the fitting.

Install Sending Unit

4 Finish the assembly by installing the sending unit. If the O-ring is in good condition, you can reuse it. Otherwise, replace the O-ring to ensure a good seal. The sending unit is held in place by a ring that tightens against the tank as the ring is rotated. Use a blunt screwdriver to gently rotate the ring, tapping on all three tabs in sequence.

Install Gas Tank Straps

5 You can use new gas tank strap insulation from CARS, Inc. to protect the gas tank from abrasion with the straps. These have an adhesive on the backside, and you simply peel them and stick them in place. You can reuse the original straps and replace the rusted fasteners at the rear with new carriage bolts and nuts.

Install Fuel Line Clamps

6 If you use a reproduction steel fuel line, you can use the factory-style clamps to hold it to the frame. However, if you use braided steel, you need to use another style of clamp, such as a plastic, two-piece clamp from Made For You Products or a padded Adel clamp. Route the fuel line a safe distance from moving parts, such as suspension components, and also away from the exhaust system. Using the clamp as a guide, use a center punch to mark locations for the mounting fastener.

Install Fuel Line Clamps (Continued)

7 Drill a hole in the frame rail for the clamp. (This frame has been boxed for added strength.) If you are drilling through a single-wall frame rail, put a piece of metal behind the frame section to keep from drilling into the rocker panel when the drill bit pushes through the frame rail. Use a number-22 drill bit for a number-10 threaded machine screw if you plan to tap threads into the frame rail.

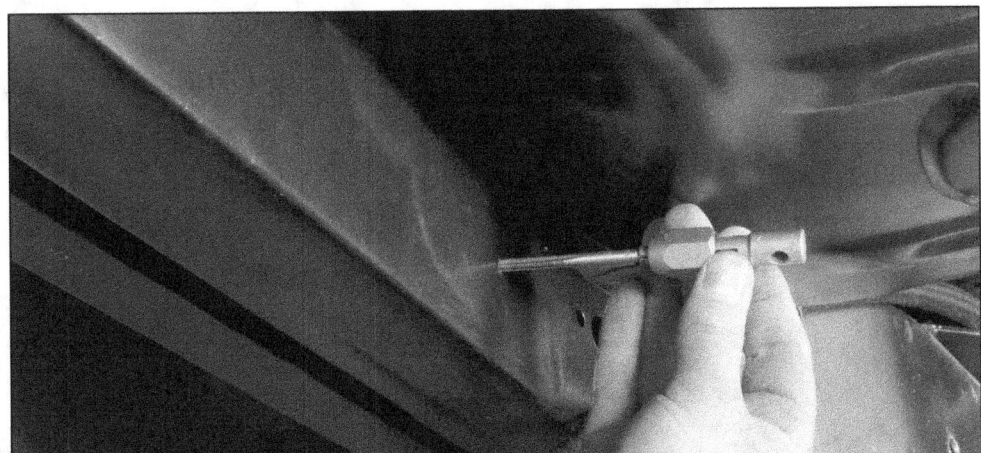

8 The inner frame section of a boxed frame is thick enough to tap it and thread the clamp screws directly into the metal. Use a 10-32 tap to cut threads into the holes. Because the holes are so close to the floor, use the sliding-bar handle for the tap, and work very carefully to keep the tap level and straight.

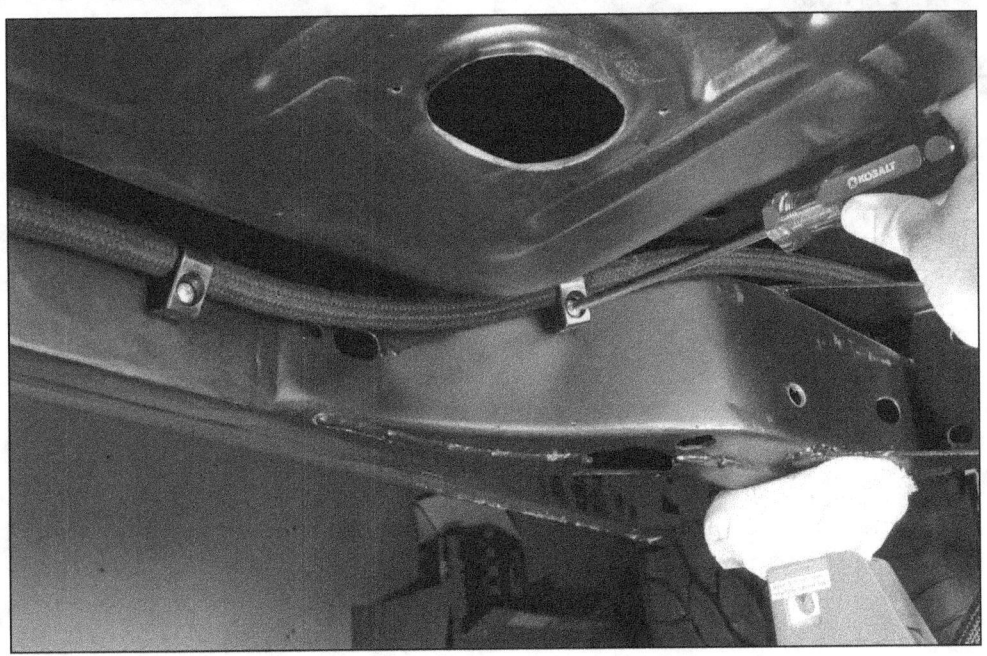

9 With holes drilled and tapped every 18 inches (closer near bends, such as this transition in the frame rail), thread the machine screws through the clamps and into the frame rail. The Made For You Products clamps are made from 6-6 DuPont Zytel nylon, which the company says does not melt, fade, stain, corrode, or discolor. They also include stainless-steel fasteners. They are also not affected by brake fluid or fuel. All of that means that they should last longer than braided-steel fuel line.

CHAPTER 9

PERFORMANCE COOLING SYSTEM

The more power your engine makes, the more heat you need to dissipate. Size and upgrade your cooling system appropriately to avoid overheating problems that can rob you of enjoying your car and possibly damage those new engine parts.

It is extremely common for a performance Chevelle to run hotter than it should. The radiators in 1964–1967 models were a bit small to start with, and the original-design radiators are very antiquated technology now. To make matters worse, most of us have made, or are planning on making, engine performance upgrades that produce more heat, requiring additional cooling capacity. In addition to taking steps to make sure your Chevelle keeps its cool, there are also opportunities to improve the performance of your car by switching from a belt-driven fan to an electric fan.

If you're starting from scratch, putting together a high-quality cooling system for your Chevelle isn't too difficult. I've seen 1,000-hp cars idling in traffic without the owner breaking a sweat, let alone a drop of engine coolant hitting the ground. The key is determining what you need and matching radiator size to airflow. It's actually more difficult if you have an existing system and you are chasing a cooling problem.

Overheating Diagnosis

There are a couple of rules of thumb to help diagnose an overheating problem. If your Chevelle keeps its cool on the highway but overheats in traffic, you have an airflow problem. If your car overheats under highway and traffic conditions, your radiator isn't up to par. This is also true if your car runs cool until you get into situations where you're making a lot of power, such as on a racetrack. Based on these two

This is a pretty typical cooling system in a car that has seen decades of upgrades. The clutch fan is from a later GM car. The shroud was lost somewhere in the process of upgrades. The radiator is a generic replacement type. Sit in typical summer car-event traffic with this combination and you will be watching your temp gauge more than the cars around you.

guidelines, there are ways to correct your situation.

The first thing to do is make a note of when the overheating problem began. Was it after a major performance modification? If so, this isn't a surprise, and you should keep reading. However, if you didn't make a significant change, you may have a smaller issue you can reverse, or a part in your cooling system may be failing.

The most common tuning issues that create an overheating problem are when the ignition timing has changed by 5 to 10 degrees or a recent switch to a carburetor or fuel-injection system has made the engine run much leaner. Even if you didn't make a change, check the ignition timing and look for possible causes that changed the air/fuel mixture, such as a clogged fuel filter.

An overheating problem at idle and slow speeds is almost always a result of insufficient airflow through the radiator. This is most common with a belt-driven fan and a broken or missing fan shroud. Air always takes the path of least resistance, and, without a fan shroud to force the air to be drawn through the radiator, it goes above and below the radiator instead. If you have most of the fan shroud in place, but are missing a section or have a broken shroud, most of the air is pulled in through this section.

This problem goes away once you get above about 40 mph, because the air is rammed through the radiator and the fan isn't doing much at that point. Even with a proper fan shroud, a belt-driven fan may not pull sufficient air through the radiator at idle to cool a high-performance car.

The fan blades used on non-air-conditioned cars in the 1960s were not as aggressive at moving air. The later fans used with fan clutches are better for moving air, but they also suck a lot of power from the engine.

A final element is how thick the radiator is and the condition of the core. At the end of the muscle car era, a four-core radiator was the answer for any high-performance application. The problem is that this is very restrictive to airflow. And if the core is damaged—with a fair number of fins pushed flat, closing out airflow—it is not possible to improve the cooling without replacing the radiator.

Electric Fan

Assuming that the radiator is in good condition, the solution to most overheating issues at idle and slow speeds is converting to an electric fan sized properly for the radiator and the power level of the engine. Unlike a belt-driven fan, an electric fan can spin at full speed even when the car isn't moving, and with the engine idling. In addition to solving your cooling problem, switching from a belt-driven fan to an electric one also improves performance by completely removing the mechanical load of spinning the fan from the engine. This means more power to the wheels, and even a fuel economy gain. Removing a belt-driven fan that mounts on the water pump also reduces the load on the pump. This can lengthen the life of the bearings in the water pump. These are the reasons nearly every new vehicle sold today is equipped with electric fans.

Not all electric fans are equal, and choosing the right one makes a huge difference in your ability to keep your Chevelle cool. First, an electric fan used as a primary fan should be mounted behind the radiator to pull air through it. Second, it should have an incorporated, rectangular fan shroud covering as much of the radiator core surface as possible. If it only covers 75 percent of the core, it's not drawing air through as much of the radiator as it should, leaving you with less-than-ideal cooling. Also, the least-expensive fans are referred to as basket fans. They have round shrouds only slightly larger than the fan blades themselves. These do not do a great job of moving air though the radiator and really should only be considered as an auxiliary fan to be mounted on the front of radiator in addition to a belt-driven fan on the backside.

There is also confusion about whether dual fans are better than a single electric fan. The best setup is the one that draws more airflow and covers more of the radiator surface. Dual electric fans look cool, but if a radiator is primarily square in shape, like the ones found in early Chevelles, a single fan that fits the radiator well is the best solution. And a single fan is less expensive, because you are only paying for one electric motor and one fan. The radiator that fits in 1968–1972 Chevelles is wider than it is tall, and a dual electric fan setup fits these radiators better.

Finally, the airflow needs to be sufficient for your engine. If you're producing up to 500 hp, an electric fan rated at 2,500 cubic feet per minute (cfm) of airflow with a full shroud is generally sufficient to keep it cool. Above 500, you want a fan that can pull at least 3,000 cfm. If you have a turbocharged or supercharged car and will need boost for any longer than a blast down the drag strip, you need something in the range of 4,000 cfm to run consistently cool.

Converting your Chevelle from a belt-driven fan to an electric fan can free up horsepower and clean up the engine bay. Switching to an electric fan removes the mechanical work of spinning a fan from the engine, delivering more engine power to the rear wheels. Electric fans also do a better job of cooling a car in traffic because the airflow is the same regardless of engine speed.

Belt-Driven Fan

If you're not ready to convert to an electric fan, there are a few versions of belt-driven fans to consider. For maximum airflow to overcome an overheating problem, it's hard to beat a steel seven-blade fan, with or without a fan clutch.

Stock Versions

Stock fans can be found in the salvage yard, and a favorite upgrade for small-block Chevelles is converting from the original short water pump to a long-style one. This accepts fans and clutches used on GM cars from the 1970s, and also makes alternator and power steering brackets far easier to find and replace. However, it does not properly place the fan in the original fan shroud.

Aftermarket Versions

Another option is the seven-blade steel fan from Flex-a-lite. This has the same design as an original clutch fan, but is designed to mount directly to the water pump or a spacer without the need for a clutch.

There are performance options for belt-driven fans too. Flex-a-lite invented the flex fan, where the blades are curved at lower engine speeds to move more air, but flatten out at higher engine RPM to reduce the drag on the engine. This six-blade Flex-a-lite provides a very good combination of cooling capability and increased engine performance.

Flex Fans

Generally, a flex fan is not a cooling solution, but it is a popular performance upgrade. Flex-a-lite pioneered the flex fan concept in 1962. The idea was to decrease engine drag in performance applications by making the blades from a flexible material that would flatten out at higher engine

PERFORMANCE COOLING SYSTEM

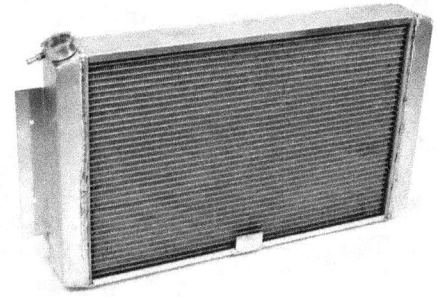

A variety of radiators are available for all Chevelles. Many are larger than what came in these cars originally, and may require drilling new holes in the core support. Unlike a lot of popular muscle cars, Chevelles have plenty of real estate to mount a good-sized radiator.

There are more radiators available for Chevelles now than ever before, whether you want aluminum or a more stock appearing brass and copper radiator.

speeds. The concept is still alive and well today, with Flex-a-lite offering three versions of the flex fan.

The best one for street applications is a series 1300, which has large blades to move as much air as possible at lower engine speeds. A low-profile version, the series 1000, has smaller blades to fit in tighter spaces. This also means less engine drag at all engine speeds, but less total airflow too. The third version is the series 400. This all-plastic fan is extremely lightweight with small blades for the least amount of drag, but it also moves the least amount of air. Flex-a-lite recommends this one for use on drag-racing cars when a belt-driven fan is desired.

Radiator

Now that you know what you need to make a good decision on a cooling fan, let's talk about radiators. The job of the radiator is to dissipate heat. The wider and taller the radiator, the better it is able to do its job. Most Chevelle owners desire a radiator that attaches to the factory bolt

I swapped the old radiator in an early Chevelle for a new Flex-a-Fit aluminum radiator and electric fan combination from Flex-a-lite. I started with a 52180 radiator, and includes the powerful 3,000-cfm single electric fan and fits 1966–1967 Chevelles. I say "started with," because I custom-ordered it with 45-degree angles on the bottom of the side tanks to fit in between the core support mounts; and the car is equipped with an LS engine, so I needed 1½-inch-diameter inlet and outlet, both on the passenger's side. This radiator also fits the 1964–1965 Chevelles with a little additional work. For owners of 1968–1972 Chevelles, the Flex-a-lite 58295 radiator and fan combination fits nicely, and it comes with a dual electric fan setup that moves 4,600 cfm of air; plenty to keep just about any engine cool. (Photo Courtesy Flex-a-lite)

holes that held the original one in place. On the earlier cars, this limits the size, making it a challenge to meet the cooling needs of more radical engines. That's one reason why some companies offer radiators that are slightly larger and require a little bit of modification to fit for much better cooling performance.

With advancement in materials and manufacturing methods, the rules have completely changed as to

CHAPTER 9

Measuring for an Electric Fan

Converting from a belt-driven fan to an electric fan can be very rewarding. First, you free up some horsepower by removing the fan from the water pump. You may also notice an increase in fuel economy. The other significant benefit is that an electric fan is a very good solution for cars that overheat at idle or stop-and-go traffic typical of hot rod events. They are also handy for quickly cooling a car in a racing environment, even if the engine isn't running.

Often, the hardest part of adding an electric fan is figuring out which one to use. Generally, you want the largest one that fits. Measure the height and width of the radiator core and then break out the catalogs to find the fan that covers as much of the surface as possible.

The other key measurement you need is the distance between the water pump pulley (with the belt-driven fan, clutch, and spacer removed) and the face of the radiator. This depth measurement is pretty important because the electric fans that move the most air require more depth.

Electric fans may come with or require a relay kit, or they may include a thermostatically-controlled activation module.

It's pretty easy to determine what size electric fan will fit. Measure the surface of the radiator core for height and width dimensions. Then measure from the face of the radiator to the end of the water pump pulley, leaving room for bolt heads and an additional 1/8 inch of clearance.

what makes an efficient radiator. As I discussed earlier, in the 1960s, every performance radiator was a four-core design. This meant that four rows of cooling tubes stacked together and attached to the upper and lower tanks. The tubes in each row were approximately 3/8 inch in diameter.

About 20 years ago, automakers learned they could produce radiator cores with 1-inch tubes made from aluminum. The aluminum didn't transfer heat as well as copper, but it was much lighter, and the 1-inch tubes had considerably more contact with the cooling fins, which increased heat transfer. Also, it was easier to pull air through a radiator core made with two of these 1-inch cores than it was to pull air through an older-style four-core radiator. Today, nearly all radiators use this design.

The Flex-a-Fit radiators have a unique construction. They include a patented radiator side tank design that greatly improves the efficiency of heat transfer while maintaining aluminum radiator construction. The patented part is an extruded side-tank profile (shown). This provides cooling fins on the inside and outside of the side tanks. On the inside, these fins significantly increase the surface contact with the coolant for better heat transfer. Outside, the fins create greater contact surface with the air. Flex-a-lite says that the side tanks are 135 percent more efficient at transferring heat than the sheet-aluminum side tanks found in most aftermarket radiators, and they are even 41 percent more efficient than a brass radiator's tanks. An added bonus is that the outer fins form channels that T-bolts fit into. This makes electric fans, mounting brackets, overflow containers, and brackets for transmission coolers easy to mount to the radiator.

PERFORMANCE COOLING SYSTEM

Project 1: Radiator Installation

Remove OEM-style Radiator

1 The old radiator was a down-flow style, meaning the tanks were located at the top and bottom of the radiator. This is the case with all original and replacement-style radiators in 1964–1967 Chevelles. The performance radiator from Flex-a-lite is a cross-flow style, with the tanks mounted on the sides. The coolant passes from one side to the other. This is a better design for cooling, and it is the type of factory radiator found in the 1968–1972 Chevelles. Here, the inlet and outlet are on the same side of the radiator, making it a dual-pass cross-flow. In this arrangement, there is a barrier welded in the side tank that holds the inlet and outlet, so the coolant must travel to the opposite side and back before it is returned to the engine. This forces the coolant to make two passes through the radiator core instead of one. This puts the inlet and outlet in the correct place for an LS swap, and it is also better for cooling.

Install Mounting Brackets

2 This radiator is not a direct fit for the Chevelle, and it is actually a bit wider than the original. To start the installation, I slid the mounting brackets into the side channels of the side tanks and snugged them so they wouldn't move too much. Flex-a-lite includes rubber isolators, which should be used between the radiator brackets and the core support. Gently lower the radiator into place and make notes about the general placement of the radiator. This will tell you what section of the core support the brackets will contact and if anything needs to be moved.

Protect Paint while Installing Radiator

3 Apply a layer of masking tape to the core support in the area where the radiator mounts to protect the paint. Also tape the cardboard that came on the radiator core surface during shipping back onto the radiator to protect it during the subsequent mock-up installations. Use a pair of Craftsman bar clamps with rubber pads to hold the radiator firmly to the core support as you finalize the mounting hole locations and bracket positions.

CHAPTER 9

Locate Passenger-side Holes

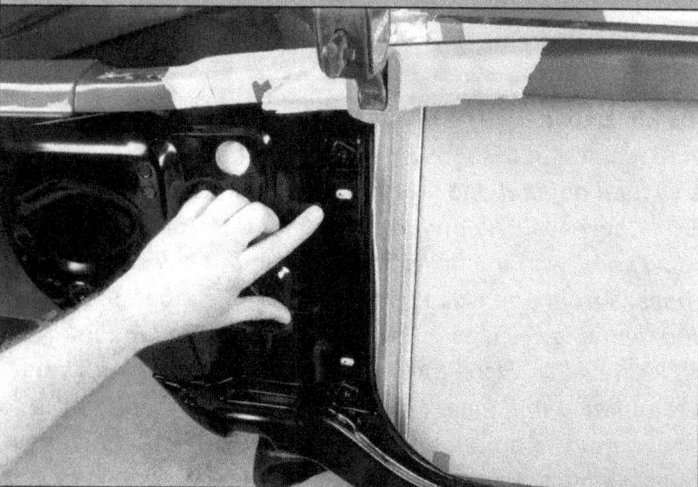

4 On the passenger's side, use two existing holes in the core support to mount brackets. These are not the original radiator mounting holes that have nuts welded in place, but they accommodate a slightly wider radiator. The universal brackets included with the Flex-a-lite radiator can slide up and down the side tank of the radiator to meet the height requirement of the mounting holes.

Drill Driver-side Holes

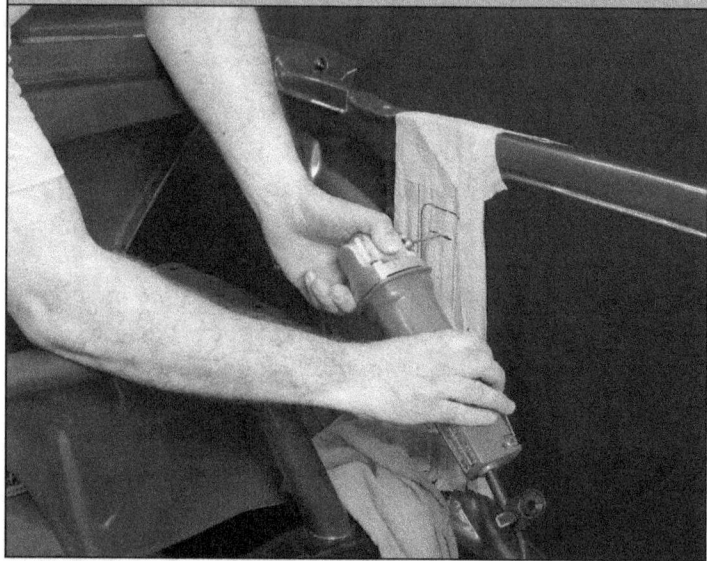

5 On the driver's side, there are no holes to line up with the bracket. With the radiator clamped in place, slide the bracket to a position that lines up with two good locations on the core support without interfering with the grille brackets or headlight buckets. Mark the holes and drill them, starting with an 1/8-inch drill bit and finishing with a 3/8-inch drill bit. Because the radiator is wider, the driver-side bracket covers the original location for the wiring harness. You could drill a large hole in the bracket for the harness, or trim away this part of the bracket. If you custom-wire the car and relocate the harness that would pass through the core support, this is not an issue.

Fit Radiator to Core Support

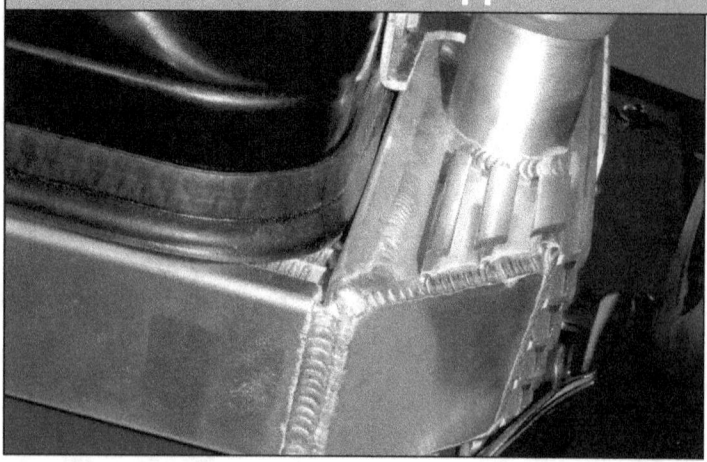

6 Here you can see the quality of the hand welds on the radiator, and the way the radiator nestles into the curve of the core support. This is the section of the core support that bolts to the frame rail; the 45-degree angle custom-ordered on the bottom of both side tanks allows the radiator to fit perfectly without hanging down below the bottom of the core support and without sitting up too high.

Install Radiator Overflow Tank

7 A 17-inch stainless-steel radiator overflow tank from Flex-a-lite includes the bracket for an easy installation on the radiator using the T-channels. This overflow has two hose fittings on the bottom. The inlet hose attaches to a short tube inside the tank. There is another tube inside which extends almost all the way to the top. This lets fluid escape the overflow tank if it gets too full.

8 Instead of using a brass barbed fitting and rubber hose to plumb the overflow tank, you can use black -4 AN hose. The first step is to thread a 1/8 NPT to -4 adapter into the water neck. Dab the threads with sealant to avoid any liquid leaks where the adapter threads into the radiator. Do not use thread sealant on the hose end of the fitting. Install a 90-degree AN fitting on the end of an approximately 26-inch-long hose. At the bottom of the overflow tank, push the hose over the end of the slip-fit tube and secure it with a worm-style hose clamp.

Select Radiator Hoses

9 With a custom engine and radiator, you can spend a few hours searching the back room of your local auto parts store until to find the perfect preformed radiator hoses. They may require a slight trimming in length, but the end result is hoses that look like they were made just for this application. You may be tempted to use the new shrink-tube-style hose clamps. These literally slide over the end of the hose and shrink when you apply heat to apply clamping force. Since this is a performance car, and you may need to remove the engine or radiator during testing and later modifications, and it may be better to paint conventional worm-style hose clamps and rotate them to hide the barrel part of the clamp.

Install Fan Control Unit

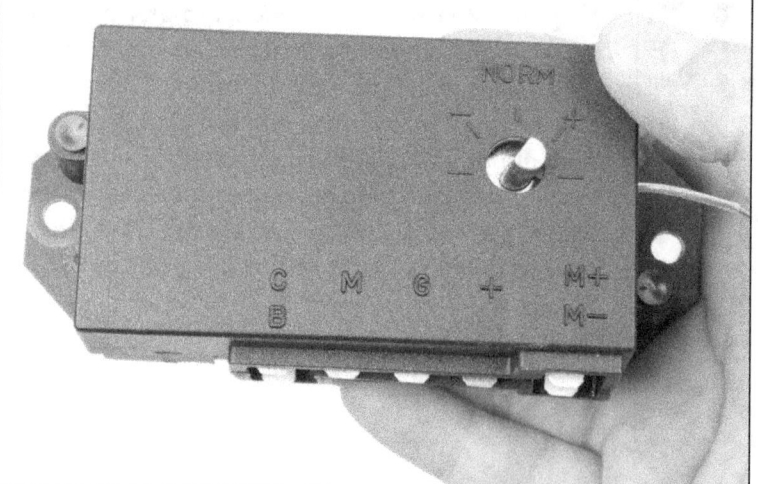

10 This Flex-a-lite electric fan came with an adjustable control unit. A temperature probe installs in the radiator core, and the fan turns on and off automatically. By turning a knob, you can adjust when the fan turns on, from approximately 160 to 240 degrees. The control unit also acts as a relay, so no additional relay is required. Wiring the module is simple: Terminal B is wired directly to the positive side of the battery; C is an optional trigger wire that connects to the air-conditioning clutch wire to turn on the fan whenever the air conditioning is on; M is an optional override terminal that lets you turn the fan on or off whenever you want with a switch; G is connected directly to the negative post of the battery, and positive should be connected to a keyed 12-volt circuit; M-positive goes to the positive side of the electric fan, and M-negative connects to the negative side of the electric fan. Wire and connectors are included with the controller.

Fill Radiator with Coolant

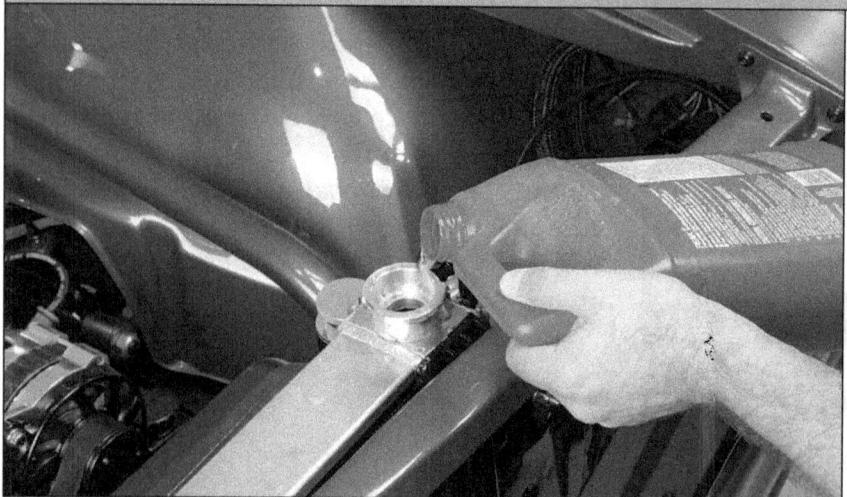

11 The final step is filling the radiator with water, starting the engine, and letting it come up to temperature. Start with straight filtered water instead of anti-freeze. That way you don't waste anti-freeze if you find a leak somewhere or need to remove part of the cooling system. Start the engine and let it come up to operating temperature. Check for leaks and rotate the knob on the electric fan controller to set the fan to turn on at the desired temperature.

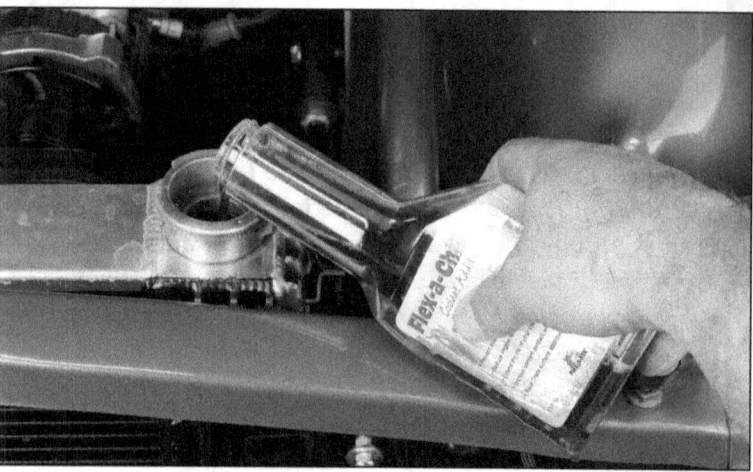

Once you are satisfied that everything is working properly and you don't need to take it apart, drain the radiator and add a few gallons of antifreeze. With an aluminum radiator, it is important to use an additive that protects the aluminum from corrosion. Under normal use, electrolysis starts immediately, corroding the aluminum radiator, as well as the aluminum cylinder heads and water pump, from the inside out. You can install a zinc anode as a sacrificial protection, but a better solution is to add a bottle of Flex-a-Chill from Flex-a-lite. This coolant additive was developed specifically to protect aluminum from corrosion, and Flex-a-lite recommends it for its radiators.

CHAPTER 10

PERFORMANCE EXHAUST

While some of the projects covered in this book may seem more fitting for a higher-end buildup, creating a performance exhaust system is something that benefits every Chevelle. The exhaust is one of two systems attached to the engine that can significantly restrict an engine's ability to make power, and it's also one of the easiest systems to upgrade. The other system is the air inlet, but that's another story. Best of all, a complete high-performance exhaust system doesn't require a personal loan to purchase and install.

In addition to having a huge impact on performance potential, the exhaust system also creates the signature sound of your Chevelle. This is often overlooked when picking the type of system and specific components. It's worth your time to find a few cars that you like the sound of and ask the owners about the exhaust systems. The engine in your car has an affect on the tone, and this needs to be taken into consideration as well. If you have a 200-hp 283, it's not going to have the crisp, deep exhaust note of an 11:1-compression, 600-hp big-block,

An exhaust system defines the characteristic sound of your Chevelle and can have a significant impact on the performance.

CHAPTER 10

The exhaust manifolds that came on the 1964–1972 Chevelles restricted flow, putting a crimp in performance right from the factory. The exhaust manifolds in recent times, such as these for a late-model Corvette, are much less restrictive, but still reduce engine noise and help carry the heat farther downstream.

no matter what you do. But some choices alter the exhaust sound, and you can give your car the desired persona with its exhaust system.

Headers or Manifolds

Starting at the engine, you need to make a choice between headers and exhaust manifolds. The traditional choice has always been headers, but if you're building a more mild-mannered car with a late-model engine, don't rule out exhaust manifolds. Many of the manifolds that come stock on the new LS series of GM engines, for example, flow very well. They also keep things a little quieter, especially mellowing the tinny sounds found with most headers.

For most small-block applications, you have a choice between 1⅝- and 1¾-inch primary tubes, usually ending in a 3-inch collector. There is a philosophy that says that headers with primary tubes that are too large will rob low-end torque from the engine. Going back to our 200-hp 283 example, this would probably be true. But if your small-block makes more than 350 hp, I recommend 1¾-inch primary tubes.

When you build a big-block Chevelle, most of the available headers have either 1¾- or 2-inch primary header tube diameter. Similar theories exist about matching tube diameter to the power output of the engine; smaller tubes retain low-end torque in a lower-horsepower engine, while larger-diameter tubes are best for engines producing higher power levels.

One of my favorite engines made 890 hp at around 7,000 rpm, and still made 540 ft-lbs of torque at 1,800 rpm. And it used 2¼-inch custom-built primary tube headers. Reduced torque is relative when talking about more radical engines with turbos and nitrous, which are becoming more common.

Most people focus on the mufflers when they think about what connects to the headers. That is a significant exhaust system decision, but the exhaust-tubing diameter and several other elements also play a huge part in the final sound and power potential of the system. When considering the exhaust diameter behind the collectors, there isn't a performance Chevelle in existence that I would use anything smaller than 2½-inch tubing on.

I don't subscribe to the idea that smaller-diameter tubing is okay after the mufflers either. While it may not be necessary to maintain the exhaust pipe diameter throughout the whole system, downsizing the tailpipe tubing changes the sound characteristics, adding or amplifying a raspy sound. And although 2½-inch tubing is a good choice for most Chevelles. When you push the 500-hp level, you should think about 3-inch tubing, but then routing and ground clearance become challenges. And if your engine makes more than 700 hp, you need to carefully consider what your priorities are with your exhaust, as a 4- to 5-inch diameter is best for power, but can distract from the street manners of the vehicle.

Tailpipes

Tailpipes are another big decision. Just 15 years ago, the decision would have been to either exit just behind the rear wheels or route the exhaust to the rear bumper. But with larger-diameter systems, as well as louder cars in general becoming

PERFORMANCE EXHAUST

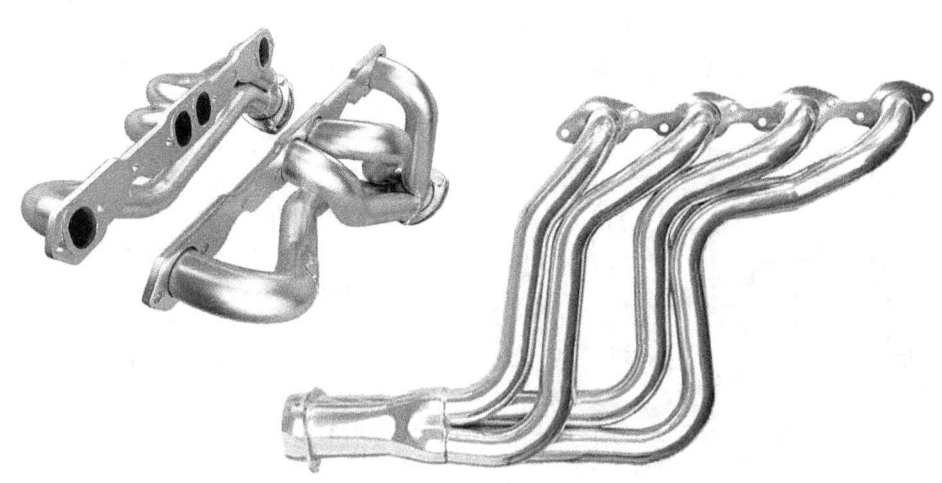

Long-style headers (right) have long been the choice for maximum performance. Recently, though, shortie headers and mid-length variants have become popular to maximize ground clearance. This helps considerably if you are building a Chevelle that sits extremely low. (Photo Courtesy Hedman Headers)

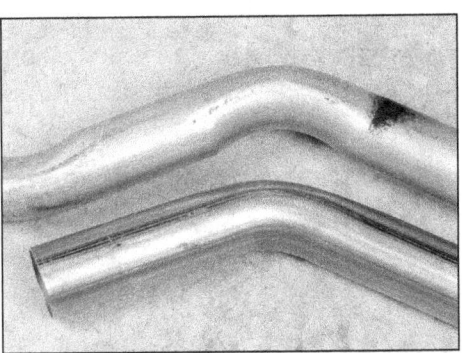

Mandrel-bent tubing (bottom) is the only way to go for a performance exhaust system. Compression-bent tubes (top) significantly decrease the cross-section area of the tubing and disrupt the flow, both of which hurt performance.

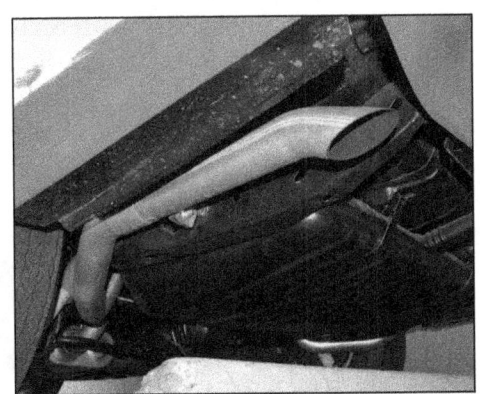

Most people opt for a full exhaust system that includes tailpipes. A quality, high-performance exhaust shop can build a complete system with up to 3-inch tubing all the way to the rear bumper.

popular, a lot of people are opting to dump the exhaust before the rear axle. Tailpipes introduce significant bends into the system, which quiets the sound considerably. Bends also create restrictions, although this is after the mufflers, so the affect on power is usually minimal.

With engines making less than 500 hp, the decision to end at the rear axle or to use tailpipes is mostly about the desired sound. Ending at the rear axle produces a louder, performance sound. Using tailpipes quiets the system and makes the engine sound milder.

Exhaust Tubing

A very important consideration for exhaust performance is the type of bend used in the tubing. Most exhaust shops have tubing benders that work by compressing the inside radius of the bend. For low-performance applications, this is okay, but it's detrimental in a performance exhaust system because it decreases the diameter of the tubing, restricting flow. It's easy for a 2½-inch tube to effectively become a 2¼-inch tube or even a 2-inch tube in a tight compression bend.

A mandrel bend is one that maintains, or comes very close to maintaining, the diameter of the tubing throughout the bend. The equipment needed to do this is very expensive.

However, high-performance exhaust shops purchase mandrel-bent tubing, cutting and welding sections together to create a custom exhaust that fits your car without unnecessary restrictions caused by compression bends.

The next decision with exhaust tubing is whether to install a crossover tube. This connects the left and right banks of a dual-exhaust system, allowing the alternating pulses of the individual cylinders firing to make use of the entire internal volume of the exhaust system. The decision is easy: If you can afford it and fit it, make a crossover tube part of your plans. It makes a significant difference in low-end torque without any detriment to high-RPM horsepower. It also changes the sound of the exhaust, usually giving it a deeper sound, but not taking away the crisp sound of a well-built system.

Mufflers

Finally, what most people see as the central part of the exhaust system is the mufflers. It's true that mufflers do make a large difference in power, and they definitely contribute to the signature sound of the car. Performance muffler designs start in two camps: those with an insulated packing material and those without. Mufflers such as those from Borla, DynoMax, and MagnaFlow use an insulated packing material to decrease overall sound and create a smooth, mellow sound. These can have a variety of internal designs to either minimize sound or increase flow characteristics.

Flowmaster is the best known manufacturer of mufflers without insulated packing material. These use metal dividers inside the muffler to cancel sound waves, reducing overall noise. They have a sound that is more metallic in nature. Decades ago, this was the best way to make power, so the sound of an exhaust with Flowmaster mufflers is usually associated with more extreme performance cars. However, the racing mufflers—those with insulated packing material and those without—from leading manufacturers all flow extremely well now, allowing you to choose your sound without limiting your power-output potential.

A crossover tube should also be considered a must in a performance system. The most popular style is an H-pipe (shown), but some builders prefer an X style that connects the two exhaust tubes at a single point.

These two Flowmaster mufflers illustrate that there is more to choosing mufflers than simply the inlet and outlet diameter. These both connect to 2½-inch tubing, but the 40 Series (left) minimizes the chamber size, resulting in a louder exhaust tone. The 50 Series (right) has larger volume, which reduces the overall sound level and produces a deeper tone.

Project 1: Performance Exhaust Installation

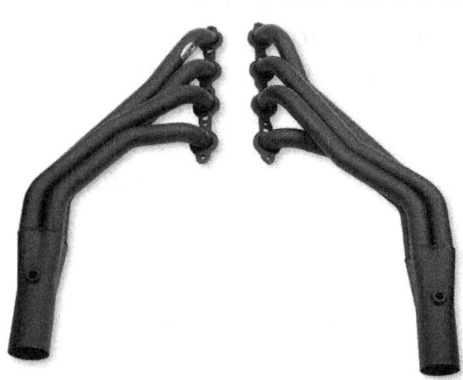

A popular installation is a set of Hooker Darksides full-length LS engine swap headers with the company's new black ceramic coating. The system behind the headers is formed from 3-inch aluminized tubing, a crossover tube, and Flowmaster 40 Series Delta Flow mufflers. This system is ideal for an engine that makes between 500 and 700 hp. If you want a quieter system, you can choose Flowmaster 50 Series mufflers, or mufflers of another brand, and add tailpipes. The Hooker headers are now available with a black satin ceramic coating for corrosion resistance. The coating is rated for 1,700 degrees F, making it suitable for supercharged or nitrous applications. Ceramic coatings help control under-the-hood temperatures. These coatings keep the heat in the exhaust system and route it farther back in the car.

Raise Car to Fit Headers

1 On a Chevelle, the headers almost always need to be installed from the bottom, which means you need to raise the car until the frame is about 24 inches off the ground. Use jackstands to secure it. If you are also installing tailpipes, place the rear jackstands under the rear axle so the distance between the axle and the body is the same as when the car is sitting on the ground. The headers are inserted at quite an angle to fit between the frame rails and the engine. Of course, this is easier with two people, one working from below and the other on top to grab the header and start the bolts into the cylinder heads. It is very typical to need to install the starter and the passenger-side header simultaneously.

Modify Headers for Fitment

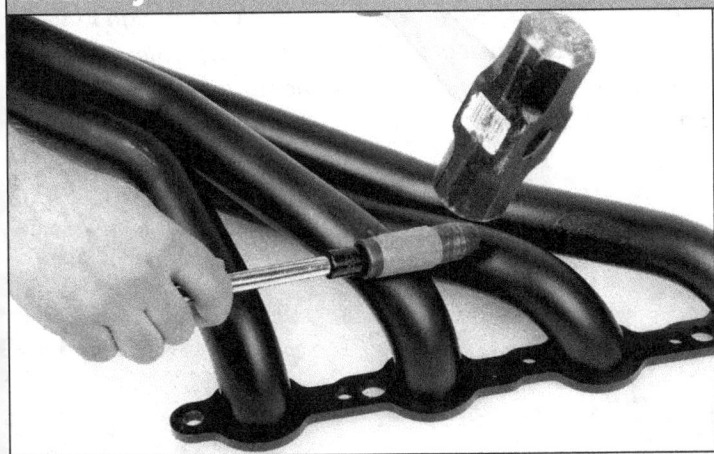

2 Sometimes you need to dent a header tube to clear chassis or steering components in a Chevelle. This is not ideal for flow, but necessary for proper fitment. With a hammer to hit it, use a large-diameter deep socket to make the dent as smooth as possible. You can wrap the socket with a sheet of shipping foam or masking tape to minimize the damage to the paint or coating on the header tube. Using a heavy hammer lets you use less force and gives you more control over the work. Also, make sure that the header flange that bolts against the cylinder head is not tweaked in the process. Possible interference points are near the steering shaft and both frame rails.

Insert Header Bolts into Block

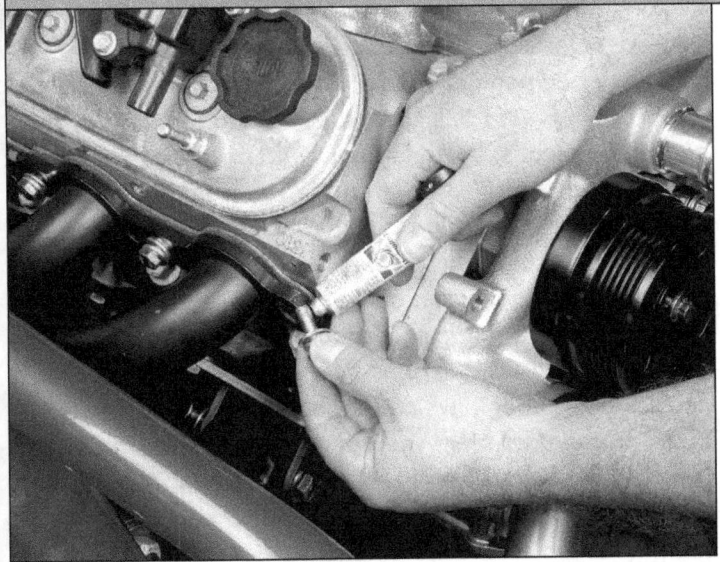

3 When inserting the header bolts into aluminum cylinder heads, coat the threads with anti-seize to keep the bolts from tearing the threads out of the heads when you need to remove them. Because of the heat cycling and vibration, you need to tighten these bolts again after the first 500 miles, and check them periodically after that. If you are switching from exhaust manifolds to headers, you may also need to change the spark plug wires, as these often contact the headers. Wires with 90-degree boots are required with most cylinder heads having straight spark plugs. Angled spark plug heads usually require straight plug wires, or ones with adjustable ends to create a 15- to 45-degree bend.

CHAPTER 10

Install Collectors

4 I took this Chevelle to Great Lakes Customs where Greg Csernai showed how he builds a performance exhaust system. These Hooker LS swap headers came with slip-on-type collectors, which are great for racing applications. On the street, the slip fit gets corroded over time and makes it very difficult to remove. It is recommended that a traditional three-bolt collector be welded onto the end to make disassembly of the system for engine or transmission removal in the future much easier.

Determine Muffler Position

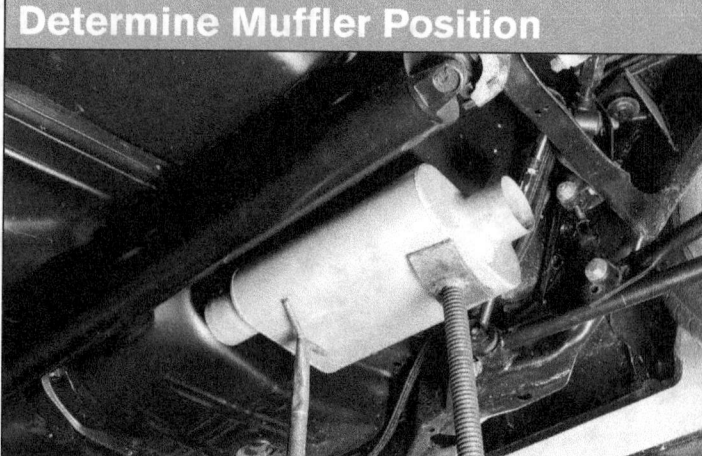

5 Position the mufflers in the car and then connect the headers to the mufflers with the tubing. All Chevelles have a generous and natural location for two mufflers in the section of the floorpan under the rear seat. Locating the mufflers here lets you tuck them high in the chassis to maximize ground clearance. Typically, you use mufflers with side inlets to raise the muffler as high as possible and connect the inlets near the driveshaft tunnel.

Build First Exhaust Section

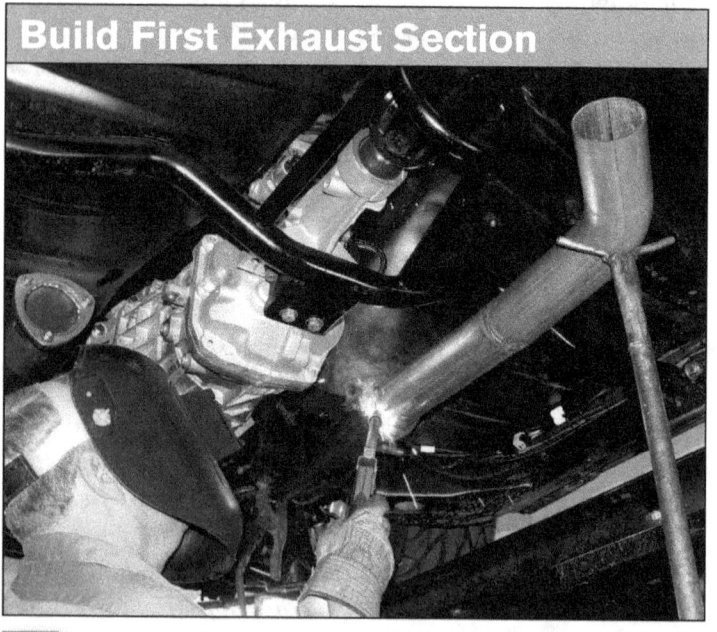

6 With the first muffler in position, start the section of exhaust tubing from the header. A straight section of about 18 inches brings the exhaust back under the raised portion of the transmission crossmember. Then weld a 45-degree mandrel-bent piece in place to bring the exhaust inward, near the driveshaft. Greg uses a MIG welder to tack the sections of exhaust together and then moves each section to a welding table to TIG-welds the pieces together.

Fit Exhaust Tubing to Mufflers

7 A pneumatic expander evenly stretches the exhaust tubing, or in this case, the inlet of the muffler. This allows the pieces to slip together and have 2 to 3 inches of overlap at the muffler for strength. You weld this junction in addition to being slipped together. The overlap at the muffler adds strength, which is important because the mufflers are the heaviest part of the entire exhaust system. Manual versions of tubing expanding tools allow you to do this at home. If building a complete system at home, you need an expander, a welder capable of working on aluminized or stainless steel, multiple jackstands to support the car, mufflers and tubing, a reciprocating saw if you need to cut an old system off the car, and a chop saw or band saw to make clean cuts.

Finish Tubing to Mufflers

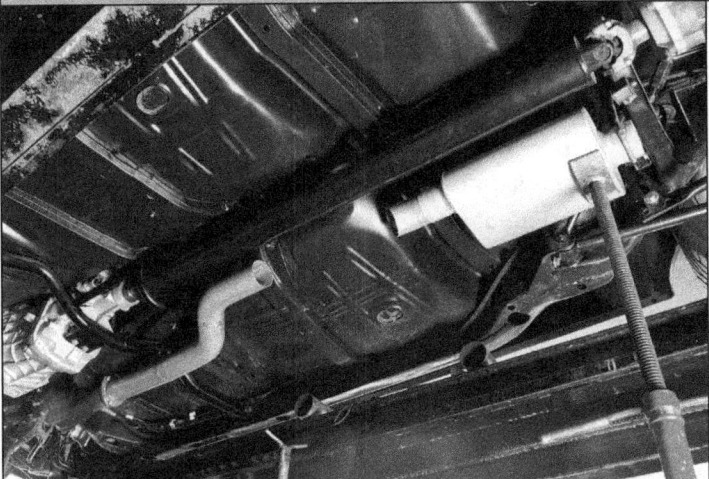

8 The final bend at the inlet of the muffler is the most challenging. It's less than a 45-degree angle, so a mandrel bend has to be cut in the bend and section-welded together to make the tubing fit perfectly. Up to this point, most of the work is such that a do-it-yourselfer could tackle it. But this is where having a pro do the work pays off. In order for the system to be TIG-welded without leaks, the junctions of these sections must fit together perfectly flush.

Install Muffler

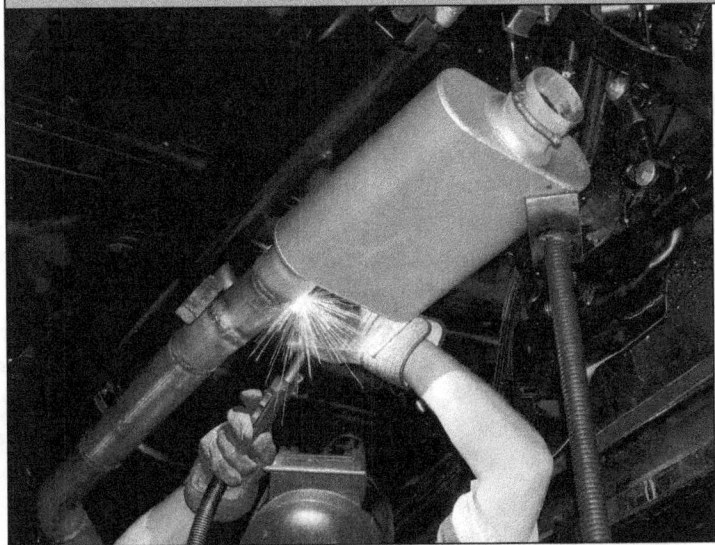

9 Consistency in the tubing routing is important for a system to look good and not contact anything under the car. Use small blocks of wood to position the tubing a safe distance from the driveshaft. Using the same block when you construct the opposite side of the exhaust ensures an equal distance. The height of the exhaust is a balance between ground clearance and providing enough space away from the floor pan to avoid rattles and the transfer of excessive heat. It's best to have a gap of at least 1 inch between all of the exhaust components and the floorpan for heat dissipation.

10 With one side complete, you build a mirror image on the opposite side. This system ends just before the rear axle for a visceral, race car sound that represents the 500-plus-hp engine under the hood quite well. Completing the system with tailpipes exiting behind the rear wheels or at the rear bumper would quiet the system considerably and change the tone of the system to a more traditional muscle car sound. Use rubber mounts, similar to what new cars use. On this car, vibration isn't really a concern, but most people appreciate the reduced vibration that this type of mount offers. The muffler mount should be attached to the Chevelle's factory crossmember that attaches to the suspension upper control arms. This frame structure can support the weight of the exhaust system.

Install Cross-over Tube

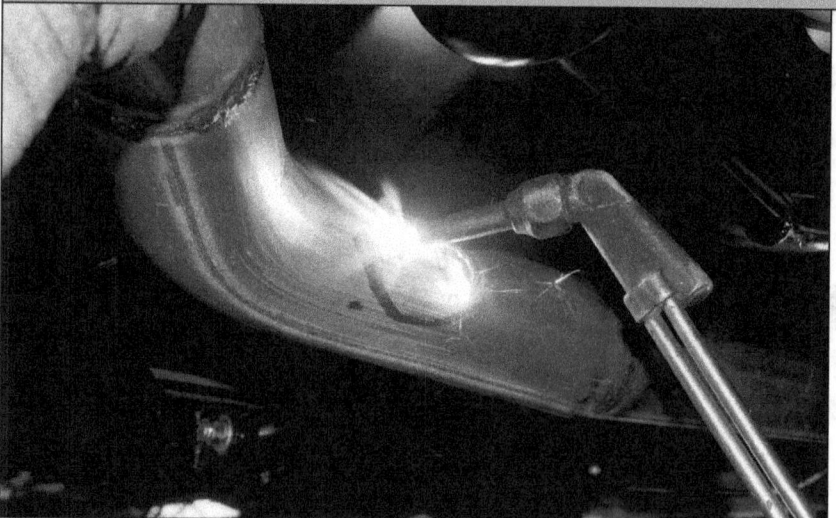

11 Once both sides of the dual exhaust are built and completely welded, fabricate the crossover tube. Leave room for the crossover in the overall design, but add it last so that the exhaust can be routed perfectly before connecting the two sides. Start by cutting a section of tubing to connect the left and right sides near the tailshaft of the transmission. Using a marker, trace the circumference of the tube onto the exhaust system and use a torch to cut holes through the tubing.

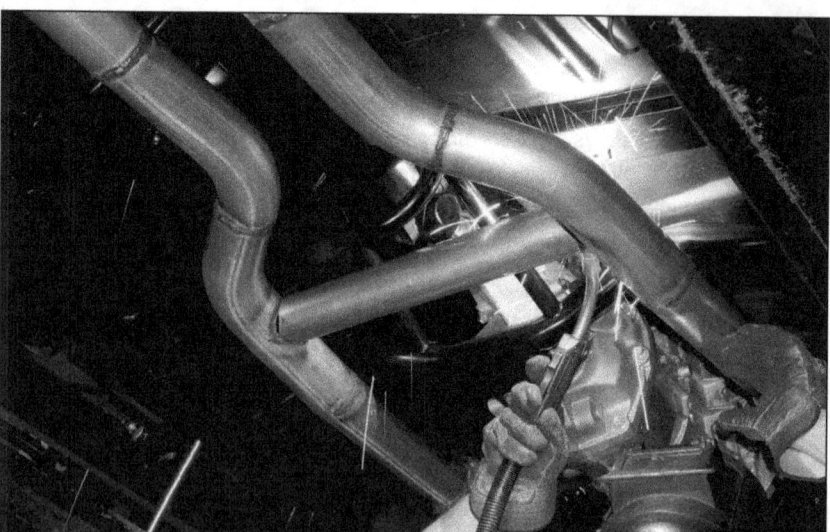

12 The fitment of the tube for the crossover is pretty challenging to get completely flush. Sand the aluminized coating off the tubing where you need to weld, allowing you to use a MIG welder to fill the gaps, as well as create leak-free junctions. Once all of the welding is done, paint the junctions with a high-temperature paint that comes close to matching the natural finish on the aluminized tubing for a finished look. The difference in sound between a car with and without a crossover tube is a bit shocking.

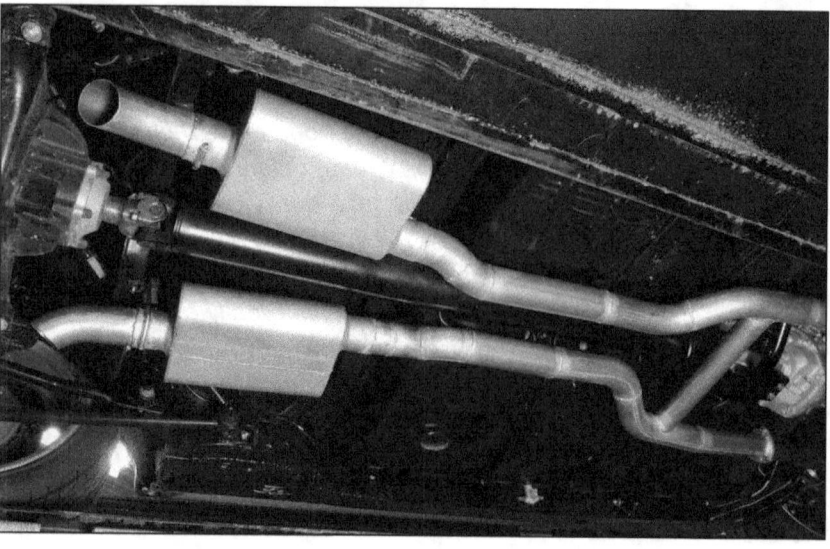

13 The crossover makes the tone of the system deeper and smoother. If you drive your car before and after the installation, you will find a huge improvement in torque with the crossover at engine speeds below 2,000 rpm without limiting high-RPM power. If you end your system in front of the rear axle, angle the exhaust tips outward. This decreases the amount of dirt and debris that the exhaust kicks up as you drive. With the system completed, you can remove it from the car and have it ceramic-coated by Jet-Hot Ceramic Coatings or other companies for great looks, lower temperatures, and extremely good corrosion resistance.

CHAPTER 11

OVERDRIVE TRANSMISSION SWAPS

Building a modern performance muscle car *without* an overdrive transmission is extremely rare. Basically, you only run across this if a person is trying to keep the car original, or if it will be used almost exclusively as a race car that wouldn't benefit from a lower final ratio of 1:1 in the transmission.

The primary reason an overdrive is desirable is to lower the engine speed on the freeway. This also gives you the opportunity to choose a higher numerical rear-axle gear ratio for improved launch without completely limiting your freeway cruising speed. Also, most overdrive transmissions have more gears than the 4-speed manuals and 3-speed automatics that Chevelles came with, so the first-gear ratio is steeper, providing better launch performance.

All of this adds up to a much improved driving experience. The engine is less stressed on the highway, which means you're less stressed, and the ride is quieter with lower engine speed. A higher numerical first gear makes it easier to pull away from a stop in everyday driving, and it quickens launch times in

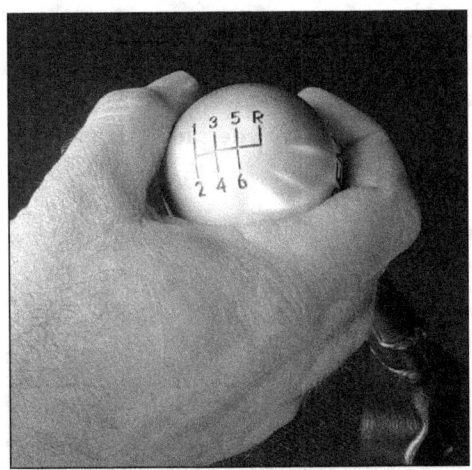

An overdrive transmission is one of the most rewarding upgrades you can make to your Chevelle. In addition to the potential strength upgrade, the drop in engine RPM on the highway can make your car a joy to drive at speeds over 60 mph.

all types of racing. Stepping up to a 5- or 6-speed manual provides more gearing options for a road course and even lets you build your car with ratios more tailored for the exact type of driving and racing you like to do.

The only real downsides to installing an overdrive transmission are cost, size, and, in some cases, complexity. Each of these factors varies greatly between automatic and manual overdrive transmissions.

Automatic Transmissions

There are plenty of overdrive automatic transmissions in the salvage yards, with GM rear-wheel-drive production applications spanning more than 30 years. Naturally, you never know exactly what the condition of a salvage-yard component is, so a rebuild may be part of the price equation. The earlier TH200R4 and TH700R4 transmissions are less expensive than the later 4L60E, 4L65E, and 4L80E, because they do not require an electronic controller, basically a stand-alone computer controlling the transmission.

TH200R4

The TH200R4 was initially shunned by the performance world because it seemed to be weaker than a TH350, and it was one of the first metric GM transmissions. It actually has proven to be durable, and many feel that it's as strong as the larger TH700R4 transmission.

Other upsides are that it is usually the least expensive of the automatic

CHAPTER 11

General Motors has used several automatic transmissions over the past several decades that are good swap candidates. Choices include the TH200R4, the TH700R4 and its electronic cousin the 4L60E, and the 4L80E.

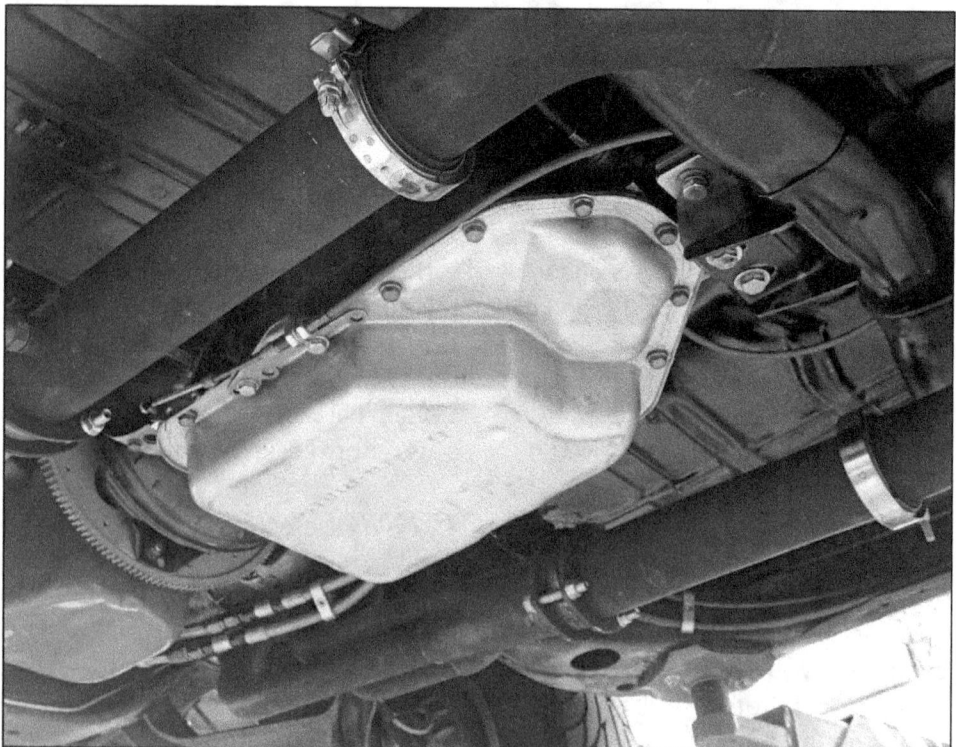

The TH200R4 is popular because it requires very few changes to the car if you're replacing a Powerglide, TH350, or TH400. It's an affordable overdrive that fits under the factory floor sheet metal and is strong enough for moderate performance engines. They can be built to withstand high levels of power.

overdrive transmissions, and it is relatively easy to retrofit into a Chevelle. It has a .67:1 overdrive and a 2.74:1 first-gear ratio, making it a close-ratio automatic overdrive transmission, which is desirable for drag-race-style acceleration, and can be advantageous on autocross and road courses. Generally, people use a slightly larger numerical rear gear ratio with this setup.

The TH200R4 has the traditional (pre-LS) bellhousing bolt pattern and uses the same flexplates and 27-spline slip-yoke as a Powerglide or a TH350. It's also nearly the same overall length as these early automatic transmissions, although the rear mount is located approximately 6 inches farther rearward. You can purchase a new crossmember specifically made to bolt this transmission in a Chevelle from Bowtie Overdrives, and a variety of other companies, or you can slide the original crossmember back in the open C-channel frame and drill new holes in the frame rails. It accepts a traditional rubber or polyurethane transmission mount.

The best news is that this transmission doesn't require any floor modifications. You need to modify your factory shifter with a conversion kit from ShiftRight, or install an aftermarket shifter for a TH200R4 available from B&M, Hurst, TCI, and others. The last thing you need to do is install a throttle valve (TV) cable. This connects to the carburetor or throttle body and is how the transmission knows the engine load. The best way to do this is with an aftermarket cable and bracket made for the type of carburetor or fuel-injection system on your Chevelle. Cables and brackets are available from B&M, Lokar, and others. While the adjustment of this cable is not an exact

OVERDRIVE TRANSMISSION SWAP

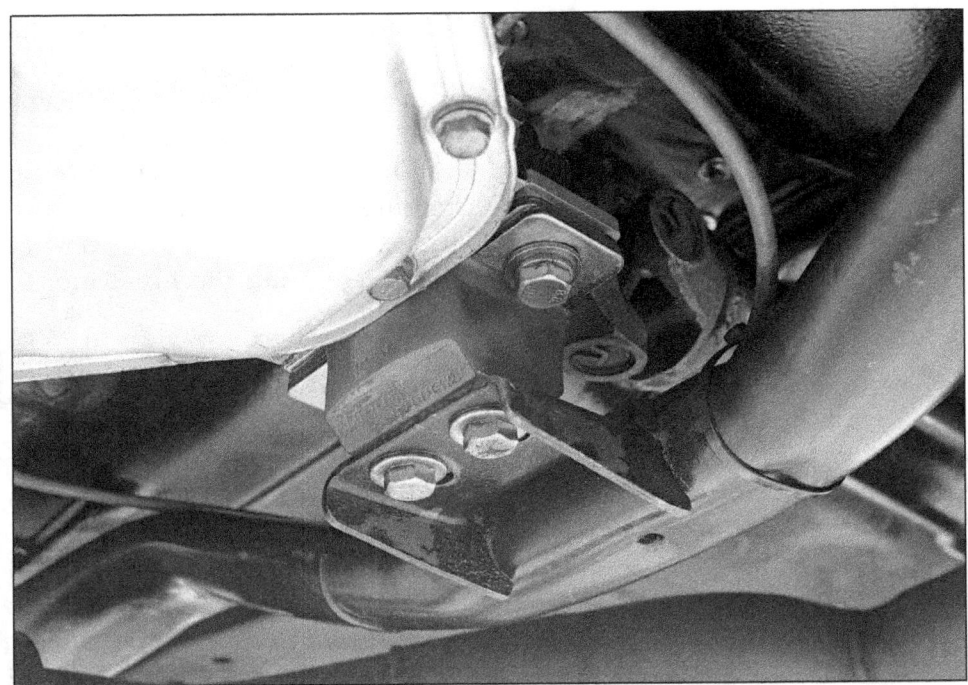

All of the automatic transmissions accept a traditional GM transmission mount. The bolts going into the transmission are usually metric, but otherwise it's the same mount originally used on Muncie and TH350 transmissions.

You can scrounge salvage yards looking for useable transmissions. You can also purchase them brand new, usually with desirable upgrades to work great in your older muscle car. This is a new 4L60E from TCI, and the company offers it in several versions to meet various performance needs.

science, it is critical that the cable be installed and the length be adjusted to the correct range. If it's not, the line pressure in the transmission will be off and damage will occur to the transmission.

TH700R4, 4L60E, 4L65E and 4L70E

The 4L60E is essentially a computer-controlled version of the TH700R4, so installation is very similar. There are also 4L65E and 4L70E versions with different internal parts, which were later incorporated into the 4L60E. The installation details of these transmissions are the same. The 4L60E requires an electronic controller to vary shift firmness and shift points as well as torque converter lockup, while the TH700R4 uses a TV cable to moderate shifts and a simple wire connection to control the lockup torque converter.

The rear mount is only about 1 inch farther back compared to a TH350's, and these transmissions also accept a traditional rubber or polyurethane mount. Early Chevelles may need the toe panel on the passenger side of the floor tunnel to be hammered slightly for clearance.

4L80E and 4L85E

The 4L80E is a much larger transmission with stronger internal components. The 4L80E was thought to be the modern, overdrive version of the TH400 when it first hit the streets. From a strength and performance perspective, the 4L80E is definitely a player. Its downsides are size and weight. It is a computer-controlled transmission, so you also need to run a transmission controller.

There are now stand-alone systems, such as the TCI EZ-TCU controller, that make this simple. These systems plug into the transmission

CHAPTER 11

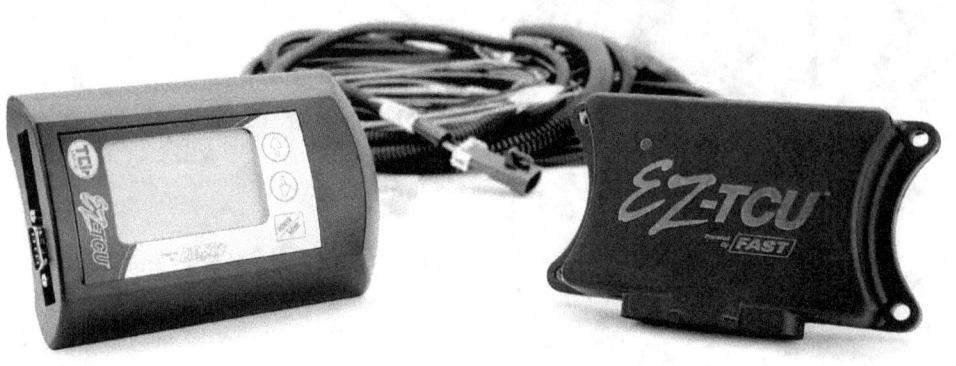

The 4L80E is a completely computer-controlled transmission, which means you need a stand-alone controller. TCI designed an easy-to-use system that lets you set up and tune the transmission shift characteristics with a simple handheld interface.

and offer an easy-to-use handheld interface, asking you basic questions and doing the rest of the work for you.

Anyone who has worked with a 4L80E will tell you it is a massive transmission. Fully dressed with torque converter and fluid, it weighs approximately 240 pounds, while a TH400 weighs about 180 pounds. And that size also means massaging the floor with a sledge hammer for clearance. On the 1968–1972 Chevelles, I've been told that you only need to add clearance near the transmission lines, while older Chevelles require more work. However, you don't need to cut out the sheet metal and fabricate a new tunnel as you do for some of the larger overdrive manual transmissions. You need to move the crossmember rearward approximately 9 inches, and I have heard cases of the heavy transmission bending stock crossmembers.

There is also a variant of this transmission called the 4L85E with some stronger internal components. The exterior and the installation is the same.

TCI 6X

One of the coolest automatic overdrive transmissions currently available is the TCI 6X 6-speed. This transmission is based on the 4L80E but gives you six forward gears. Much like a modern 7- or 8-speed BMW or Mercedes transmission, it essentially engages overdrive in first and second gears to create a close-ratio 6-speed that's great for drag racing, autocrossing, and road racing.

TCI rates this transmission up to 850 hp, making it a very stout choice. The TCI 6X 6-speed must be used with the TCI EZ-TCU controller, which lets you easily program shift points.

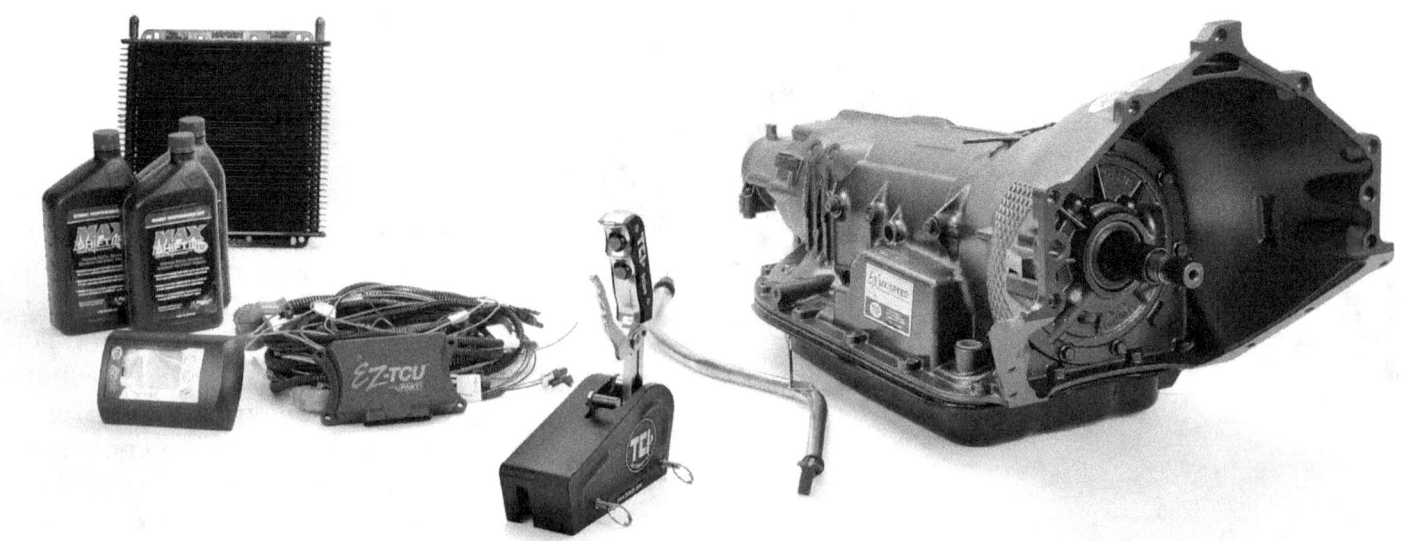

TCI has taken the 4L80E to the next level, converting it to a six-speed automatic. The TCI 6X available in a complete kit that includes a shifter, controller, cooler, and even transmission fluid. A steering-wheel-mounted paddle shifter is an optional upgrade.

Manual Transmissions

Moving into manual transmission options, this is a good time to be a fan of shifting your own gears. These days there are more boxes that can tolerate high power and heavy cars and still offer great shifting and overdrive gears. Tremec, the company that supplies General Motors, Ford, and Chrysler with transmissions for their modern muscle cars, also offers versions for Chevelles. At this time, Tremec offers three overdrive manual transmissions in the aftermarket. The T-5 and TKO are 5-speeds, while the T-56 Magnum is a 6-speed. Each of these transmissions is significantly different from the others, and comes with its own set of installation requirements.

Tremec has three transmissions that cover the needs of just about any Chevelle owner looking for an overdrive manual transmission: two 5-speeds, and its newest transmission, the T-56 Magnum 6-speed.

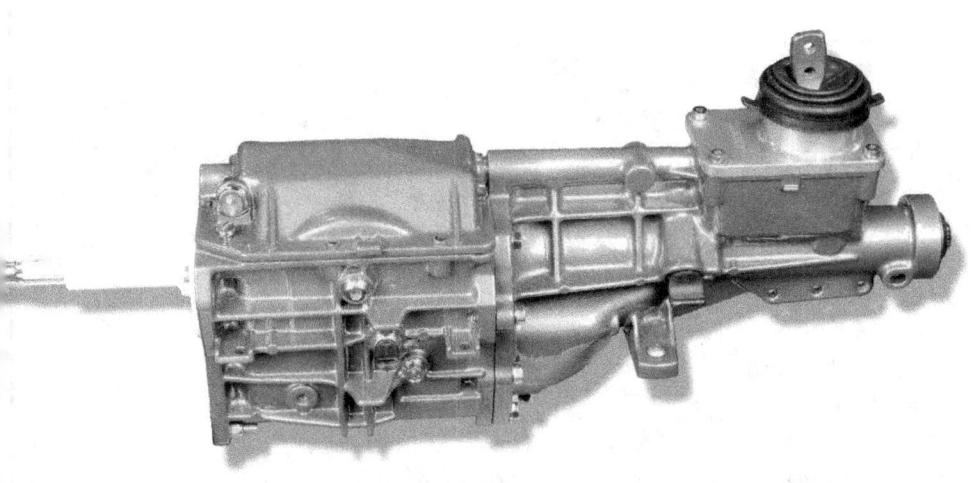

The oldest design in the Tremec lineup is the T-5 5-speed. This transmission has been in production since the early 1980s and has evolved into the compact, reliable transmission offered today. Its biggest drawback is a conservative torque-input rating of 300 ft-lbs.

The T-5

The Tremec T-5 has been produced for a very long time and was original equipment in third-generation Camaros and Firebirds, as well as the popular 5.0-liter Mustangs. The current version offered by Tremec has been upgraded for strength; however, it is only rated for use behind engines making 300 ft-lbs of torque or less. It is the smallest of the Tremec transmissions, and it can be swapped into a Chevelle without major floor surgery but you need to cut a hole in the floor for the shifter, even if you have an original 4-speed car.

It is available with only one set of gear ratios, featuring a 2.95:1 first-gear and a 0.63:1 overdrive. Another significant advantage is that it can bolt up to a Muncie-style bellhousing, allowing you to retain your existing bellhousing and mechanical clutch setup. It is also the most economical of the Tremec aftermarket transmissions.

TKO500 and TKO600

The next box in the Tremec lineup is the TKO 5-speed, which is a completely different transmission than the T-5. There are two versions of the TKO available: the TKO600, with a torque input rating of 600 ft-lbs, and the TKO500, with a rating of 500 ft-lbs. Within each of these models, multiple gear ratios are available. The TKO is a significant step up in strength and options, as far as the gear ratios go. However, it is larger than the T5 and requires cutting of the transmission tunnel.

Companies such as American Powertrain offer installation kits for these transmissions that include a curved sheet-metal section that can be welded in to raise and widen the transmission tunnel.

The TKO uses a late-model bolt pattern at the bellhousing, so a new bellhousing or scattershield is required. You can use a mechanical throwout bearing or convert to a hydraulic clutch system.

T56 Magnum

The big daddy of the Tremecs is the T56 Magnum 6-speed. It's rated at 700 ft-lbs of torque and offers six gears in a box that is fantastic to shift. There are several combinations of gear ratios available, including a 2.66:1 and 2.97:1 first-gear ratio, and a choice of either a 0.63:1 or 0.50:1 sixth gear. Both fifth and sixth gears are overdrives in the T56 Magnum.

Like the TKO, it uses a late-model-style bolt pattern at the bellhousing. It is also larger than the TKO, requiring even more floorpan work to fit. But if you're building the ultimate performance pro-touring Chevelle, this is the transmission you want.

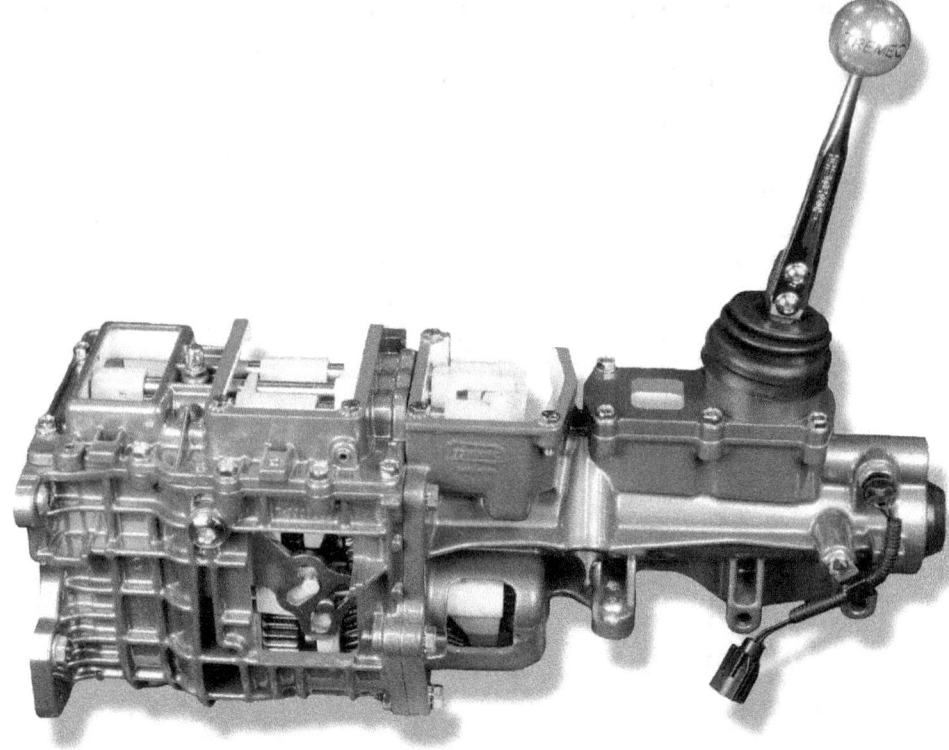

The TKO 5-speed is a significant step up in performance, with many available gear ratios available, and much stronger internal components. It's offered in two torque ratings (based on the gear set) of either 500 or 600 ft-lbs.

Tunneling

Just about any 5- or 6-speed manual transmission swap requires significant transmission tunnel work. These modern gearboxes are much taller and, overall, more bulky than the svelte Muncie 4-speeds and Saginaw 3-speeds that originally resided under vintage Chevelle floorpans. To fit most of the transmissions, about two thirds of the original tunnel must be cut out and enlarged, raising the height of the tunnel and extending the tunnel rearward in the car.

American Powertrain offers a tunnel panel that you can work with to make this change. It's a curved section of sheet metal that is the correct length for Tremec TKO and T-56 Magnum transmissions. You need to cut out the top section of the factory tunnel and massage the metal edges to meet the shape of the new tunnel section.

If you're handy with sheet metal, you can form your own custom tunnel. The floor panel, held in the photo, is from American Powertrain. The one welded into the car was fabricated by ABC Performance for a perfect fit.

OVERDRIVE TRANSMISSION SWAP

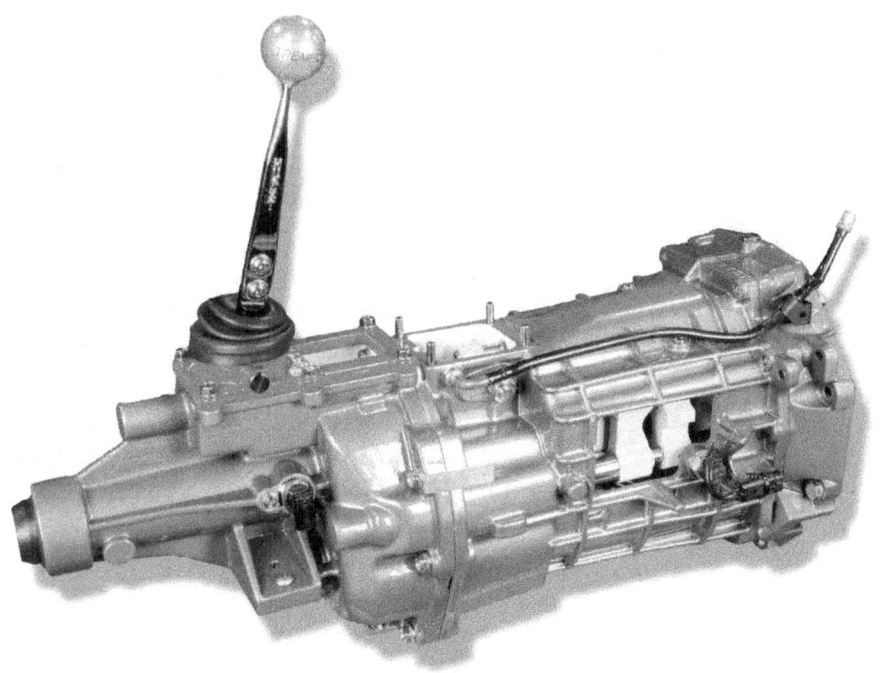

The T-56 Magnum is the newest Tremec transmission. It's a massive transmission, but it's also the only Tremec aftermarket transmission with six forward gears and it is practically bulletproof with a torque rating of 700 ft-lbs.

The Gear Vendors Solution

Installing a Gear Vendors unit behind your existing transmission is another way to add an overdrive to your muscle car. It is an auxiliary overdrive/underdrive that bolts to the rear of your transmission. It has a planetary gearset (like an automatic transmission), and can be used to create stepped gears between your current gears in addition to providing a 22 percent overdrive when used with your 1:1 top gear. The Gear Vendors unit can be set up to shift in and out of overdrive automatically, or you can control it manually.

Gear splitting is one very important feature of the Gear Vendors product. It can help considerably with acceleration, especially to fill in the gaps between second and third gears on a TH350 or TH400, and between second and third, as well as third and fourth gears, on a manual 4-speed transmission.

For autocross and road racing, there's an even bigger advantage during downshifting. When you downshift, the percentage of gear change is much larger than when you upshift, making the change in engine speed much greater. By using the Gear Vendors unit to split the gear as you downshift, you make the change in engine speed smaller, causing less upset to the chassis and retaining more control over the car.

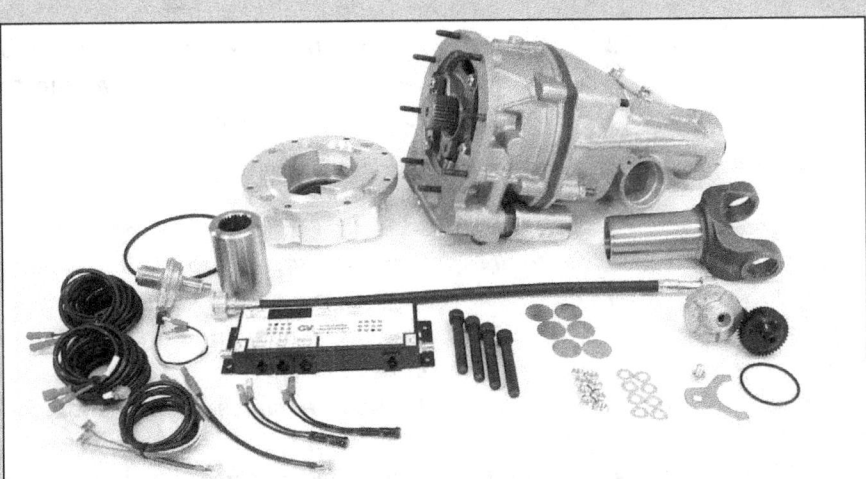

Gear Vendors has an auxiliary overdrive/underdrive that bolts onto the rear of your existing transmission.

CHEVELLE PERFORMANCE PROJECTS: 1964–1972

Project 1: Clutch Installation

Select Clutch

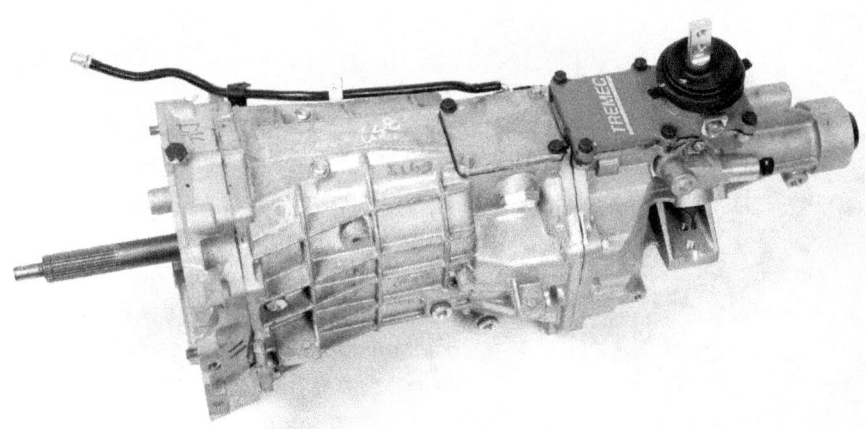

1 Our car uses the Tremec T-56 Magnum 6-speed version with a 2.97:1 first gear and a 0.50:1 sixth. The 2.63:1 first-gear version is popular because it is a close-ratio version. However, this car will see such a variety of use, including high-speed road courses, that the 0.50:1 sixth will be more valuable. Also, the 2.97:1 first should help considerably with launches, provided there is sufficient traction. You can also custom-order a Tremec Magnum, swapping one or both of the overdrive gear ratios.

Select Installation Kit

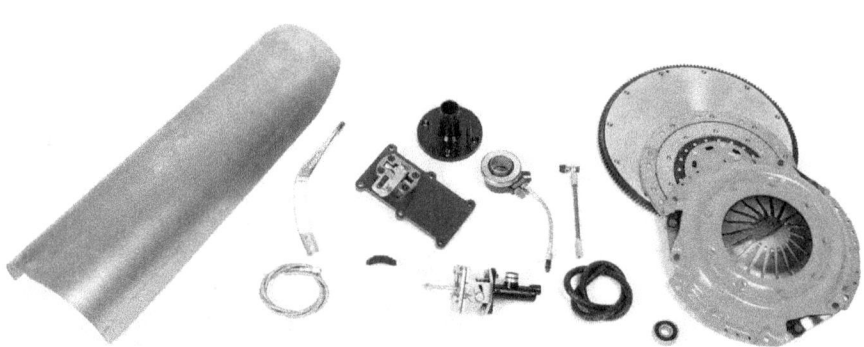

2 We used an installation kit from American Powertrain. The company offers kits for all of the Tremec transmissions to make retrofitting the transmissions into early muscle cars easier. It can also mix and match parts for your specific conversion. For example, the conversion for this car called for an LS engine flywheel and throwout bearing, hydraulic clutch conversion, but no crossmember, because our car has boxed frame rails and we will be using the matching ABC Performance crossmember.

Install Pilot Bearing

3 There are quite a few things to do before hoisting the transmission into place. The first is to prep the back of the engine. For LS engines, there are two different pilot bearings. They have different thicknesses, and the thick one keeps the Tremec transmission from sliding all the way flush against the bellhousing. Coat the flywheel bolts with Red Loctite, and bolt on the flywheel, torquing all of the bolts in a criss-cross pattern initially to 15 ft-lbs and then 75 ft-lbs.

Align Clutch Disc

4 The clutch assembly goes together like any traditional clutch, using the provided clutch-disc alignment tool to center the disc to the throwout bearing while you install the pressure plate. American Powertrain has its own line of Science Friction 10½- and 11-inch discs that include copper-impregnated organic material for performance street use, full-face Kevlar for high-power applications, and Full Circle Ceramix for up to 845 hp with the appropriate pressure plate.

Install Pressure Plate Bolts

5 Use ARP pressure plate bolts. There's a lot riding on these bolts, and ARP has designed them specifically for this type of application, with heads designed to give accurate torque readings. Tighten the bolts in a criss-cross pattern. Initially torque them to 15 ft-lbs and then to the final 55 ft-lbs specification. Some people recommend using Red Loctite on the threads.

Select Hydraulic Clutch Conversion

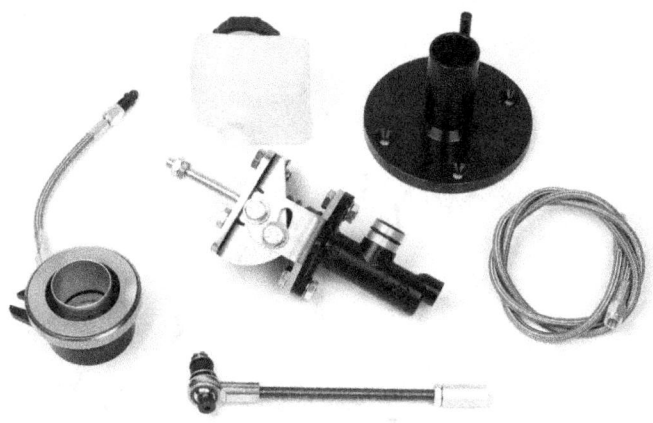

6 Converting a Chevelle from a mechanical to a hydraulic clutch can be intimidating, but the kit from American Powertrain makes it easier. The conversion at the transmission is pretty straightforward, but the challenge comes with mounting a clutch master cylinder on the firewall and connecting it to the clutch pedal at a point and angle that works with the pedal travel. The kit includes a Wilwood master cylinder that can be used either with the reservoir mounted on the cylinder or with it mounted remotely. The two key parts of this kit are the adjustable master cylinder mount bracket and the adjustable pushrod that connects to the pedal with a Heim joint.

Install Throw-out Bearing Collar

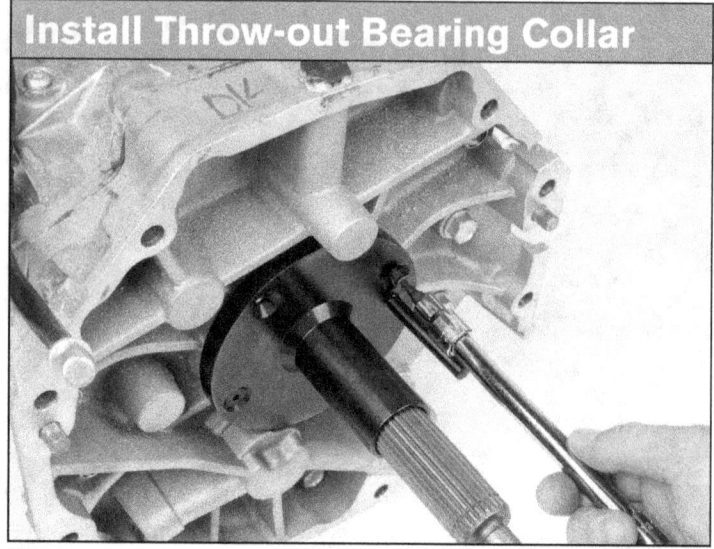

7 The American Powertrain hydraulic clutch conversion includes the components you need at the transmission and also for the clutch master cylinder. The hydraulic throwout bearing rides on the transmission collar. American Powertrain provides a collar with a location pin to keep the throwout bearing from spinning and to align the hydraulic lines for routing out of the bellhousing.

Take Throw-out Bearing Measurement

8 To set up the American Powertrain hydraulic clutch system properly, measuring the distance between the face of the throwout bearing and the fingers on the pressure plate is critical. This determines the gap between the two components when the clutch is released. Make sure that the throwout bearing is fully seated on the transmission collar and that it is fully compressed. Bolt the bellhousing onto the transmission. Use a straightedge to measure the distance between the face of the throwout bearing and the face of the bellhousing. You need to be very precise in this measurement, and check it at three different places on the throwout bearing. The measurement should be the same at all three places. If not, the throwout bearing is not seated correctly or is partially extended.

Take Throw-out Bearing Measurement (Continued)

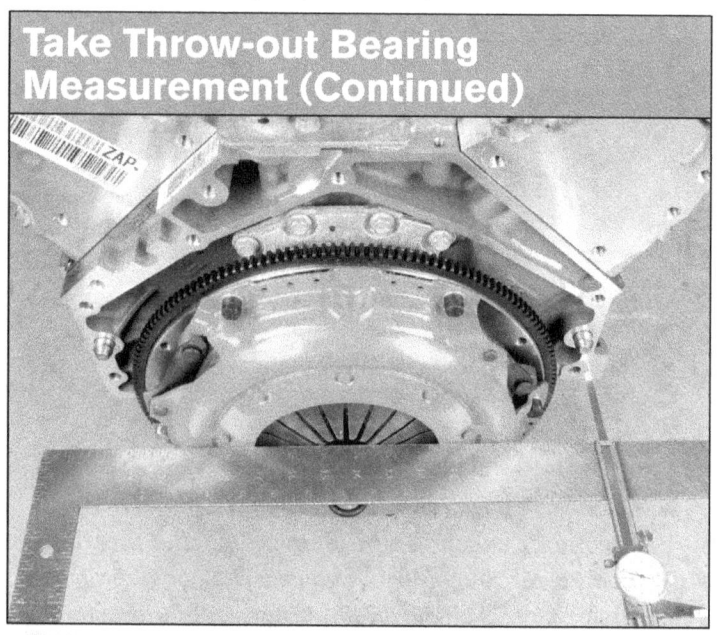

9 Using a straightedge, measure from the bellhousing mounting face on the block to the tips of the pressure plate fingers where the throwout bearing rides. Take measurements on the passenger's and driver's side of the block to make sure you have the straightedge square on the clutch fingers. If you use a scattershield with a block plate, bolt the block plate to the back of the engine and measure from this surface.

Set Air Gap

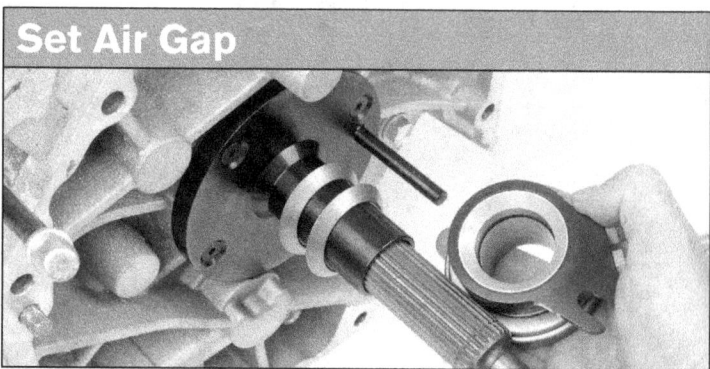

10 Subtract the second measurement from the first to find your air gap. Too much air gap, and the throwout bearing isn't able to disengage the clutch. Too little, and the clutch is partially engaged when the pedal is at rest, causing the clutch to slip. An air gap of .150 to .200 inch is what American Powertrain calls for, but the company says you can run as little as 0.100 inch of air gap. The kit includes conical shims that fit over the American Powertrain transmission collar to reduce the air gap. If the air gap is not large enough, American Powertrain offers a 1/4-inch spacer to install between the bellhousing and engine block. If you do not have enough air gap and are using a bellhousing without a block plate, switching to a scattershield and using the block plate adds between .200 and .250 inch of air gap.

Install Bellhousing

11 Speaking of bellhousings and scattershields, if you are installing a TKO or Magnum, you most likely need a new one, as these do not use the old Muncie-style transmission bolt pattern. The QuickTime scattershield is required for many racing classes, and a good idea if you plan to drive your car aggressively. As the name suggests, these are designed to contain a pressure plate or flywheel if they come apart. The QuickTime scattershields are machined properly and fit well. These are QuickTime scattershields for the TKO and Magnum using hydraulic clutches. The one on the left fits an LS engine, while the one on the right fits Gen I small- and big-block engines.

12 Often, a scattershield has to be installed with the headers loose, because they typically have a larger mounting flange than a production bellhousing. With a swivel socket and a long extension, you can reach every bolt from the underside of the car. If you have rubber or polyurethane engine mounts, do not let the engine tilt unsupported with the transmission removed. This can damage the engine mounts. Attach a lift plate to the intake, and use an engine hoist to keep the engine close to its installed driveline angle.

Mount Master Cylinder

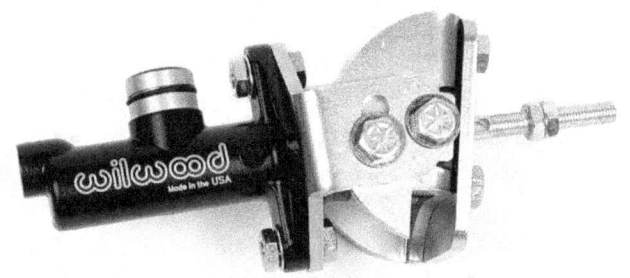

13 The other half of the hydraulic clutch system is the master cylinder, which needs to be mounted on the firewall and connected to the clutch pedal. American Powertrain supplies a Wilwood master cylinder and an adjustable firewall mount bracket. This bracket is key to the installation, because the master cylinder needs to be mounted at a downward angle on the firewall to keep the angle between the cylinder bore and the pushrod within system limitations. The master cylinder can have a reservoir mounted directly on top or remotely with the provided parts. In a Chevelle, the reservoir hits the brake master cylinder, so you need to mount the reservoir separately on the firewall.

14 The American Powertrain bracket is designed to locate the master cylinder on the firewall where the original mechanical linkage for the clutch came through. The two parts of the bracket sandwich the firewall for strength. You need to either cut the lip off the firewall where the bracket mounts or use shims between the bracket and the firewall so that the bracket bolts tightly against the firewall. You do not want any flex or movement here.

Install Linkage and Clutch Pedal

15 Inside the car, the linkage and Heim joint that are part of the American Powertrain kit bolt to the clutch pedal where the original clutch linkage connected. The new linkage is adjustable, and you thread the rod to make the engagement point where you want it in the clutch pedal travel. Finally, bleed the clutch. This is a two-person job, with one person pumping the clutch pedal and the other releasing air from the system with a valve found on the second steel-braided line coming off of the throwout bearing. The process is very similar to bleeding brakes.

Project 2: Transmission Installation

Install Speedometer Drive

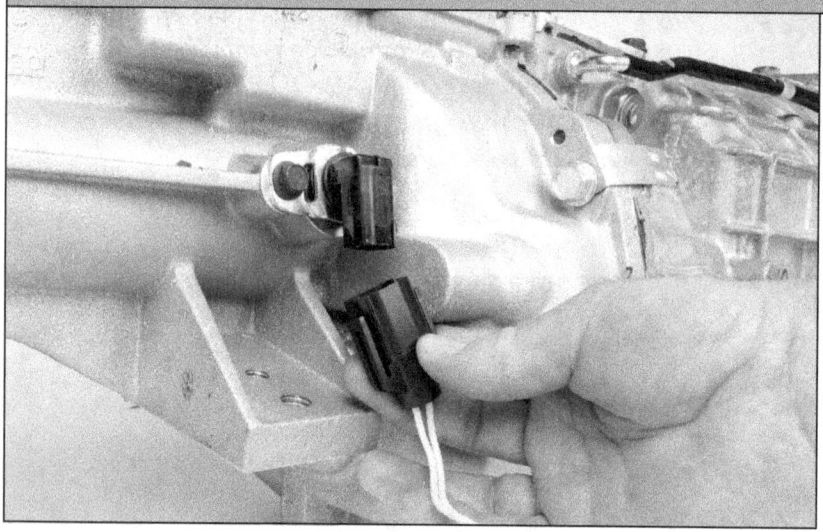

1 You will make the electrical connections to the transmission after it is installed, but it's good to be familiar with the locations of the connections before the transmission is tucked up inside the transmission tunnel. The Tremec TKO and T-56 Magnum have electrical and mechanical speedometer outputs and an electric one. The connection for using an electric speedometer is on the passenger's side of the tailshaft housing. American Powertrain provides a connection for this that allows you to wire it to an aftermarket electronic speedometer. This is a pulse-type speedo sending unit; you connect one lead to the speedometer and ground the other lead.

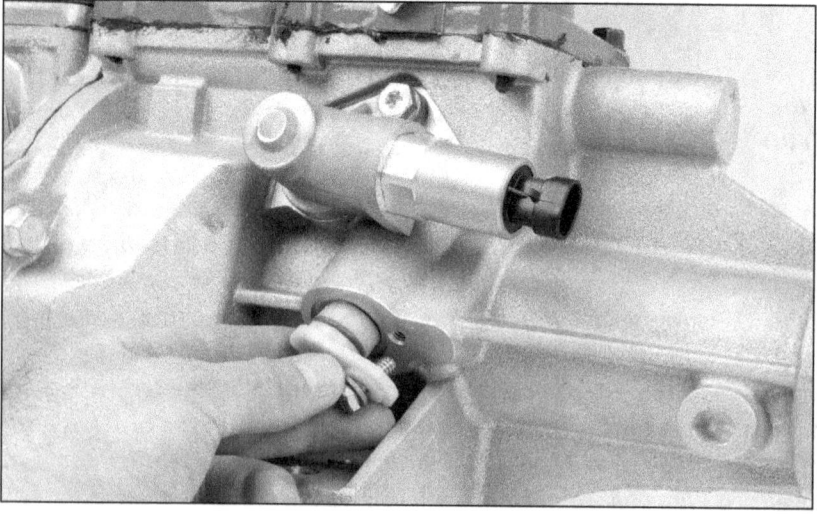

2 On the driver's side of the tailshaft is the mechanical speedometer output. If you do not use a speedometer cable, you need to install a plug, available from American Powertrain. On the T-56 Magnum, just above this connection, is a reverse-gear detent solenoid. There is a bit of pressure on the shifter to keep you from selecting reverse instead of fifth. By supplying 12-volt power to the solenoid, the pressure is removed, letting you slide into reverse more easily. If you are using a tall shifter, it isn't really necessary to power this solenoid, as you have enough leverage to engage reverse.

Install Shifter Plate

3 American Powertrain offers a shift plate that moves the shifter to the mid position on the transmission and moves the shifter to the left. This mimics the position of the 4-speed shifter these Chevelles originally had. You need to modify the floor for transmission clearance, so you may want to mock-up the trans/shifter/seat location before deciding in which position to mount the shifter. There are also many styles of shifter handle to choose from, including a muscle-car-looking Hurst kit from American Powertrain.

Install Hydraulic Lines

4 Before lifting the new transmission into place, tighten the hydraulic lines to the throwout bearing. The lines that American Powertrain sells are braided steel for better protection and appearance. Tighten them firmly, but do not over-tighten them. The precise machined flare does a very good job of sealing. Route the lines through one of the notched openings in the transmission case. There are three to choose from on the driver's side of the transmission, allowing you to route the lines according to your header and exhaust locations.

Install Transmission in Car

5 Most people do not own a transmission jack, so the act of hoisting the transmission into place usually involves two or three people lifting and shoving. Have the transmission bolts and tools ready and handy so you can quickly hold the transmission in place with the bolts once it is raised. Also have a jack ready to support the rear of the transmission once the transmission bolts are tight. If you place the jack on the transmission mount as shown, you need another jack under the mid part of the transmission when it's time to install the crossmember and transmission mount.

CHAPTER 11

Choose a Crossmember

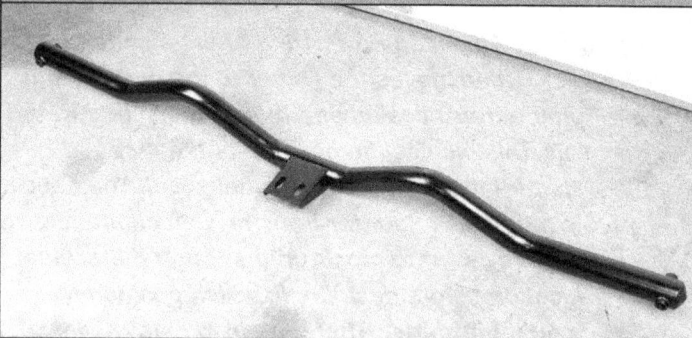

6 American Powertrain offers crossmembers for the Tremec transmissions that fit in a non-modified chassis. The frame on this car is boxed using an ABC Performance Frame Boxing Kit (see Chapter 1 for details), so we also used an ABC Performance Transmission X-Mbr. This crossmember is made from round 1¾-inch mild steel tubing with a 1/8-inch wall thickness. This is plenty strong to support the heavy transmissions, and looks nice and smooth.

Measure Driveline Angle

7 The Transmission X-Mbr is available either with (shown) and without an integrated driveshaft loop. Both come with weld-on mounting tabs that weld in place on the inside of the boxed frame rails. Before welding the mounting tabs to the frame rail, you need to set your driveline angle; the angle at which the engine and transmission are installed in the chassis. You can measure it at the bellhousing flange on the engine or the flat surface at the end of the transmission tailshaft. These measurements are perpendicular to a reference point in the chassis, which is the bottom of the frame rails, so you have to subtract 90 degrees from what you measure. These cars had a pinion angle of 4 to 6 degrees originally, meaning that the driveline angled downward 4 to 5 degrees from the front of the car to the rear, relative to the frame rails. The current thinking for performance and lack of driveline vibration is to get the driveline angle in the 1- to 3-degree range.

Install Crossmember

8 The ABC Performance Transmission X-Mbr is also curved to provide room for up to 3-inch dual exhaust to run under it without losing too much ground clearance. The Tremec transmission accepts a traditional rubber or polyurethane transmission mount. These transmissions use automatic transmission fluid. I recommend you use Mobile 1 synthetic, and change the fluid after the first 500-mile break-in period.

CHAPTER 12

WIRING UPGRADES

Many people don't give the wiring system in their Chevelle a thought until something goes wrong. The reality is that the whole original electrical system was designed to handle less amperage draw than that of just one decent electric fan and a high-output stereo. Compounding the issue is that the resistance within the wire increases as it ages. This makes it more difficult for the wire to handle the loads it was designed for, let alone the substantially higher demands of additional electrical add-ons.

Naturally, there are quite a few solutions available to bring the electrical system in your Chevelle up to par. And the best place to start is with an all-new harness. That may sound drastic, but considering that the factory fuse block isn't capable of supporting all of the aftermarket add-ons you want, and that the old wiring is probably decaying and butchered, it's a very good place to start.

Wiring Harness

Aftermarket harnesses are available in various styles to fit the different ways a performance car may be built.

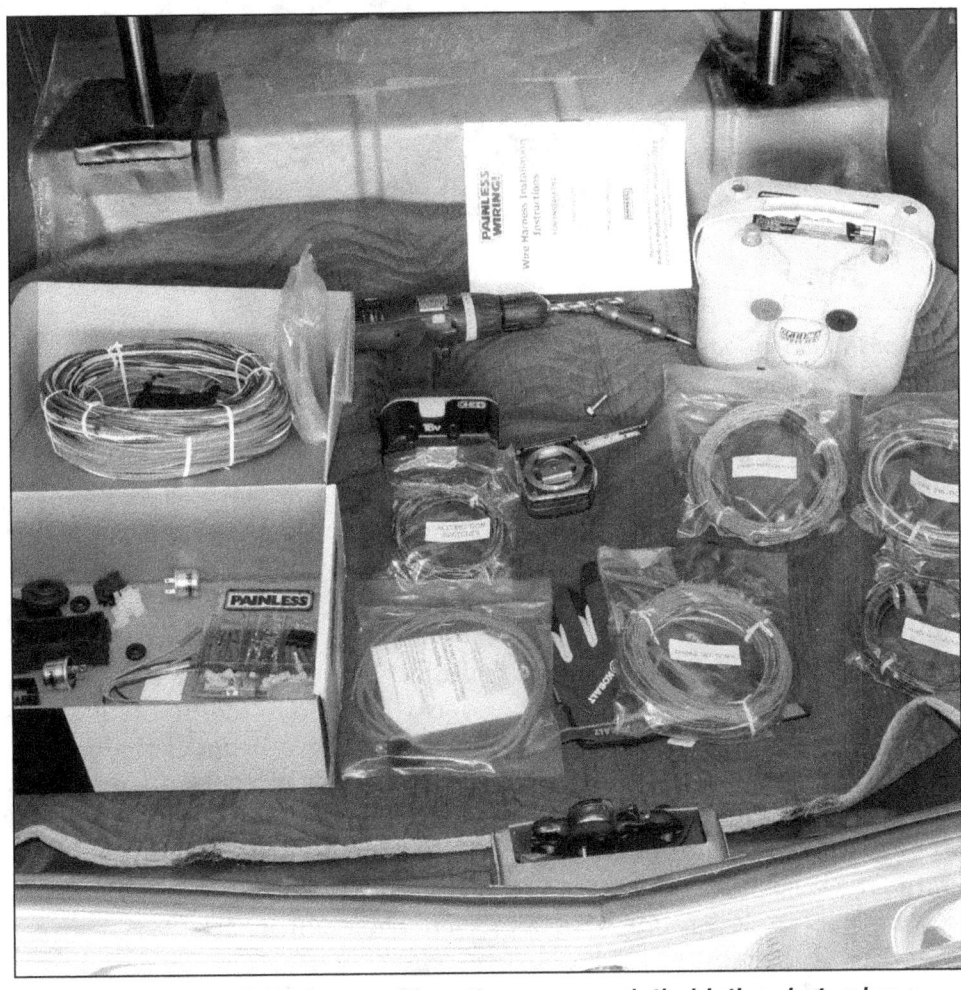

Replacing all the wiring in your Chevelle may seem intimidating, but using a quality harness and upgrade components makes it manageable. Having new wiring, a fusebox that can handle a variety of components, and making use of relay circuits will make your Chevelle reliable.

CHEVELLE PERFORMANCE PROJECTS: 1964–1972

CHAPTER 12

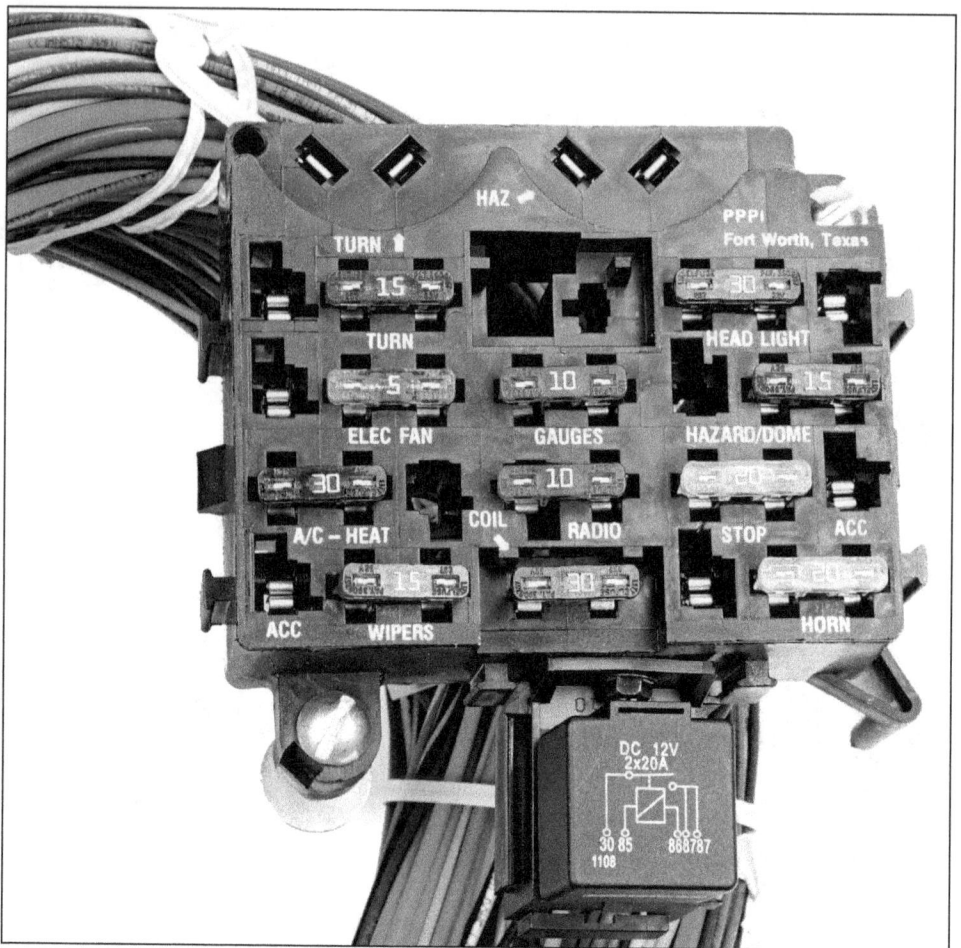

One of the advantages of using a new wiring harness is having additional circuits for fuel injection, electric fans, and other conveniences that are common on a Chevelle built to current standards. This avoids the need for complicated and problematic add-ons to the electrical system.

Relays are your friend when it comes to powering accessories that draw more than 5 amps continuously. These significantly shorten the run of high-amp wiring needed to power the component, which is safer and reduces the amperage drop caused by longer circuits run through switches.

Some are meant to be reproductions with the same number of circuits, all original-style connectors, glass fuses, and so on. These are a good choice if you are doing a numbers-matching restoration. The other styles have additional circuits for modern electrical gadgets, such as fuel pumps, fuel injection, fans, and big stereos.

The fuse blocks in aftermarket harnesses accept the modern ATO fuse, which are less prone to breaking when you remove them and easy to find replacements for. Some of them are designed to install like the original fuse block did, and the wires generally follow the path of the original harness. These styles make upgrading the electrical system fairly easy.

A third type of new harness is a universal fit or specialty. This style lets you relocate the fuse block altogether, to hide it under the dash or in the trunk with the battery. This harness requires a bit more work to install, as it is more universal and custom in nature, fitting a broad variety of vehicles.

Battery

Relocating the battery to the trunk is a great project that lets you shift a chunk of weight to the rear of the car and helps unclutter the underhood area. But when you do so, you need to increase the diameter of the battery cables to compensate for the drop in amperage over the longer length of cables.

Starter Solenoid

It's also extremely wise to change to a Ford-style starter solenoid, mounted near the battery, to improve cranking performance. The original GM starter solenoid mounted on the starter draws much higher amperage and is prone to overheating.

You can overcome these problems by using a Ford-style solenoid, which draws less amperage and can be mounted away from extreme heat sources. This also increases

WIRING UPGRADES

Phantom Key System

If there's one electrical gadget I really like in new cars, it's the push-button ignition system that only requires the key fob be in the vehicle to start the car. Painless Performance Products recently introduced its Phantom Key system. A push button with an LED light ring replaces the function of turning the key in the ignition switch.

The system comes with a rack of relays, a control module, wiring harness, and two remote fobs. It uses radio-frequency identification technology to recognize that the proper key fob is present, letting you start the vehicle by pressing and holding the push button. The system ties into your parking lights to flash when the ignition system is armed and disarmed with the proximity of the key fob. You can also control power door locks, as well as a trunk release or other single-action electrical device with the remote. The system looks a bit intimidating, but is actually easy to install.

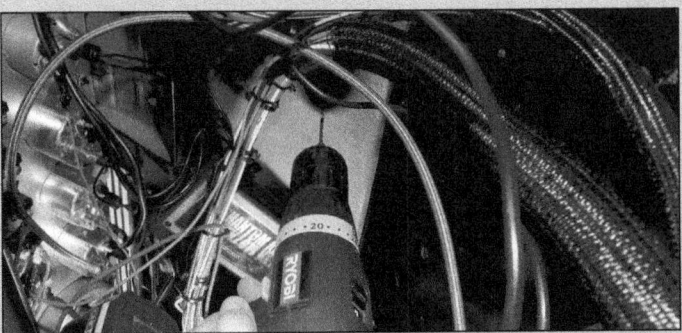

The best place to mount the relays and module is under the dash. Make sure that the wiring harnesses reaches the desired location before drilling holes. You can drill holes and screw the relays and module to the underside of the windshield wiper cowl area so that the fasteners don't show on the firewall.

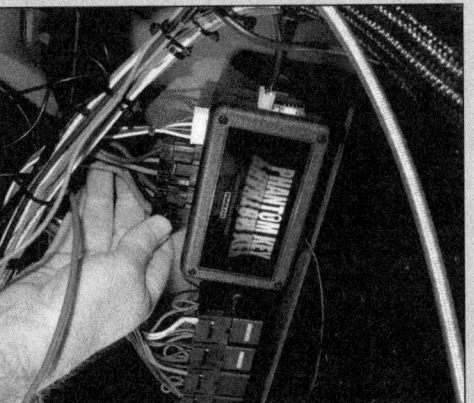

The wiring harnesses snap into place. There are a few different ways you can wire the system, depending on whether you want the push button to control power to the accessories or only the ignition and starter. You also need to splice into the parking light circuit to provide an external signal that the system has been activated or deactivated by the key fob.

There is a programming sequence to follow when you power up the system for the first time. After that, you can lock and unlock the doors with buttons on the remote, and even pop the trunk if you install an electric release solenoid. A sliding cover on the remote keeps you from pressing buttons accidentally. When you approach your car, the lights flash, and the LED ring in the stainless-steel push-button illuminates, letting you know that the system is active. Push the button once to turn on the accessories. Put your foot on the brake, and hold the push button down to engage the starter. When you want to turn off the engine, you simply push the button again.

High-Quality Battery Cables

Poor-quality battery cables can give you relentless trouble, and that's exactly what you find with most off-the-shelf battery cables. This is especially true if you move the battery to the trunk, requiring 15 feet of battery cable instead of just 3 feet. Amperage drops as the length of wire increases. The higher the amperage, the larger the drop. To combat this, you need larger-diameter wire.

The size of the copper stranding is measured according the American Wire Gauge (AWG) standard, commonly referred to as gauge. The thickness of the copper goes up as the gauge goes down. Battery cables range from 6-gauge for inexpensive, low-performance cables to 2/0 (pronounced "double ought"), which is ultra-thick. The 1/0 and 2/0 cables found at welding supply stores are very pliable and easy to work with because they typically have finer strands of copper and softer insulation. Larger-gauge cable is also heavier, and using 1/0 gauge to relocate the battery to the trunk (adding at least 15 feet for the positive cable) can easily add 5 to 6 pounds to your car. That isn't a big deal in a street car, but it's not desirable in a race car.

The ACCEL Lightning battery cable is a lightweight alternative to a traditional copper battery cable. The core is made from copper-clad aluminum for a weight reduction of 50 percent compared to the same-size copper-only cable. It's available in 4, 2, and 1/0 gauge, with the 1/0 being the best choice for battery cables. The cable is very pliable and lightweight.

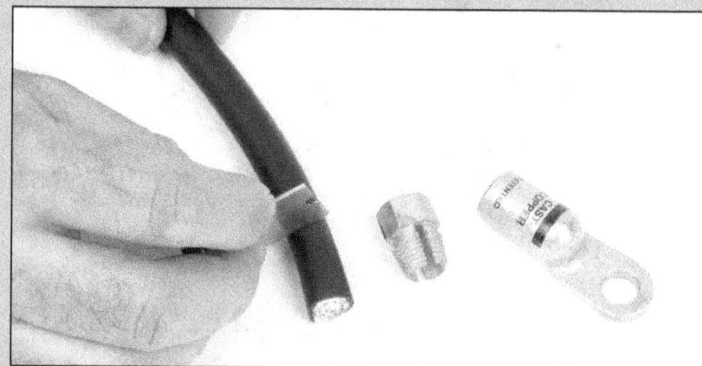

ACCEL sells thread-together battery-cable ends for its Lightning cable. Cut the cable to length, and use a razor blade to trim insulation by carefully cutting around the circumference of the cable.

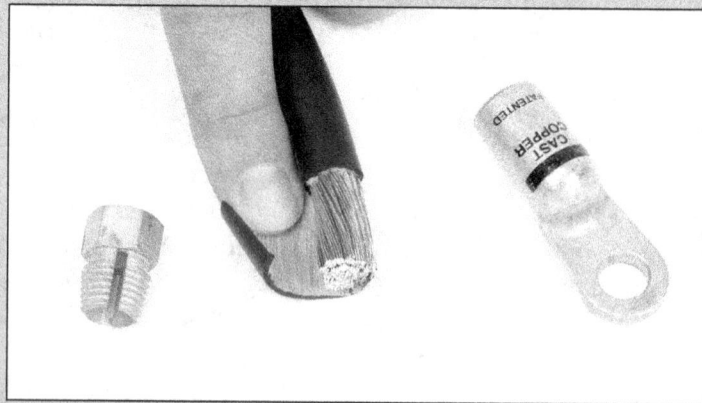

Slit the section lengthwise and peel it from the copper-clad aluminum strands. The amount of insulation you remove should be about 1/8 inch longer than the threaded collar (left in photo). The ACCEL battery cable ends are a compression fitting; once threaded together, they clamp on to the end of the battery cable for a very strong connection and excellent conductivity. They do not require any special tools to install, which is a bonus. They are not reuseable, however, so be careful not to accidentally destroy one before building all the battery cables.

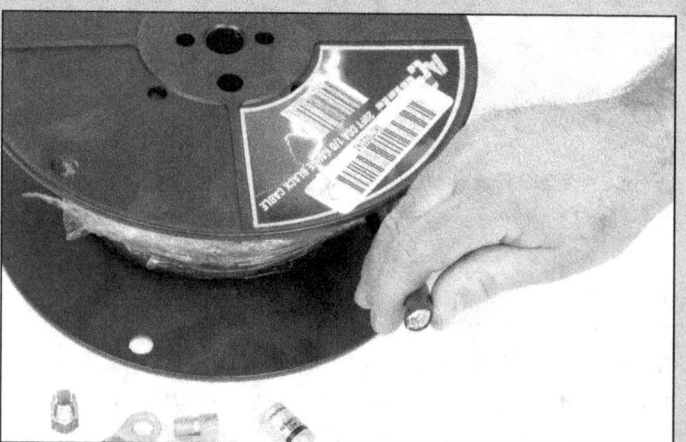

ACCEL Lighting Battery cable is sold in 20- and 100-foot spools. A 20-foot roll is plenty for building a positive battery cable in a trunk-mounted battery application. You may need a few feet more if you also have a master disconnect switch, depending on exact battery placement and routing of the cable through the car.

WIRING UPGRADES

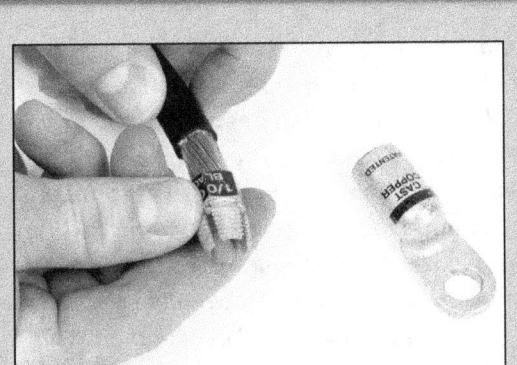

Carefully slide the collar over the strands. It's helpful to twist the collar slightly, and it is common to have a few strands push out as you slide the collar all the way down. You want the copper-clad strands to stick out of the end of the collar between 1/16 and 1/8 inch, or it it will pull off the end of the cable when you tighten the lug.

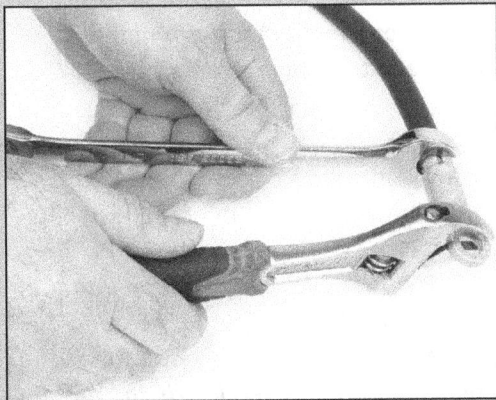

Use a wrench to hold the collar in place and an adjustable wrench to twist the lug on until it bottoms on the collar, or comes very close to bottoming. This is a compression fitting, so it gets harder to turn as you tighten it.

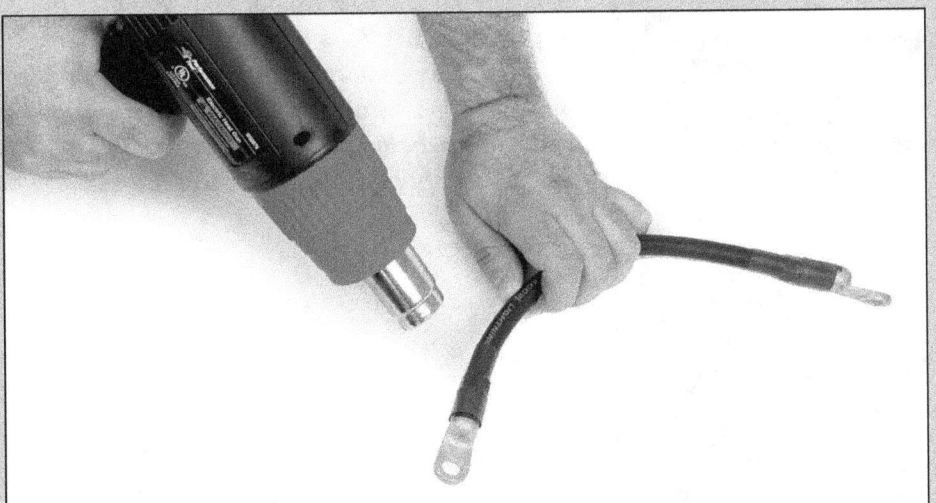

For a very professional look, you can apply shrink tubing over the end of the cable and battery lug. ACCEL sells this to fit its product, or you can use regular shrink tubing, as long as it is the correct size. The best way to apply shrink tubing is with a heat gun, rotating the wire or cable as you apply steady and even heat.

vehicle safety, because the positive battery cable is only powered during cranking; not during normal vehicle operation.

Relays

Relays improve safety and provide higher amperage to electric components that draw larger loads. In the 1960s, every electrical circuit had the full amperage running from the fuse block to the dash, through a switch, and then to the component. Relays allow you to run low-amperage current into the car and through the switches and keep the high-amperage line running between the battery and the device as short as possible for minimal amperage drop.

In addition to using them to activate fuel pumps and electric fans, you can also install a relay or two to increase headlight brightness. Not only will you enjoy brighter lights, but it's also a great visible proof of the improvement that comes with keeping the high-amperage line as short as possible.

Master Disconnect Switch

Depending on the type of racing you want to do with your Chevelle, the installation of a master disconnect switch might be required. These switches are mounted in the rear panel of the car and allow someone to turn off the entire electrical system from outside in the event of a crash. Shutting down the electrical system stops the engine, turns off the fuel pump, and can even stop an electrical fire. These are great safety devices and I recommend them, even if the type of racing you do doesn't require them.

CHAPTER 12

Project 1: Wiring Harness Installation

Select Harness Kit

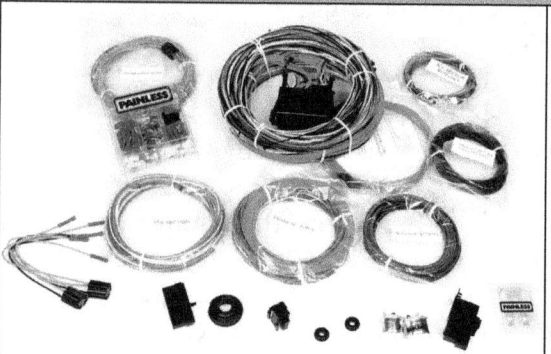

1 *Painless Performance makes a large variety of wiring harnesses. The most popular for a street machine is a replacement-style harness that mounts the fuse block in the stock location and routes the wires in a manner similar to the original harness. The harness shown here (PN 10130) is a 14-circuit, remote-mount, micro-fuse version. It uses mini fuses and has a very compact fuse block, measuring 3 x 3½ x 2 inches. This lets you mount it under the dash, under a seat, in a hidden compartment, or in the trunk. It has all of the circuits required for a street vehicle and sufficient leads to power fuel injection and air conditioning. The harness also comes with two headlight plugs, but you need two more from Painless Performance or another source for 1965–1970 Chevelles. All of the headlight plugs are installed by the customer. They do not come attached to the harness. An assortment of connectors and grommets, a steering column harness connector, flashers, and a maxi fuse that protects the whole system are included.*

Lay Out Wiring and Organize

2 *Rewiring a car with one of these harnesses isn't difficult. The sections attached to the fuse block are divided into the primary groups and are zip-tied together. You need to organize the wires and determine where each section is routed inside the car. Since this is a universal harness, you may need to group the sections a little differently than how Painless Performance sends them. Create mini sections before installing the harness, so you know exactly which wires are routed to certain components and areas of the car.*

Determine Route of Wires

3 Every wire in a Painless Performance harness is labeled with the section, wire number corresponding to the instruction manual, and where the wire should be routed. This makes it much easier as you follow wires through the car. With the fuse block location selected, you can determine how you route the wires and where you may need to drill holes to pass through the floor or firewall. You can mount the fuse block to the battery box in the trunk, and route the wires through the interior under the backseat and carpet. The only wires that need to exit the interior are for the engine bay and front lights.

Install Maxi Fuse

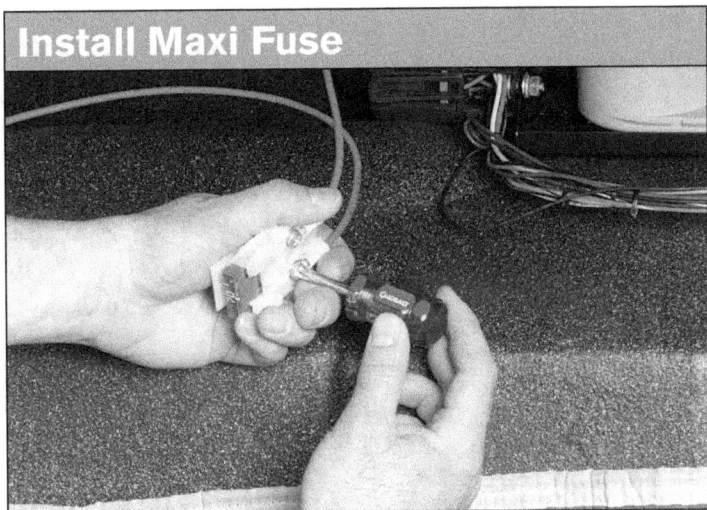

4 The maxi fuse protects the entire electrical system. It installs in the 10-gauge primary power wire that connects the fuse block to the positive side of the battery. The use of a maxi fuse or primary fuse breaker is common in new vehicles to protect against an electrical fire or major meltdown if there is a significant short in the system.

Install Wiring for Steering Column

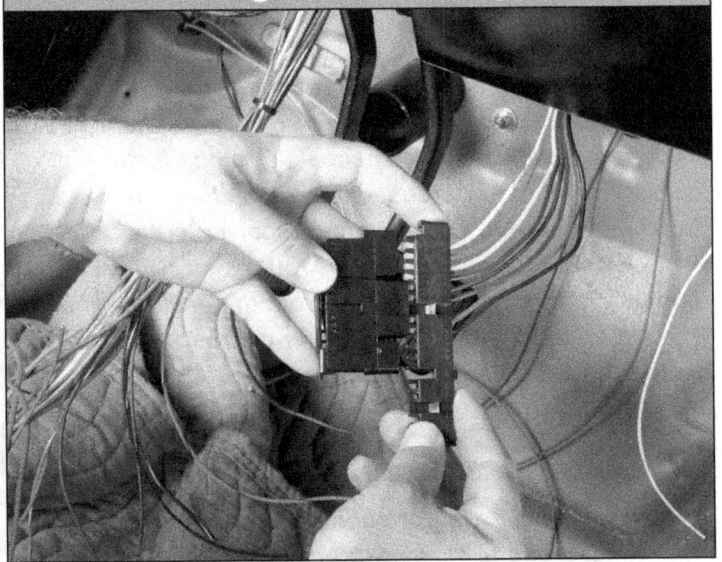

5 The Painless Performance harness comes with two styles of GM steering column connectors, which accommodate the most common aftermarket columns. If you have a 1967 or earlier factory column, you have to retain your column connector and do some adapting. It's fairly straightforward to determine which wire in the new harness connects to the appropriate terminal in your factory column harness. With a later-model or aftermarket column, determine which style of connector is needed and then put the terminals on the wires and insert them into the connector.

Wire High-output Alternator

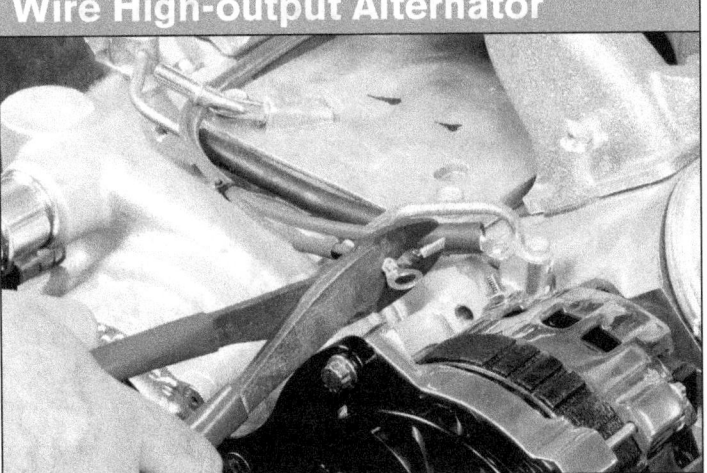

6 It's a good idea to ditch the original low-output, externally regulated alternator when you are building a modern Chevelle. Generally, you want an alternator that can produce more than 100 amps to power an electric fan, air-conditioning system, fuel injection, fuel pump, and so on. You can use a 12-si style, which utilizes a case design from the 1970s, and bolts into brackets that fit on a small-block or big-block Chevy. You can also opt for a one-wire alternator, which generally requires specialty brackets to retrofit. With the Painless Performance harness, if you have an alternator that produces more than 65 amps, you need to run two 10-gauge wires from the output pole on the alternator to handle the power.

Install Starter Solenoid

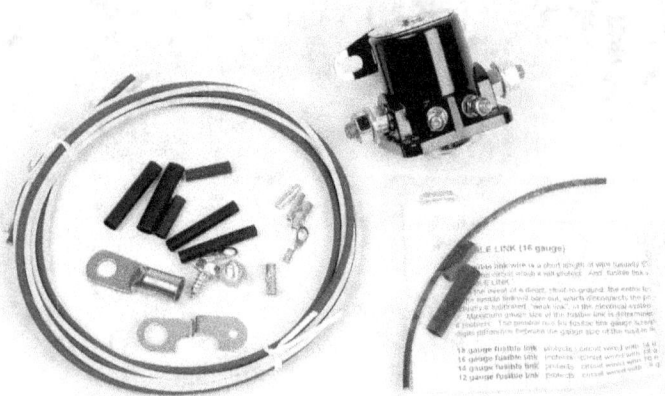

7 One GM circuit design that is commonly replaced is the starter solenoid. The GM design, until the last few decades, was a larger solenoid mounted on the starter in an area prone to heat soak. The M.A.D. Enterprises Start'm Up Kit includes a Ford-style solenoid and the wires, terminals, and other parts you need to install the remote-mount solenoid; it alleviates the GM hard-start problems associated with the original design. If you have a trunk-mounted battery, this solenoid can be mounted in the trunk near it; doing so provides a safety advantage as well as improved starter cranking. The large positive cable connected to the starter is only live during cranking, eliminating the risk of a direct battery short through this cable during driving.

Install Headlight Relay Kit

8 There is an easy way to improve the performance of your headlights, whether you have stock 35-watt headlights or have upgraded to 65-watt sealed halogen or xenon bulb replacements. The original circuit design has power traveling from the fuse block, through the headlight and dimmer switches, and then to the headlights. Along with a long length of wire that reduces amperage through resistance, the headlight switch also reduces the available amperage. Painless Performance offers headlight relay kits for two- and four-headlight systems that remove these drops in amperage, providing more power to the headlights for brighter operation. This route also removes a relatively high-amperage circuit from the dashboard and through an old light switch for safer operation and to extend the life of the switch.

Install Headlight Relay Kit (Continued)

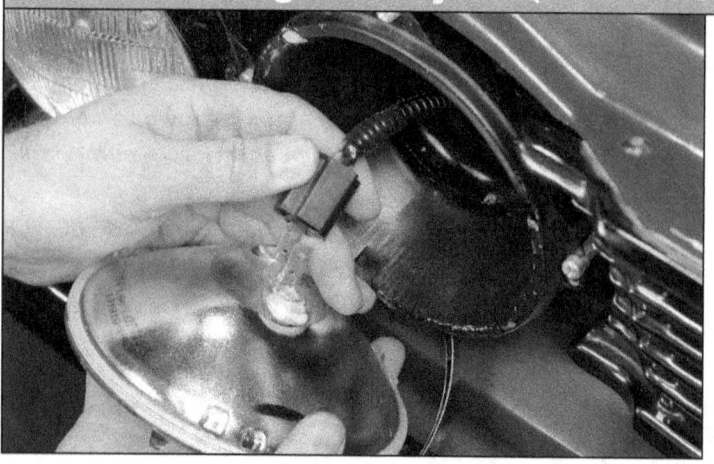

9 The Painless Performance headlight relay kit comes with plugs to connect directly to the headlights. For activation, it connects to one of the original three-prong headlight plugs, which tells the kit when to turn on the low beams and when to turn on the high beams. The power for the relay kit should connect directly to the battery if the battery is under the hood, or to a junction block if the battery has been relocated to the trunk. Even with brand-new bulbs, wiring harness, and a headlight switch, installing this headlight relay kit makes an improvement in lighting performance. And with an older wiring harness and switch, the difference is even greater.

WIRING UPGRADES

Install LED Taillights

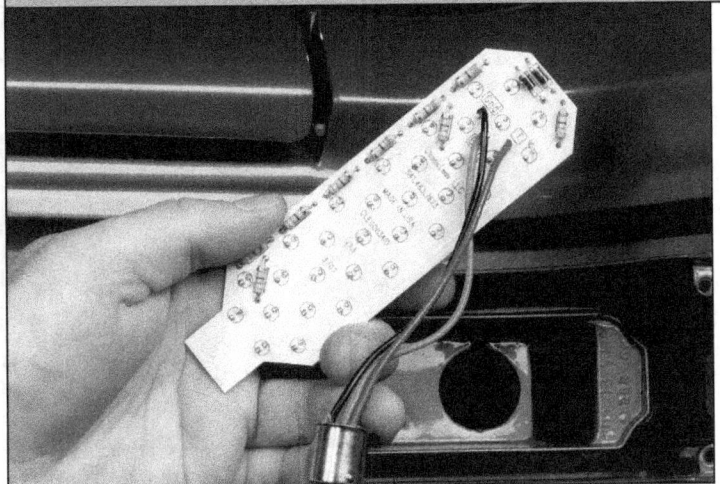

10 At the rear of the car, you may want to consider upgrading to light emitting diode (LED) lights. These direct-fit LED taillights are available from National Parts Depot (NPD) for all years of Chevelles. LED lights use very little power and produce very bright light. They also illuminate very quickly, changing a lazy-looking turn signal or brake light into a crisp, modern look. The kits from NPD provide a circuit board shaped to fit in the Chevelle taillight housing. They come with a plug that is meant to be inserted into the wiring harness socket, but it's difficult to insert and turn. It may be best to cut off the plug and hard-wire it to the taillight wiring harness. LED lights last much longer than standard incandescent light bulbs.

Install PowerBraid Loom

11 To make your entire wiring system look its best, you can cover the harnesses with loom. The standard wire loom is a plastic, corrugated tube with a slit that lets you slip the wires inside. This is okay, but it retains moisture and dirt. Painless Performance offers its PowerBraid loom that lets air, moisture, and dirt pass through, but provides protection for the wires against abrasion and looks nice. Individual rolls of PowerBraid are available, as well as a Chassis Harness Kit (shown) that provides what you typically need to cover exposed sections of wire in a complete harness installation.

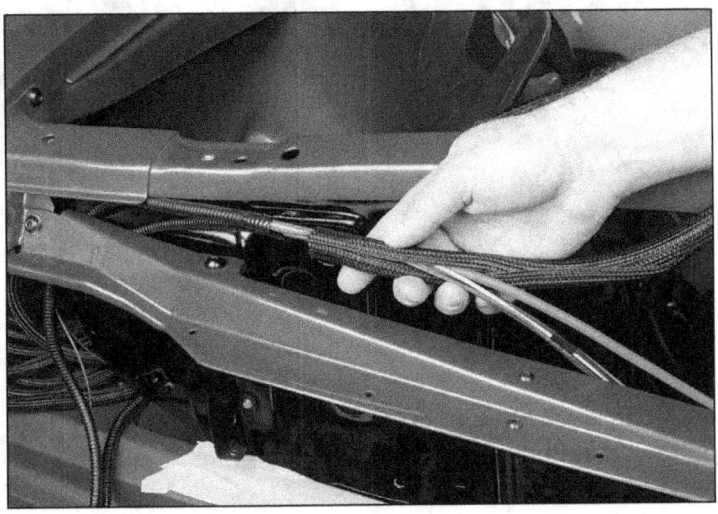

12 The Painless Performance PowerBraid is easy to work with. You slip the wires in a slit that runs lengthwise, like a corrugated plastic loom. The Chassis Harness Kit includes shrink tubing and stretch tape to neatly wrap the ends and keep the loom from fraying.

CHEVELLE PERFORMANCE PROJECTS: 1964–1972

Project 2: Trunk-mounted Battery Tray Installation

Fabricate Trunk-mounted Battery Tray

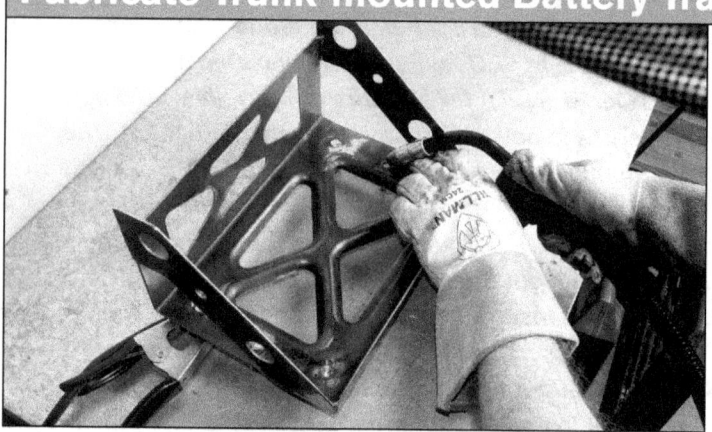

1 An extremely popular modification for street and performance Chevelles is to move the battery to the trunk. This moves weight farther back in the chassis for better weight transfer in drag racing and a more balanced front-to-rear weight ratio in autocross and road racing. It also removes a significant amount of clutter from the engine bay. I use an Optima AGM battery, so there are no corrosive fumes to vent. If you are using a conventional battery, it must be mounted in a battery box and vented outside of the vehicle. There are a variety of battery boxes. You want one with a metal base to mount solidly to the floor, and preferably to the frame or roll cage. This one is from JEGS and is sold as a weld-in unit, so the first thing to do is weld bolts to the base to attach it to the car.

2 Using the metal battery-mount base as a template, determine where the bolts should be located to attach to the trunk floor in desirable locations. Make sure you're not drilling into wiring, fuel lines, the fuel tank, or other critical components before finalizing your desired battery location. If you do not want bolt heads inside the battery mount (because they will abrade the battery) drill 3/8-inch holes and weld the bolt heads flush with the bottom of the battery tray. You can use these holes in the battery box as a template to drill your trunk floor before welding the bolts to the box. Also weld around the bottom of the bolt heads.

3 The top tabs on the JEGS battery box are meant to sit over a frame rail and be welded in place. If you are not installing the box this way, cut off these tabs and use an abrasive disc to round the corners of the battery box. Also use the abrasive disc to smooth the weld puddles on top of the mounting bolts.

Mount Starter Selenoid to Battery Tray

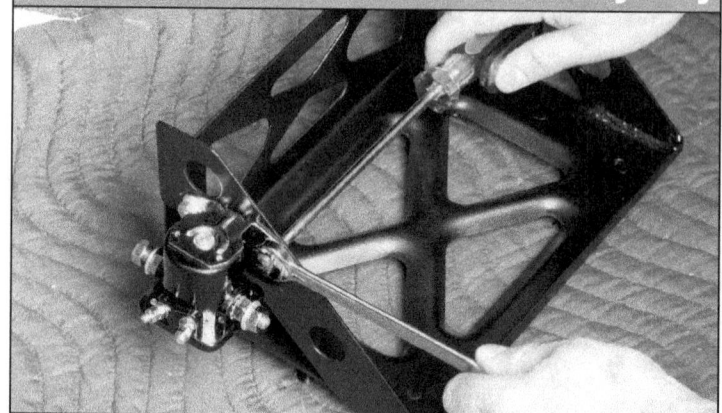

4 A coat of paint protects the metal battery tray from rust. Install a M.A.D. Enterprises Start'm Up Kit solenoid to the battery tray, using rounded Phillips-head 1/4-inch screws to protect the battery from abrasion. Mounting the solenoid here keeps the live positive cable very short. Also mount the Painless Performance fuse block to the battery box, again keeping the primary power wires very short.

Install Power Distribution Block

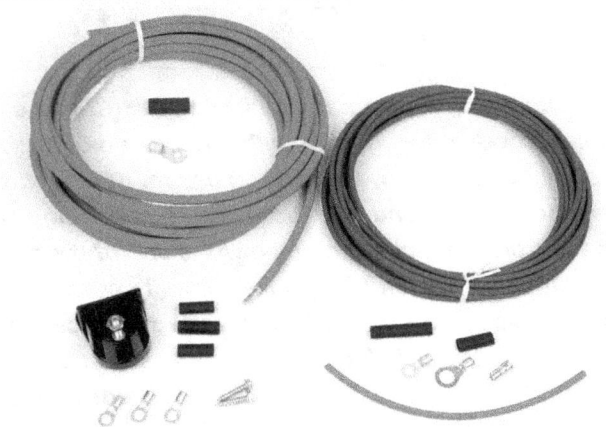

5 One of the issues that arise when moving the battery to the trunk is how to provide high-amperage power under the hood for accessories such as an electric fan and even the Painless Performance headlight relay kit. The solution is to install a junction block powered by direct, but protected, battery power. This trunk-mount battery helper kit from M.A.D. Enterprises includes a junction block, fusible link, terminals, shrink tubing, 22 feet of red 8-gauge Tuff-Wire, as well as 22 feet of blue and yellow 14-gauge Tuff-Wire.

6 Tuff-Wire uses high-quality automotive copper strands and high-temperature, abrasion-resistant insulation. If you've ever used inexpensive replacement wire whose insulation can nearly be removed by scraping it with your fingernail, you can appreciate how robust this wire is. The insulation is also non-flammable, and it doesn't easily degrade if it comes in contact with gasoline or oil. The red wire in this kit provides electricity to the junction block at the front of the car; at the junction block, you can connect your higher-amperage, constant 12-volt accessories. Use the blue and yellow wires to connect the Start'm Up Kit when mounted in the trunk.

Install Junction Box

7 You can add a second junction block from M.A.D. Enterprises to create a common ground for under-the-hood accessories. Both junction blocks are mounted behind the outer headlight, making them accessible but nearly hidden. The ground circuit in a trunk-mounted battery application can be created by using the frame rail or cage or both. It's critical that the electrical systems be properly grounded and that there is a ground strap between the engine and the frame rail. Many electrical problems can be traced to a poor body or chassis ground.

Mount Battery Tray in Trunk

8 If you mount the battery above the rear axle, you can build a panel later to hide this entire area. A more common location is over the passenger-side frame rail, farther toward the rear of the car. The farther back it is mounted, the better for weight transfer. If you use an open battery box (shown), NHRA requires that a rear firewall be installed of .024-inch steel or .032-inch aluminum, including the rear package tray. Alternatively, you can use a sealed steel or aluminum battery box and vent the box outside of the body. We used a group 34 Optima RedTop battery. In addition to featuring an outstanding 800 cold cranking amps, this battery features the Optima Spiralcell technology, which uses glass mat separators and spiral-wrapped lead. This design is spill-proof and resistant to damage caused by vibration, making it ideal for racing applications and severe street use.

CHAPTER 12

Project 3: Master Disconnect Switch Installation

Select Master Disconnect Switch Kit

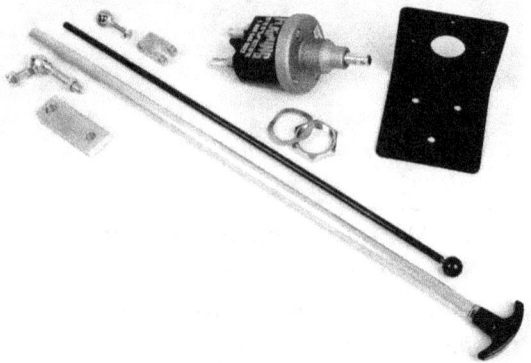

1 A master disconnect switch is required by NHRA and other sanctioning bodies for vehicles with a relocated battery. They are a good safety device on any vehicle you use for competition. They don't have to be large and ugly, however. The Flaming River Big Switch master disconnect switch (shown) is one of the best switches. It engages solidly, and is spring-loaded to snap into the "off" position once you start turning it. It is rated at 250 continuous amps. It's sold as just the switch and mounting bracket, or with a lever kit that includes a push-pull rod kit (which includes the aluminum rod and T-handle shown here), the switch-mount bracket, and one Heim joint and aluminum block. The Flaming River lever kit is nice, but there is an even smaller rod that still meets NHRA requirements from Jerry Bickel Race Cars. This steel rod comes with a small black knob and small Hemi joint and aluminum bracket to connect to a universal switch.

2 The first thing to do is determine where to mount the switch and where the rod protrudes through the rear of the car. Typical installations include through the rear sheet-metal panel. Some skip the push-pull rod and just install the twist-style switch in the rear bumper. (We want to make ours as subtle as possible, as this is primarily a street car.) On a 1966 Chevelle, there is reinforcement behind the taillight to which you can mount the switch bracket, and an access hole lines up perfectly with the reverse light lens. This also lets you simply replace the lens if you want to remove the switch later. Spend sufficient time determining the switch mounting options and the alignment of the rod to make sure you only need to drill one hole.

3 This shows the routing of the rod and where you will mount the switch bracket. The only parts of the Jerry Bickel Race Cars kit used here were the rod, knob, and quick-release pin. The rod is cut to length once you have the bracket mounted. You also need to use a tap to thread the inside of the steel rod to thread over the Heim joint provided with the Flaming River lever kit. Also drill a hole in the aluminum switch block midway between the switch shaft and the hole provided by Flaming River. This reduces the travel of the rod, letting it stick out of the rear of the car less when in the "on" position.

WIRING UPGRADES

Select Master Disconnect Switch Kit (Continued)

4 Remove the switch from the bracket and use the bracket as a template to mark and drill the mounting holes. The mounting surface for the switch must be secure. Check your support to make sure that rust hasn't weakened it or its attaching points. Also be careful not to drill into wiring or hit other items behind the support when drilling. Attach the bracket using lock washers to keep the fasteners from vibrating loose. Install the switch with the provided nut and wave locknut.

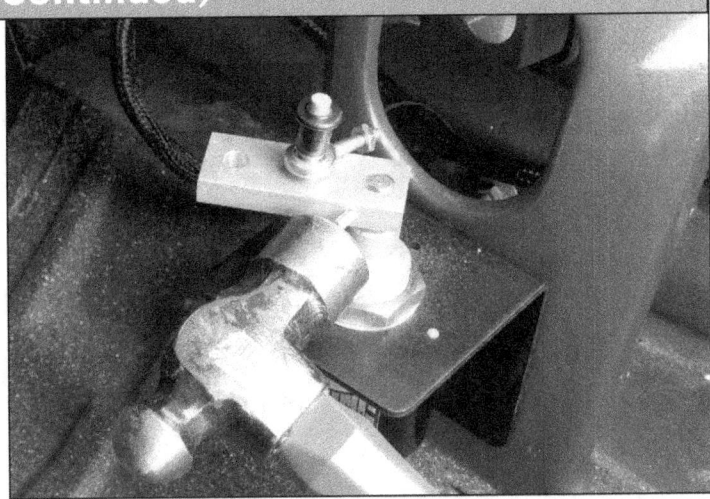

5 The switch is pinned, so it can only be installed in two positions. Install it the same way you mocked it up. Install the aluminum block and drive the roll pin into place to lock it onto the switch shaft. With the switch in the "off" position (the rod is closer to the body in the "off" position compared to the "on" position), mark and cut the rod to length. Leave a gap of just over an inch between the knob and the taillight lens so you can comfortably grip the knob and pull it into the "on" position.

6 Operate the switch to make sure there is no binding or interference. If you use kits from two different companies, the locknut on the Heim joint may interfer with the aluminum block. Drill a new hole, which provides the needed clearance and still keeps the movement and travel acceptable. You need to splice the switch into the positive battery cable. If you've installed a Ford-style starter solenoid, this is the cable that connects the battery to the solenoid. You should also install battery terminal covers over these battery cable connections to protect against an accidental short when moving items in and out of your trunk. These are available from Flaming River or an electrical supply store.

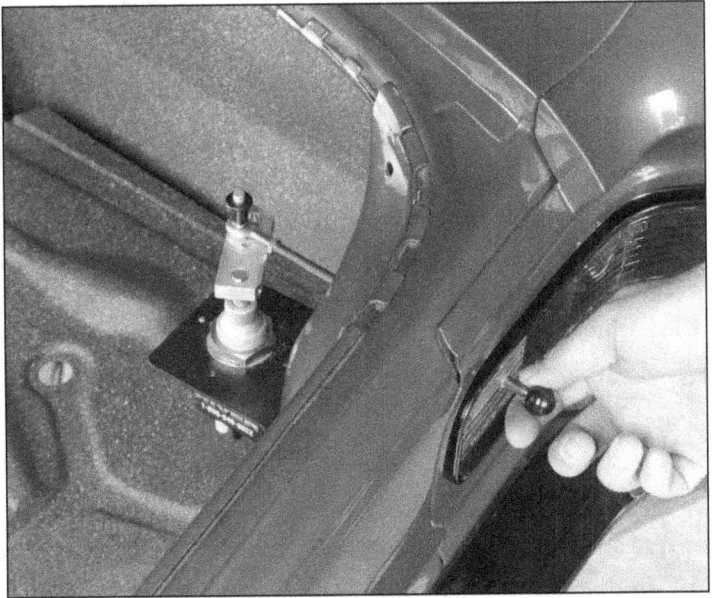

7 The finished installation is very clean outside the car. The small knob is barely noticeable. Both kits come with decals that say, "Push Off," which is required on NHRA-sanctioned drag strips. You can also make a magnetic sign, which is more noticeable when you're at a racetrack and easy to remove when you're not.

CHAPTER 13

PERFORMANCE INTERIOR

For many people, modifying the interior of their Chevelle is one of the most difficult parts of the car buildup to plan. There are quite a few areas that you may want to upgrade, but making changes to the classic lines and details of the interior without considering the overall theme of the car can quickly disrupt the design and style of the car. The end result can be a finished product you're not happy with. As with the overall exterior styling of your car, you have to plan and envision what you want the theme of your interior to be in addition to functional upgrades.

There are four basic interior areas that you want to consider upgrading for better performance: seating (including safety belts), safety cage, dash, and sound deadening. Installing a cage is the most involved and makes the biggest change in the interior. All of the other projects are manageable in a day or a weekend. Before you dive into these or any other interior upgrades, though, think through the style you're trying to achieve with your car in addition to the specific performance upgrades you would like.

In many ways, the factory Chevelle interior is a blank slate. While the exterior of these cars has become the symbol of the muscle car era, the interior reminds us that these were in fact family cars with some performance options.

Seating

Chevelles were family cars when originally produced, and seat technology was far from a science. A wire frame, some springs, foam and other stuffing, and upholstery were all that was needed. Today, I generally want a seat that offers control (keeping you in place as you turn corners) and comfort. There are also safety concerns. A performance or racing seat

PERFORMANCE INTERIOR

There's a lot you can do and still retain the styling cues found in the original cars. The basics of a performance interior are massive gauges, seats that provide lateral control, safety harnesses, and a safety cage in the more extreme cars.

A unique approach to adding a cage but keeping the car as street-friendly as possible is the RideTech Tiger-Cage. The cage bolts in, making it easier to take out in the future. The door bar design is low, making entry and exit much easier than a traditional, NHRA-legal cage. One of the biggest advantages is that you don't have to find a professional chassis shop to put a cage in your car. (Photo Courtesy RideTech)

is built to keep you in place, even during an impact, and almost all of them are designed to work with 5-point safety harnesses.

Speaking of safety harnesses, the next time you get into your Chevelle and click the 40-plus-year-old seat belt around your waist, think seriously about how much you trust a nylon strap of that age. If you do any competition driving with the vehicle, you also want to think about the considerable safety added with shoulder belts, keeping your torso away from the steering wheel and your head away from the windshield in a crash. There's a reason all new cars come with three-point seat belts and that five-point safety harnesses are required in most pro-level competition cars.

Safety Cage

There are some realities to deal with when you add a cage to your car. Most cages make getting in and out of a car a bit challenging, and they generally make the back seat impossible for anyone to access except children and extremely limber adults. But a cage provides crucial safety in a high-speed crash or rollover (both of which are a real possibility if you plan to drag race or road race your Chevelle) and it provides a significant improvement in chassis stiffness, which is a performance advantage for any type of racing.

Most cages compromise the interior, but there are a few things you can do to minimize this. One thing you can do is make removable or swing-out door bars. This makes getting in and out of the car much easier for front-seat passengers. And it's possible to do a swing-out bar in a way that still meets NHRA rules. While NHRA rules don't apply for autocrosses and road courses, these rules are a very sound guideline for building a safety cage for most types of racing.

Another option that makes a cage extremely livable is a bolt-in system called TigerCage from Ridetech. The tubing in the TigerCage is all stainless steel, and the cage bolts to key chassis points and uses clamps to attach tubing within the system.

Dash

Most people don't want to replace the entire dash, but would like some space for serious performance gauges. Depending on how you want to use your car, you may also want room for a new-style radio, or combination radio and navigation system, as well as controls for an aftermarket air conditioning system.

The key here is to add modern performance equipment without looking like you just started hacking and adding things to the original dash. If you're skilled at custom fabrication, you can modify your existing dash, or build an insert from scratch. For the rest of us, there are a few popular aftermarket options that make installing large gauges and modern conveniences a bolt-in exercise.

Covan's Thunder Road makes dash inserts for 1964–1972 Chevelles (there are actually six different parts to fit this range of years) that come with or without a variety of Auto Meter gauges. The panels are made from molded ABS plastic and are available in either black or carbon fiber finish. These are meant to bolt in place, replacing all of your original gauges. Radio options vary, and the original controls for heat and air conditioning are left untouched.

There is another option for 1966–1967 Chevelles from ABC Performance. This dash bolts in, replacing your entire dash shell and opening up the gauge area, allowing you to fit a 5-inch-diameter speedometer and tachometer. Even though the dash bolts in place, each one is custom-built, so you can specify the radio, vents, air conditioning controls, and switches you want mounted and in what location.

The 1968–1972 Chevelles have a generous-size gauge insert. Installing a Covan's Thunder Road panel to hold a rack of large, performance gauges is relatively easy. The 1964–1965 Chevelles also have good options. Only the mid-year cars require major dash surgery to fit large gauges. (Photo Courtesy Covan's Thunder Road)

Most people are driving their Chevelles more and want a less fatiguing experience. Covering the floor with sound deadener reduces the overall sound level and really improves the sound quality. It also limits the transfer of heat from the exhaust to the interior.

Sound Deadening

Sound deadening doesn't make your car any faster or handle any better; in fact, it does just the opposite because you are adding a fair amount of weight to your car. But the improvement in sound quality helps you enjoy every minute that you spend in your Chevelle.

Road noise and exhaust sound vibrates the floorpans, doors, and quarter panels when your car is running and driving down the road. Dynamat, Eastwood, and Hushmat make material in sheets that you can cut and stick to these surfaces. It deadens the vibration at the sheet metal, removing the most annoying noise from the drive and reducing the overall sound level. If you cover the inside of doors and quarter panels, as well as the roof, you can have doors that sound like those on a Mercedes when you shut them, and create an interior that's downright enjoyable in traffic or cruising down the highway for hours on end.

Custom Seat Installation

There are quite a few performance seat options for a Chevelle. Most of them offer very good lateral control for cornering, comfort, and access holes for use with a five-point harness. However, only a few of them are available with custom mounting brackets to bolt them directly into your Chevelle and still have an adjustable slider to move them fore and aft in the car. With a welder and some very basic fabrication skills, you can adapt most seats to mount on the original seat slider mechanism.

Before I get started, I want to make clear that Kirkey manufactures these seats for racing applications only and does not intend for use on the street. Kirkey also does not recommend the use of stock sliders and adjusters as I show here. Kirkey says these can fail in a high-speed crash.

This is a set of Kirkey Racing Fabrication 41V Series Vintage Class Bucket seats. These aluminum, low-back, racing bucket seats provide a cool retro race car look with outstanding lateral support. The open and nearly flat window openings of the 1964–1967 cars look disrupted with high-back buckets, although a seat with a headrest is much safer in an accident. They are also 66 pounds lighter than the original bucket seats (not including the original seat frames that we reused). You can order these seats with the Kirkey snap-in upholstery and universal mounting brackets.

The first step is to determine if the seats and brackets fit with the original seat sliders, and also position you in roughly the right place. Consider height, as well as distance from the pedals and steering column. This combination puts your hips a little higher in the car than you may like, but it is worth it to be able to use the sliding mechanism.

Bench-seat cars had a slightly different floor in the early Chevelles that didn't have the holes and nuts for bucket seats. The floor is about 3/8 inch low on the inside front seat mount for the driver's side, so you need to create a mount for this side that you weld to the floor.

Use 1/4-inch steel strapping and 1/2-inch square tubing from Tractor Supply Company to build a square frame. Weld the frame together and bolt it to the original seat sliders. The Kirkey universal seat mounts bolt to the top of the frame.

The Kirkey universal brackets give you quite a bit of adjustability to raise and tilt the seats by moving the mounting bolts to different holes. For street driving, you may want to have a little recline in the seats, but sit them up straight for competition. With the upholstery snapped in place, the seats are far more comfortable than they look. An additional layer of closed-cell foam may even make them perfect for cross-country driving.

CHAPTER 13

Proper Safety Harness Installation

For protection in a crash, and the best control over your car during racing, you need to be held securely in your seat. Production seat belts have limitations based on the realities of belting up every time you get into a vehicle. Also, remember that seatbelt use was only mandated by most states in the past 10 years, and many of the cars we're talking about in this book only came with lap belts. Whether you're interested in drag racing, autocrossing, or road racing, aftermarket safety harnesses should be on your shopping list.

The standard in safety harnesses is a five-point system made from 3-inch-wide webbing. Since these are designed for racing, they have an SFI specification rating. Check the classes you're interested in competing in to make sure you get the proper SFI-rated belts. These safety harnesses are quick-release, with a single mechanism that releases all five attachment points in a single motion. Some are the traditional lever (latch and link), but a rotating knob (cam lock) is also popular.

Safety harnesses come with a variety of hardware to attach to the floor. The belts thread through the hardware and then loop through a tightening buckle. This buckle securely holds the belts; adjustment in length is managed through another mechanism at the end of the belt closer to the latch. The NHRA rulebook says that they must attach to the floor with the nuts, bolts, and washers provided.

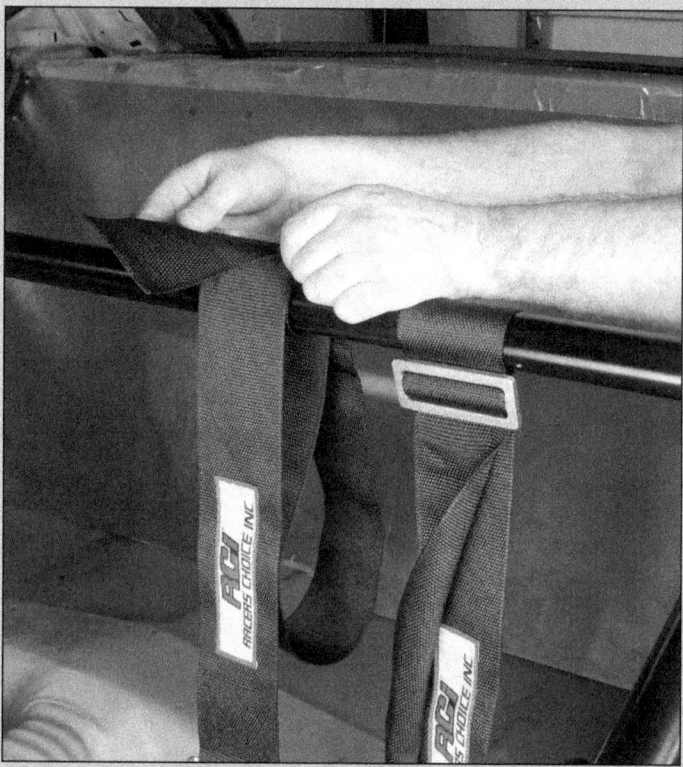

The most common mistake I see with safety harness installation is improper mounting of the shoulder belts. The belts must be anchored behind the driver, level with his shoulders, or not more than 4 inches below that point. To do this, you really need to have a roll bar or roll cage with a cross brace just behind the front seats. And you should have the seats and seat frames mocked-up in the car to determine the shoulder height when this bar is welded in place. If you run the shoulder straps straight down to the floor, a hard impact can compress your spine or allow you to slip out of the shoulder harnesses.

PERFORMANCE INTERIOR

Project 1: Roll Cage Installation

Whether to cage your Chevelle or not is a big decision. There's no question that a roll cage makes a significant difference in chassis stiffness, which contributes to better drag-strip launches and much better handling, and improved safety is a given. However, installing a cage is a big undertaking and compromises the ease of getting in and out of the car, as well as almost entirely cutting off access to the backseat. I worked with Tony Grzelakowski at ABC Performance on the design and installation of this cage in an early Chevelle.

Replace Body Bushings

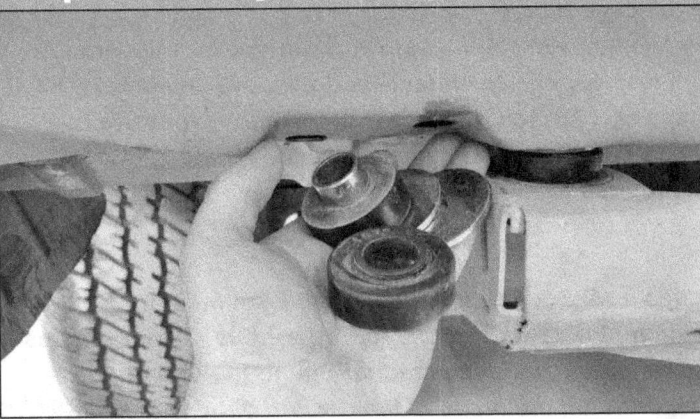

1 For strength and integrity, the right way to install a cage in a Chevelle is to weld it directly to the frame. So the first step is to actually replace the body bushings. Once the cage is welded in place, they are nearly impossible to change. If you install a set of ABC Performance solid body bushings, they should never wear out and they provide increased chassis stiffness. The bushings are CNC-cut from T6061 billet aluminum. They have the proper steps machined to seat in the various frame and body holes perfectly.

Take Measurements

2 Building a custom cage is part science and part art. There are measurements to be taken, angles to work with, and metal to be bent. But you have to make sure it looks right as well. You have to decide how much cage you want or need. If you will be drag racing, there are specific NHRA rules concerning this, and you should reference the rulebook to make sure you comply with the current regulations. This cage is as much for chassis stiffness as safety, so it is a 10-point cage, but four of those points are under the hood. The interior looks like a traditional six-point cage.

The first tube you bend is the main hoop that mounts just behind the front seats. It's ideal to locate this a few inches behind the driver's head. The bar will be hidden behind the junction of the door and quarter windows, so it is as stealthy as possible. Use a plumb bob to ensure that the line you are envisioning is straight up and down.

CHEVELLE PERFORMANCE PROJECTS: 1964–1972

CHAPTER 13

Bend Roll Cage Tubes

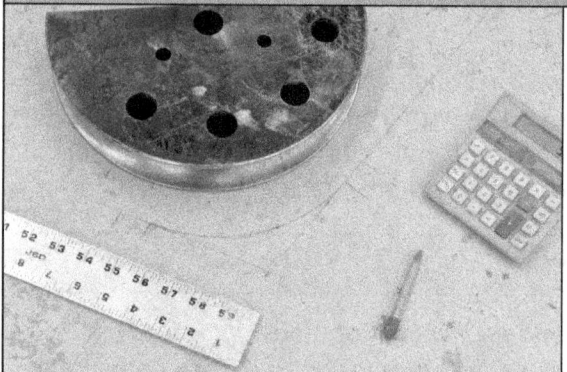

3 The bends in a roll cage are made with a tubing bender. The arc of the bend depends on the specific dies that you use with your bender. You have to factor these bends into your calculations and recheck the dimensions after you've added in the radius. Tony uses long straightedge to map out each piece of the roll cage on the floor before cutting or bending the tube. Or, use metal electric conduit to test the shape and length of each piece before bending up a section of expensive roll cage tubing.

There are two types of steel tubing you can use for roll bars and roll cages. The less-expensive material is drawn-over-mandrel (DOM) mild steel. NHRA requires all DOM tubing to have a wall thickness of .118 inch. Chrome-moly is more expensive but much lighter, and the required wall thickness varies from .049 to .83 inch, depending on where the tubing is located in the cage. A DOM cage can be MIG-welded, while chrome-moly requires TIG welding.

4 Tony uses a JD Squared bender, which is an industry standard. A selection of dies is available for the various diameter tubes. Slip the tubing in place, and then manually bend the tubing and ratchet the bender until the angle of the desired bend is achieved. (JD Squared also offers hydraulic rams to work with the bender to take the manual part out of this process.) There are a couple of things to watch with any bender. One is where the bend actually starts in the bender. Make a test 90-degree bend with each size of tubing you use in your cage. Mark where it sits in the bender, and then measure from this point to where the bend actually starts when you pull the tube out after bending it.

The other nuance is spring-back. The steel springs back a little bit after you release the pressure. To get a 90-degree bend, you may have to go to 95 degrees. It's very difficult to undo a bit of the bend, so start by going a few degrees past your mark and then increase it 2 to 3 degrees at a time until you get the desired angle.

Cut Roll Cage Tubes

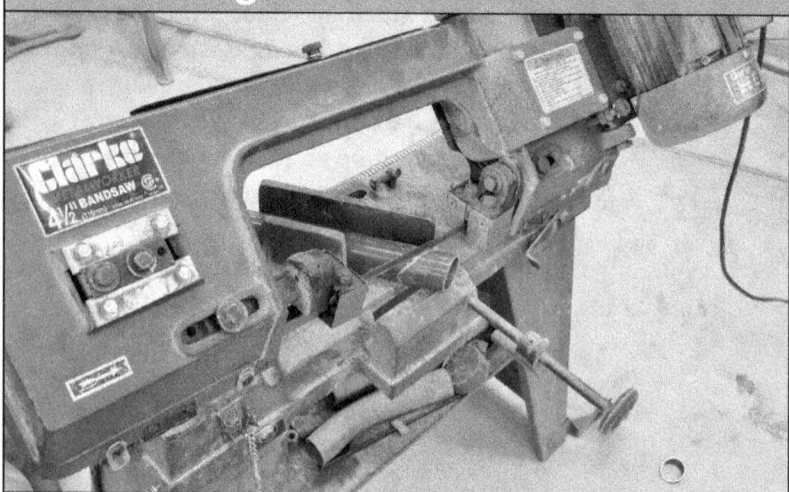

5 You can use a band saw or a chop saw to cut the tubing. With either tool, you need to clamp the tube firmly before making the cut. Several of the cuts require an angle like the one on this main hoop to match the angle of the top of the frame rail. Make the first cut about 2 inches longer than what you think it needs to be and then work toward the final length. You can't put material back on the tube, so it's very important not to cut too much.

Trial Fit Main Hoop

6 This is the main hoop after a few trims and trial fits. It's lining up well with the design that Tony measured and sketched on the shop floor. It's easiest to start in the center of the tube and work toward the ends, finishing one side at a time. Remember to always make the bends in a symmetrical pattern, so that the bend's start and stop points are the same on each side.

7 It's easiest to build a cage with the headliner removed from the car, but it can be done with the headliner in place. You need to use a metal shield to protect the headliner when welding. If the car does not have a headliner, you need to know where the headliner will sit. Tony used masking tape pulled taut between two headliner bows to mimic the location of the headliner. Also make sure you're leaving enough room to install window trim, the dome light, rearview mirror mount, and anything else that may be blocked if you get the tubing too close to the roof.

Tack Weld Main Hoop in Place

8 After several trial fitments and trimming, you are ready to tack-weld the main hoop in place. Since all Chevelles are full-frame cars, you need to cut access holes through the floor and weld the cage directly to the frame. Tony trimmed this hole large enough to weld all the way around the tube when it's time to do the final welding. For now, double-check your measurements front to rear, and side to side, and then tack-weld the main hoop in place.

Bend Rear Bars

9 Once the main hoop is in place, you can either do the rear down bars or the front bars. The front bars are the most difficult, so I prefer to do the rear bars first. Using a long piece of welding rod or electrical conduit, bend the basic shape of one of the tubes. You want to follow the roof and headliner shape, leaving enough room at the rear window for trim installation, and pass through the package tray and trunk floor to contact the frame. These bars triangulate the main hoop, giving it stability in a rollover, and also tie in the rear section of the frame where the springs and shocks mount, providing very good suspension stability.

Cut Holes in Floor for Rear Bars

10 You need to cut holes through the floor, and probably through the package tray, too, depending on whether someone has already cut holes for 6 x 9-inch speakers. This car has a coil-over suspension tubular crossmember to tie into. If your rear suspension is the stock style, your holes and bars need to be farther outboard to hit the top of the frame rails.

Fit Rear Roll Bars

11 Transfer the shape to a piece of tubing. For these tubes, you can use the welding rod you bent as a guide right over the tubing in the bender. I recommend getting one of these bars completely done before starting on the other. At this point, the lower end of the bar is still a couple inches too long, and you need to cut about 6 inches from the top. This end has a fish mouth, making the cutting of the bar a little trickier.

Create a Fish Mouth

12 Before you trim the lower end of the bar, you need to trim the top end that meets the main hoop. The trick here is to cut the tubing long enough so that the top and bottom of the tube fits over the radius of the main-hoop tube. Using a tubing notcher, cut the top end of the rear down bar in a fish-mouth shape. This fits over the main hoop and allows the tube to be welded all the way around. You can angle the way the bar is held in the fixture to recreate the angle that the bar fits against the hoop in the car. Ours is pretty close to 90 degrees. It takes a lot of care to get this cut right, and to not remove more material than needed. Once this end is done and fits the main hoop well, fit the other end to the frame rail.

Clean Up Tube Ends

13 Finish all tubing ends with an abrasive disc. This cage is chrome-moly and TIG-welded, which requires extremely tight fitment between the tubes. You can use the abrasive disc to fine-tune the gaps, removing high spots so that the tubes fit very tightly together. Patience and double- or triple-checking your measurements and work along the way avoids frustration and wasted tubing. Tack the rear down bars in place to add stability to the main hoop before you start on the front section of the cage. This keeps the main hoop from moving and lets you fit the front bars perfectly.

Choose Location of Front Tubes

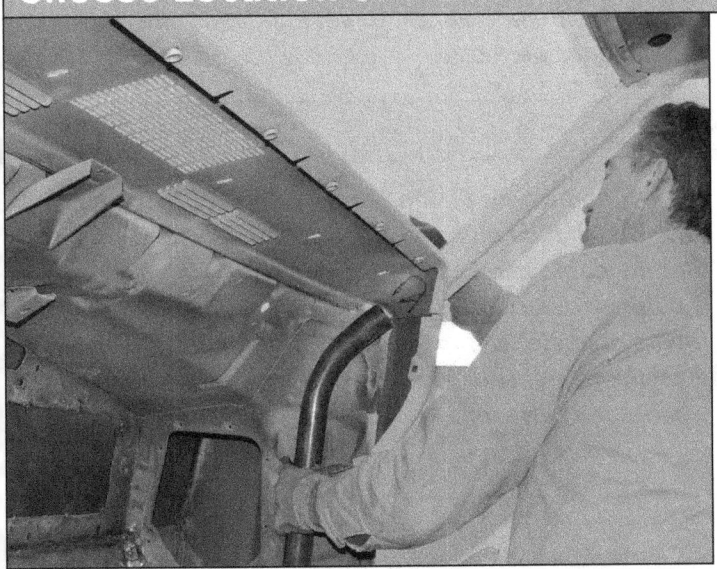

14 The front bars in a cage present a number of choices. First is whether to pass the bar through the dash or in front of it. Some people don't want to cut holes in the dash, and it's a lot of work to get the tubes to go through the dash and around and through everything necessary to hide the rest of the cage inside the dash. However, going through the dash allows you to hide the bars behind the A-pillars and make it easier to get in and out of the car by having the bars connect to the frame farther forward, out of the door opening. It's a personal choice, and there isn't a right or wrong way to do it. If you go through the dash, you need to determine where the holes should be cut, considering the angle of the A-pillars and the transition to the frame rails.

Cut Holes for Front Tubes

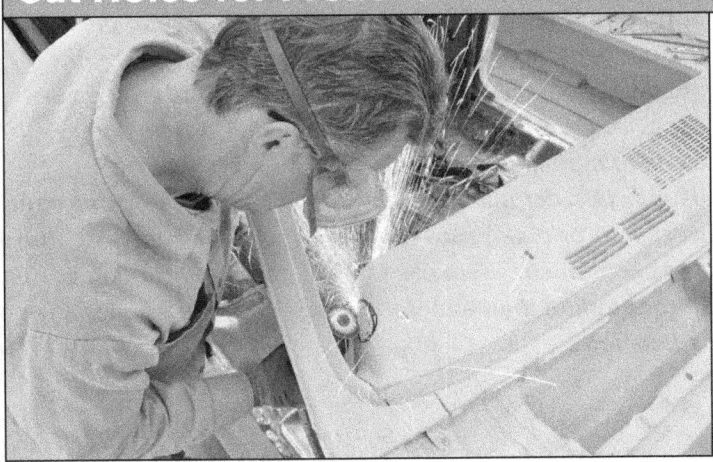

15 Use a cut-off wheel to start the hole, and then use a rotary file to turn the square hole into an oval. Because of the curve of the dash, this hole is much longer than it is wide. And you probably need to trim the hole several times as you fit the bar. Keep the hole as tight to the bar as possible if you plan on welding them together when you're finished. If you don't want to weld them, leave a 1/4-inch gap all the way around the bar to allow for vibration and movement. The dash pad can cover the transition for a finished look.

Choose Front Bar Design

16 There are also two methods of constructing the front part of the cage. One way is to use two bars that run from the main hoop down to the frame rails on each side. A third bar is welded in place at the top of the windshield to connect these two tubes together.

The other way to do the front section is to create a halo bar that starts at the main hoop, runs across the top of the windshield, and then connects to the opposite side of the main hoop. Down bars then connect the halo to the frame rails along the A-pillars. Because of the radius of the 90-degree bends at the windshield, it's difficult to get a halo-style bar to fit as tightly to the car, but it's generally easier to create the front half of the cage with the halo style. A super-tight fit makes the cage nearly invisible when finished. Tony worked three bends into this down bar, all in different planes, to get it to follow the roof and A-pillar lines perfectly.

Fit Front Tubes to Cage

17 For the tight fit of a properly finished fish mouth, each tube must be hand-fit in the exact location that the bars intersect. Moving this bar up 2 inches requires a different angle on the fish mouth, and the tubing diameter changes slightly through the curve. Mark everything, measure at least twice, and trim slowly until you get the perfect fit.

18 Before tacking the front down bars in place, make sure you've left enough room to get the kick panels and any other trim in place. Tony also trimmed away the bottom part of the dash mount. Weld the tube to the dash mount, reinforcing this mount, and also eliminating the possibility of a squeak. A cage vibrates quite a bit as the car drives down the road. Any place that a tube comes close to metal, either attach it to the metal (which is usually best for added strength and to reduce overall cage vibration) or make sure there is enough clearance so the two can't touch. There are few things more irritating or harder to find than a metal-to-metal squeak when the car is finished.

Fit Front Tubes to Cage (Continued)

19 With one A-pillar bar finished, Tony transferred the key measurement points to the second bar. A couple of precautions when you do this: First, most cars are not perfectly symmetrical, so you still need to double-check the measurements and angles as you work. Second, you need to do any left-to-right angles in the opposite direction. For example, these bars have a slight bend outward along the top of the side-window openings to line up for their drop through the dash. This bend is in opposite directions on the left and right to create the same effect on both sides of the car.

20 With the A-pillar down bars tacked in place, Tony worked on the top windshield bar. This bar is pretty tricky, because it has a fish mouth on both ends. Tony also put a slight bend in the center of the bar to help it follow the shape of the windshield opening. Use quick-release clamps to keep the bar from sliding down as you trial-fit it. Another choice you have to make is how far forward and high this bar sits. Will you have sun visors? Was your factory rearview mirror attached to the roof pane instead of glued on the windshield? Make sure you leave room for the components you want to keep.

21 When you have the bar fitting perfectly, mark a spot on one of the A-pillar down bars that are covered by the windshield bar. Drill a 1/8-inch hole in the tube. You need to do this anywhere that a tube is closed on both ends so that the gas and pressure trapped in the tubing during final welding can escape. Typically, you can drill one hole here, one where the seat brace connects to the driver's side of the main hoop, and where all four of the front and rear down bars connect to the main hoop. Then drill one hole near the base of one side of the main hoop. This should provide a pathway for all trapped gas and pressure, but look at your cage and trace the path for each tube.

Install Engine Bay Down Tubes

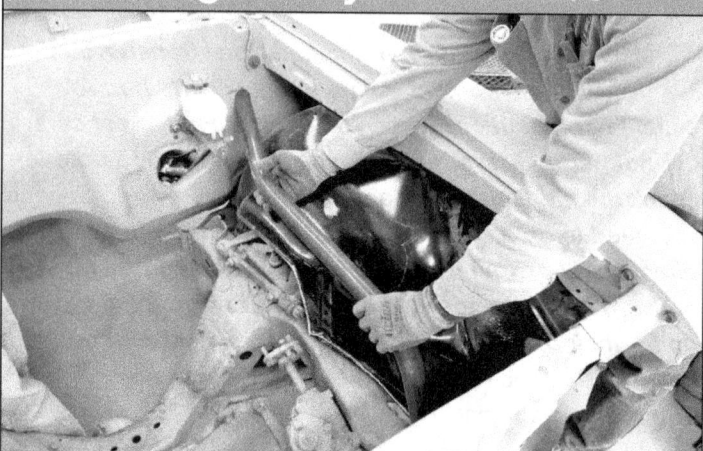

22 Next, you craft engine bay down bars. These help strengthen the front section of the frame and are helpful for chassis rigidity. It's extremely helpful to have all of your under-the-hood components, such as brake and clutch master cylinders, fuse box, radiator, and so on, installed for mock-up when you do. Tony strongly recommends to add a stringer that connects this down bar to the frame behind the upper A-arm mount to straddle the key suspension mounting locations.

Install Seat Brace Tube

23 The seat brace in this car was welded straight between the legs of the main hoop. This bar must be within 4 inches of the top of the driver's shoulders for proper safety harness location. The door bars were the last bars built for this cage. The NHRA rulebook says that the door bars must pass the driver at a point midway between the shoulder and the elbow. The easiest way to do this is to sit in the seat with your hands on the steering wheel at the 9 and 3 o'clock positions and have someone measure the position of your upper arm. You can add some shape to allow the door bar to clear the door-mounted arm rest. Also make sure that you have the seats in the car that you plan on using. Some seats are wider than others and can interfere with the door bars.

Weld All Roll Cage Tubes

24 TIG welding is a slow process, and the final steps of welding the cage can take quite a while. A variety of TIG torches can make welding in the tight locations a lot easier. Do not grind or sand any of the welds. If you need to have the chassis certified at some point, it will be rejected if any of the welds have been ground. Here, the finished engine bay down bar has the rear extension in place.

Project 2: Interior Installation

Remove Old Dash

1 For 1966–1967 Chevelles, you can fit performance 5-inch gauges with a bolt-in dash replacement from ABC Performance. It retains the classic shape of the original dash, but allows you to fit the gauges you want, as well as a single- or double-DIN radio, aftermarket air-conditioning controls and vents, etc. The first step is to remove your old dash. With the steering column removed, there are four bolts at the bottom corners of the dash and nine screws holding the dash in place. You can leave the dash assembled and disconnect the wiring once it is in this position.

Cut Out Dash for Gauges

2 Tony at ABC starts with an original core. He finds one that has had the radio holes cut out or is otherwise less desirable to someone restoring a Chevelle. To make room for the large-diameter gauges, ABC Performance cuts out the section of the dash that held the ignition, headlight, and windshield wiper switches.

Weld Dash Sheet Metal

3 New sheet metal is TIG-welded in place to create a tall surface all the way across the dashboard. There are about 15 hours of metal fabrication invested in each ABC Performance dash.

Dash Options

The top example of an ABC Performance dash retains the factory ashtray, heater controls, and glove box; these holes have all been filled in the lower example. The upper one has the headlight, ignition, and windshield wiper switches mounted on the left and right sides of the steering column; the lower one is completely smooth, and these switches can be mounted in the gauge panel, a center console, or integrated into the steering column. Whatever systems you are interested in having in your car can be added, and whatever you don't want can be removed. The dash can be shipped to you in a rough finish or completely done.

Inspect Gauges

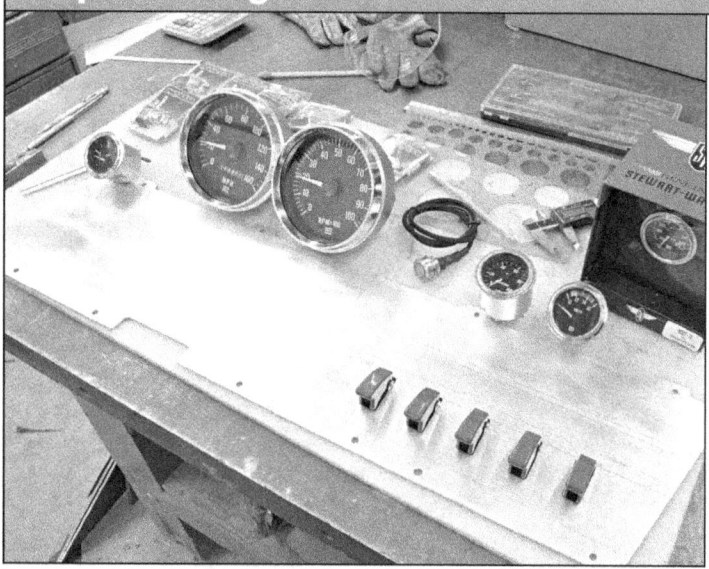

4 ABC Performance has several gauge inserts that accommodate a variety of gauge, radio, and air-conditioning vent configurations. It also offers a blank template (shown) that can be customized. This dash has a rack of Stewart Warner gauges for a classic old-style race car look. The electronic speedometer and tachometer are 5 inches in diameter, while the fuel, oil pressure, water temperature, and oil temperature gauges, as well as the volt meter, are 2 1/8 inches in diameter. A push-button ignition switch and toggle switches from Painless Performance are also mounted in the panel, further adding to the race car style.

Install Gauges in Dash

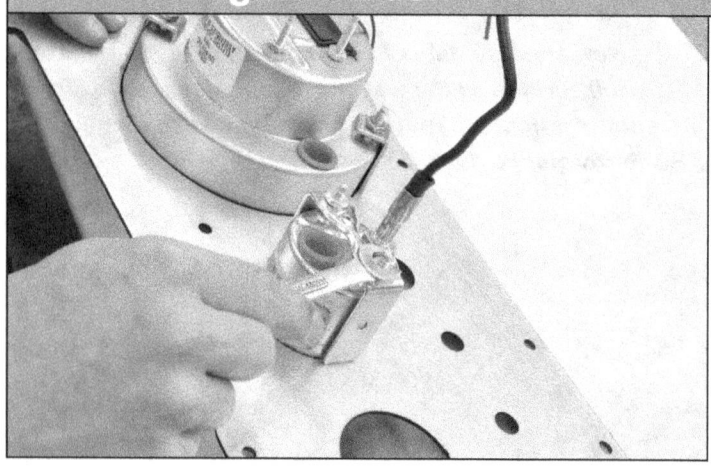

5 TJ Grzelakowski at ABC Performance laid out the gauges and switches in a pattern that looks good, cut the holes in the panel, and installed the gauges and switches. The gauges slide in through the front of the panel and are held in place with clamps that bolt to the back of the gauges. It is easiest to build a wiring harness for your new gauges before installing the dash back in the car. If you decide you want to change the layout of the gauges or make room for air vents or an in-dash GPS unit later, you can change the insert.

Install Switches

6 You can change the red toggle switch covers for black ones for a more subtle look. These are often called aircraft-style switch covers, and they are designed to shut off the toggle switch with just a quick movement of the hand. The switches themselves are mil-spec toggles from Painless Performance. They are internally sealed, and terminals with screws instead of push-on connectors. TJ also installed a Painless Performance Phantom Key push-button start system.

Select Ignition Switch

7 The Phantom Key system works like a new Challenger or Cadillac push-button start. The remote fob must be within 20 feet of the car to arm the system. Once armed, you push the button to engage the starter. The starter cranks until you release the push button. To shut the engine off, you push the button again. The kit comes with a control module, two remote fobs, a push button, wiring, and a rack of relays to control accessories such as power door locks (see page 129 for more information on this system).

Configure Dash for Your Needs

8 This is a typical ABC Performance dash with 5-inch Auto Meter speedometer and tachometer and four additional 2-inch gauges. There is room above the single-DIN radio for an air-conditioning vent. The area above the glove box requires a custom piece to fill the now taller area. ABC Performance can provide a trim piece such as the one shown covered in leather.

Install Completed Dash in Car

9 The dash installs in the factory shell using the same fasteners as the original. ABC Performance can also provide LED indicator lights for the high-beam headlights (blue light between the speedometer and tachometer) and turn signals (green lights). This is a very clean way to install large performance gauges in your 1966–1967 Chevelle and have everything integrated into your dash, rather than gauges strapped to the column, or bolted on or under the dash.

Fit Reproduction Door Panels

10 The rest of a performance Chevelle interior doesn't necessarily require custom work. You can use reproduction door panels and a headliner from CARS, Inc. to complete a race-inspired theme. These upper door panel mounts were refinished in cobalt black by Advanced Plating for a cool, dark look with reflective properties of chrome. The new door panels have the cutouts in the back board for the window and door handles, but you need to trim the vinyl.

Fabricate Dash Pad

11 You can cut a reproduction dash pad from CARS, Inc. to fit around the A-pillar bars. Custom leather upholstery can be added with detail stitching for a very nice look.

Install Sound Deadener

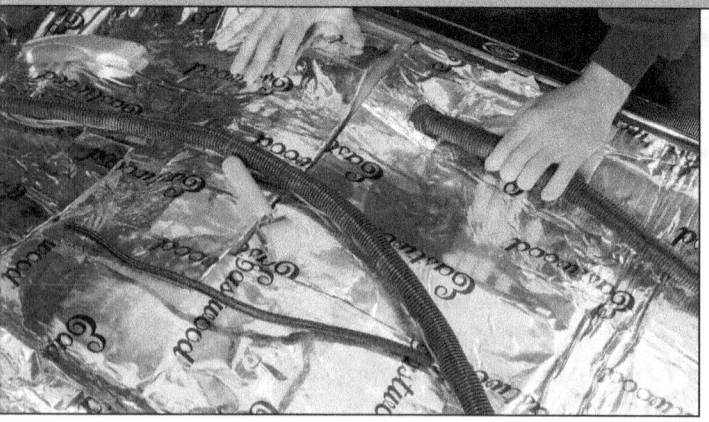

12 You can cover the floor of the car with Eastwood Thermo-Coustic sound deadener. This reduces the road noise and vibration caused by a hot performance engine and exhaust system. The butyl membrane has a peel-and-stick backing for easy installation. The top side has an aluminum face to reduce heat. This type of product adds 30 to 50 pounds to the vehicle, but is well worth the weight penalty in any vehicle you drive on the street for the improvement in interior sound quality.

PERFORMANCE INTERIOR

Install Carpet

13 *Another street concession is a good layer of carpet. This Daytona weave from CARS, Inc. has zero shag; a tight, woven appearance; and a very high quality weight of the material and a foam back, which adds further sound deadening. It does not come as a molded carpet set; you need to have it professionally installed.*

A modern performance interior for your Chevelle can be functional with performance seating, safety harnesses, roll cage, instruments, and controls. Yet, it still can have the classic styling and theme of the vintage car that you love.

CHEVELLE PERFORMANCE PROJECTS: 1964–1972   157

Source Guide

ABC Performance
Imlay City, MI 48444
810-614-3730
www.abcperformance.net

ACCEL Ignition
10601 Memphis Ave, #12
Cleveland, OH 44144
216-688-8300
www.accel-ignition.com

Advanced Plating
1425 Cowan Ct
Nashville, TN 37207
800-588-6686
www.advancedplating.com

American Powertrain
2199 Summerfield Rd
Cookeville, TN 38501
1-931-646-4836
www.americanpowertrain.com

Art Morrison Enterprises
5216 7th St E
Fife, WA 98424
800-929-7188
www.artmorrison.com

Auto Meter
413 West Elm St
Sycamore, IL 60178
866-248-6356
www.autometer.com

B&M Racing & Performance
800-544-4761
www.bmracing.com

Baer
2222 West Peoria Ave
Phoenix, AZ 85029
602-233-1411
www.baer.com

BFGoodrich
P.O. Box 19001
Greenville, SC 29602-9001
877-788-8899
www.bfgoodrichtires.com

Billet Specialties
800-245-5382
www.billetspecialties.com

Borla Performance Industries
701 Arcturus Ave
Oxnard, CA 93033
805-986-8600
www.borla.com

Bowtie Overdrives
17359 Darwin Ave Unit C
Hesperia, CA 92345
760-947-5240
www.bowtieoverdrives.com

CARS Inc.
2600 Bond St
Rochester Hills, MI 48309
248-853-8900
www.carsinc.com

Chevrolet Performance
(Formerly GM Performance Parts)
800-450-4150
www.chevroletperformance.com

Classic Performance Products
175 E Freedom Ave
Anaheim, CA 92801
714-522-2000
www.classicperform.com

Covan's Thunder Rd
866-882-3525
www.classicthunderroad.com

Dynamat
3042 Symmes Rd
Hamilton, OH 45015
513-860-5094
www.dynamat.com

Dynomax Performance Exhaust
1 International Dr
Monroe, MI 48161
734-384-7806
www.dynomax.com

SOURCE GUIDE

Detroit Speed, Inc
185 McKenzie Rd
Mooresville, NC 28115
704-662-3272
www.detroitspeed.com

Eastwood
263 Shoemaker Rd
Pottstown, PA 19464
800-343-9353
www.eastwood.com

Eaton
800-328-3850
www.eaton.com

Edelbrock, LLC
2700 California St
Torrance, CA 90503
800-416-8628
www.edelbrock.com

FAST
3400 Democrat Rd
Memphis, TN 38118
877-334-8355
www.fuelairspark.com

Flaming River Industries, Inc.
800 Poertner Dr
Berea, OH 44017
440-826-4488
www.flamingriver.com

Flex-a-lite
7213-45th St Ct E
Fife, WA 98424
800-851-1510
www.flex-a-lite.com

Flowmaster, Inc
100 Stony Point Rd, Ste 125
Santa Rosa, CA 95401
707-544-4761
www.flowmastermufflers.com

Gear Vendors, Inc
1717 N Magnolia Ave
El Cajon, CA 92020
800-999-9555
www.gearvendors.com

Great Lakes Customs
260 N. Rose St
Mt. Clemens, MI 48043
586-463-7646
www.greatlakecustoms.com

Global West Suspension
655 S. Lincoln Ave
San Bernardino, CA 92408
877-470-2975
www.globalwest.net

Holley Performance Products
1801 Russellville Rd
Bowling Green, KY 42101
270-782-2900
www.holley.com

Hooker Headers
1801 Russellville Rd
Bowling Green, KY 42101
270-782-2900
www.holley.com

Hotchkis Sport Suspension
8633 Sorensen Ave
Santa Fe Springs, CA 90670
888-735-6425
www.hotchkis.net

Hushmat
15032 W 117th St
Olathe, KS 66062
913-599-2600

Hurst
100 Stony Point Rd, Ste 125
Santa Rosa, CA 95401
707-544-4761
www.hurst-shifters.com

Inline Tube
15066 Technology Dr
Shelby Twp, MI 48315
800-385-9452
www.inlinetube.com

JD Squared, Inc
2244 Eddie Williams Rd
Johnson City, TN 37604
423-979-0309
www.jd2.com

JEGS High Performance
101 JEGS Pl
Delaware, OH 43015
800-345-4545
www.jegs.com

Jerry Bickel Race Cars, Inc
141 Raceway Park Dr
Moscow Mills, MO 63362
636-356-4727
www.jerrybickel.com

Jet-Hot Ceramic Coatings
2611 LaVista Dr
Burlington, NC 27215
800-432-3379
www.jet-hot.com

Kirkey Racing
PO Box 445
Rooseveltown, NY 13683
613-938-4885
www.kirkeyracing.com

Kobalt Tools
www.kobalttools.com
See your local Lowe's

Lokar Performance Products
10924 Murdock Dr
Knoxville, TN 37932
865-966-2269
www.lokar.com

Made For You Products
PO Box 720700
Pinon Hills, CA 92372
760-868-6962
www.made4uproducts.com

MagnaFlow
22961 Arroyo Vista
Rancho Santa Margarita, CA 92688
800-824-8664
wwwmagnaflow.com

March Performance, Inc
16160 Performance Way
Naples, FL 34110
239-593-4074
www.marchperf.com

SOURCE GUIDE

M.A.D. Enterprise
Newark, CA 94560
510-742-6780
www.madenterprise.com

Moser Engineering
102 Performance Dr
Portland, IN 47371
260-726-6689
www.moserengineering.com

MSD Ignition
1350 Pullman Dr
El Paso, TX 79936
915-857-5200
www.msdignition.com

National Parts Depot
31 Elkay Dr
Chester, NY 10918
800-524-8338
www.nationalparts.com

Optima Batteries
5757 N Green Bay Ave
Milwaukee WI 53209
888-867-8462
www.optimabatteries.com

Painless Performance Products
2501 Ludelle St
Fort Worth, TX 76105
817-244-6212
www.painlesswiring.com

Percy's High Performance
301 Highgrove Rd
Grandview, MO 64030
888-737-2970
www.percyshp.com

Performance Suspension Technology
877-226-4101
www.p-s-t.com

PerTronix Performance Products, Inc
440 East Arrow Hwy
San Dimas, CA 91773
909-599-5955
www.pertronix.com

PowerMaster Performance
1833 Downs Dr
West Chicago, IL 60185
630-957-4019

Quick Time Performance
77 Fourth Ave
Hawthorne, NJ 07506
973-513-9955
www.quicktimeperformance.com

Ridetech
350 S. St. Charles St
Jasper, IN 47546
812-481-4787
www.ridetech.com

Schwartz Performance, Inc.
1115 Rail Dr
Woodstock, IL 60098
815-206-2230
www.schwartzperformance.com

ShiftRight Transmission
450 Lincoln Hwy W
Jeannette, PA 15644
724-527-2744
www.shiftrighttrans.com

Snap-On, Inc
877-762-7664
www.snapon.com

Stewart Warner
800-447-2820
www.stewartwarnerinstruments.com

Strange Engineering
8300 N Austin Ave
Morton Grove, IL 60053
847-663-1701
www.strangeengineering.com

Street & Performance
#1 Hotrod Ln
Mena, AR 71953
479-394-5711
www.hotrodlane.com

System 1 Filter Systems
Leonard Noell Dr
Tulare CA, 93274
559-687-1955
www.system1filters.com

TCI Automotive
151 Industrial Dr
Ashland, MS 38603
888-776-9824
www.tciauto.com

Tech AFX, Inc
P.O. Box 252414
West Bloomfield, MI 48325
877-355-0137
www.techafx.com

Tilton Engineering
25 Easy St
Buellton, CA 93427
805-688-2353
www.tiltonracing.com

Trans-Dapt Performance Products
12438 Putnam St
Whittier, CA 90602
562-921-0404
www.tdperformance.com

Tremec Transmissions
14700 Helm Ct
Plymouth, MI 48170
800-401-9866
www.tremec,com

Wilwood Engineering, Inc
4700 Calle Bolero
Camarillo, CA 93012
805-388-1188
www.wilwood.com

www.ingramcontent.com/pod-product-compliance
Lightning Source LLC
Chambersburg PA
CBHW081449070526
44586CB00019B/2277